The Problem Body

The Problem Body

Projecting Disability on Film

- EDITED BY -

Sally Chivers and
Nicole Markotić

THE OHIO STATE UNIVERSITY PRESS / COLUMBUS

Library of Congress Cataloging-in-Publication Data
The problem body : projecting disability on film / edited by Sally Chivers and Nicole Markotić.
   p. cm.
  Includes bibliographical references and index.
  ISBN 978-0-8142-1124-3 (cloth : alk. paper)—ISBN 978-0-8142-9222-8 (cd-rom) 1. People with disabilities in motion pictures. 2. Human body in motion pictures. 3. Sociology of disability. I. Chivers, Sally, 1972– II. Markotić, Nicole.
  PN1995.9.H34P76 2010
  791.43′6561—dc22

2009052781

This book is available in the following editions:
Cloth (ISBN 978-0-8142-1124-3)
CD-ROM (ISBN 978-0-8142-9222-8)

Cover art: Anna Stave and Steven C. Stewart in *It is fine! EVERYTHING IS FINE!*, a film written by Steven C. Stewart and directed by Crispin Hellion Glover and David Brothers, Copyright Volcanic Eruptions/CrispinGlover.com, 2007.
Photo by David Brothers.

An earlier version of Johnson Cheu's essay, "Seeing Blindness On-Screen: The Blind, Female Gaze," was previously published as "Seeing Blindness on Screen" in *The Journal of Popular Culture* 42.3 (Wiley-Blackwell). Used by permission of the publisher.

Michael Davidson's essay, "Phantom Limbs: Film Noir and the Disabled Body," was previously published under the same title in *GLQ: A Journal of Lesbian and Gay Studies*, Volume 9, no. 1/2, pp. 57–77. Copyright, 2003, Duke University Press. All rights reserved. Used by permission of the publisher.

Sharon L. Snyder and David T. Mitchell's essay, "Body Genres: An Anatomy of Disability in Film," was previously published in their book *Cultural Locations of Disability* as chapter 5, "Body Genres and Disability Sensations: The Challenge of the New Disability Documentary Cinema" (University of Chicago Press). © 2006 by The University of Chicago. Used by permission of the publisher.

Cover design by Janna Thompson-Chordas
Text design by Jennifer Shoffey Forsythe
Type set in Adobe Palatino.

9 8 7 6 5 4 3 2

We dedicate this book to Emma, the pre-eminent Vampire Slayer.

EMMA THE VAMPIRE SLAYER BY RIVA LEHRER

Contents

Illustrations

Chapter 1: James Apperson (John Gilbert), amputee veteran. *The Big Parade.* Directed by King Vidor. MGM, 1925.

Chapter 2: Opening credits superimposed over the figure of a man with crutches who moves menacingly toward the audience until his shadowy form covers the entire screen. *Double Indemnity.* Directed by Billy Wilder. Paramount Pictures, 1944.

Chapter 3: Susy (Audrey Hepburn) tries to put out the light. *Wait Until Dark.* Directed by Terence Young. Warner Bros., 1967.

Chapter 4: Le Dr Jean Itard (François Truffaut) tests the hearing of wild child Victor (Jean-Pierre Cargol). *L'enfant sauvage* (*The Wild Child*). Directed by François Truffaut. Les Films du Carrosse, 1969. United Artists, 1970.

Chapter 5: Ken (Richard Dreyfuss) reacts uncontrollably to the hospital's medical treatment. *Whose Life Is It Anyway?* Directed by John Badham. MGM Films, 1981.

Chapter 6: Text eclipses the ill body of Vivian Bearing (Emma Thompson). *Wit.* By Margaret Edson. Adapted for film by Emma Thompson and Mike Nichols. Directed by Mike Nichols. Home Box Office Network, 2001.

Chapter 7: Bess (Emily Watson) flees torment from local children. *Breaking the Waves.* Directed by Lars von Trier. Zentropa Film Entertainment, 1996.

Chapter 8: The filmmakers procure authenticity for Maggie (Hilary Swank) by having her purchase her training bag with rolled coins. *Million Dollar Baby*. Directed by Clint Eastwood. Warner Bros., 2004.

Chapter 9: The double-amputee war veteran Lieutenant Dan Taylor (Gary Sinise) lifts himself from a seated position on the floor into his wheelchair. *Forrest Gump*. Directed by Robert Zemeckis. Paramount Studios, 1994.

Coda: Mata Hari (Greta Garbo) descends toward her executioners, as Lt. Alexis Rosanoff (Ramon Novarro), her blind lover, "looks on." *Mata Hari*. Directed by George Fitzmaurice. MGM, 1931.

Acknowledgments

Beyond all our fabulous colleagues in Disability Studies, especially the contributors to this volume, we'd like to thank Martin Boyne for his careful indexing, Sandy Crooms for her amazing editorial support, Maggie Diehl for her exhaustive copyediting, Jennifer Shoffey Forsythe for exemplary patience in vetting and giving advice regarding images, Malcolm Litchfield for his permissions advice, and Jonathan Pinto for his technical expertise. We also thank our wonderful families and our partners, Louis Cabri and Wade Matthews, for always reading. Lastly, through our work on this book, we have developed a remarkable collaborative companionship for which we are both immensely grateful.

Introduction

In this compilation we have gathered a set of essays that explore representations of disability on film. One of the quickest paths to critical acclaim for an able-bodied actor is to play a physically disabled character in a manner that a largely uninformed audience finds convincing. Filmic narrative fictions rarely ignore disability. Examples of lauded performances include those by Daniel Day Lewis (*My Left Foot*), Tom Hanks (*Philadelphia*), Sean Penn (*I Am Sam*), and Hilary Swank (*Million Dollar Baby*).[1] As David Mitchell and Sharon Snyder point out in *Narrative Prosthesis*, disability in narrative is both excessively visible and conversely invisible (15). Rather than absent, as other stigmatized social identities can be (for example, films can entirely avoid lead female or racialized roles), disability is highly and continuously present on-screen. However, it is not always agential. Often, disabled bodies appear in order to shore up a sense of normalcy and strength in a presumed-to-be able-bodied audience. In this book we follow this argument into narrative film, noting the contradiction between how many characters in films display disabilities and how seldom reviewers and audiences "notice" disability as a feature within the film. This characteristic disability haunting of contemporary film merits critical scrutiny and warrants a set of critical terms that separate disability studies from past film criticism. In what follows, we focus on critical notions of "projection" and filmic constructions of "problem bodies" to contribute such scrutiny and such terms.

Filmic narrative often aligns the bodies it represents with an elusive and ideal norm of the human body that William Blake designated "the

---

1. All films cited and discussed in the essays are listed in the Filmography at the end of the book.

1

human abstract."[2] Most bodies are presented as normative by default, implicitly—self-evidently, or so it might appear to a viewer—achieving the norm, while other bodies are designated "abnormal," failing to achieve, or even to aspire to, that norm. As Robert Bogdan, quoting his young son in his pivotal publication *Freak Show,* points out, typically, in mainstream films, when characters "look bad" they "are bad" (6). Frequently, a disabled body is represented as a metaphor for emotional or spiritual deficiency. Unlike normative filmic bodies that literally advance the plot, the disabled body often exists primarily as a metaphor for a body that is unable to do so.[3] Rarely do films come along like Crispin Hellion Glover's, David Brothers' and Steven C. Stewart's *It is fine! EVERYTHING IS FINE!* a film written by and starring a disabled actor, which presents a disabled character as exactly that—disabled, yet still a fully participating character in the film.[4] So what happens when a disabled body metaphorically becomes a site of projected identity? The essays collected in this anthology take on the poetics and politics of that question.

Projecting Disability

In this book we analyze the "projection" of disability. We include in our analysis the act of the film projector displaying disability as well as what film viewers project—in the sense of prediction—disability to be. According to Sigmund and Anna Freud, projection is an emotional defense mechanism, whereby one attributes one's own negative or unacceptable thoughts and emotions to others.[5] Rey Chow, in her book on cultural otherness, *Ethics after Idealism,* discusses the notion of fascism as "projection, surface phenomena, everyday practice, which does away with the distinction between the 'inside' and the 'outside'" (19). In writing about fascism through the lens of Freudian projection, Chow

---

2. Blake speaks, for the most part, about the human soul. But his notion that "we" need to make others poor or unhappy in order to recognize our own satisfaction speaks to the us-them relationship that normalizes the body as well as the spirit (Plate 47).

3. So, for example, in the film *Shallow Hal,* the Jack Black character "evolves" emotionally into the kind of man who could love a "fat chick," while Gwyneth Paltrow's character remains a physically repellent figure, but one who audiences must learn to see as "beautiful on the inside."

4. Although none of the films in this collection address *It is fine! EVERYTHING IS FINE!* much could be said about the representations of heterosexual masculinity in the film, as well as the ways in which the film disjunctively approaches the too-often-taboo subject of sex and disability.

5. Citing her father's book *Some Neurotic Mechanisms in Jealousy, Paranoia and Homosexuality,* Anna Freud labels projection as a "defensive method" (43) that immature egos (she speaks predominantly of children) employ "as a means of repudiating their own activities and wishes when these become dangerous and of laying the responsibility for them at the door of some external agent" (123).

insists that the more obvious meaning of projection, that is, "as an act of thrusting or throwing forward, an act that causes an image to appear on a surface" (21), shifts the discussion of a subject's anxiety mediated via expulsion (from the inside to the outside) to one where the subject's apparent lack collides with and thus forms a surface. Film, says Chow, is the external image that represents both the act of expulsion and projected otherness.

Chow's discussion offers an analysis of the ways in which film creates a literal surface upon which narrative projects identity. Spectatorship (both public cinema viewings and private DVD rentals) allows audience members to take on the unique and contradictory position of what we call the "panopticon voyeur." Film critics since Laura Mulvey[6] have outlined and analyzed the myriad ways that film audiences embody the hidden nature of the voyeur. But as the panopticon's power relies on its dwellers' *awareness* of being observed, few critics speak to the normalizing power of projected viewing audiences. Unlike the literary notion of the "ideal reader," the panopticon voyeurs of film shape and establish subject matter, cultural representations, and even changed endings (in the case of audience test screenings). For an example of how projected audiences determine race representations, one has only to look at the contrast between Disney's *Pocahontas* and *Mulan* films, both of which focus on "real" historical figures. The former, for the most part, was directed at non-indigenous audiences, and subsequent criticisms of its racism and historical inaccuracies did not affect its box-office success. For the latter, however, Disney, keen to promote films in China, strove to ensure geographical and historical accuracy. The film was, for the most part, praised for its cultural sensitivity and artistic renditions of local landmarks and a brave heroine. Although at the time of its filming, Disney did not know whether or not the Chinese government would permit wide distribution of *Mulan,* the studio treated future Chinese audiences as both subject and object, as spectators who would have a vested (and thus a controlling) interest in the bodies projected on-screen. Chow would say of these binary positions that, as subjects, spectators react to the filmic narrative also as studio projections, as viewers assumed by the industry to have a participating and controlling interest in the storyline and its unfolding. These projected viewers also act as objects: they accept the film as spectacle and their own physical selves as Disney fodder; they accept the graphic images on-screen as representative of their bodies as national story. The panopticon voyeur, then, straddles a position between passive

---

6. For explication of film and voyeurism, see critics Mary Ann Doane, bell hooks, Christian Metz, and Linda Williams.

observer and normalizing surveyor, playing a role both in the film's ultimate screening and in how a film projects its characters.

Disability activists frequently point out that those who live long
enough eventually become disabled; the statistical probability that a por-
tion of life will be lived with a disability increases with age. This disability axiom strategically implicates a wide public under the disability
rubric with the political goal of broadening an activist base.[7] In keeping
with this axiom, we argue in this book that there are many ways of living
with disability. Narrative film presents some of those ways. How experience is represented textually and how that representation is projected
onto and via audiences are both central aspects of the experience itself.
That is, the *representation* of disability does not exist separate from disability itself. Accordingly, we propose that—disabled or not—when "we"
all watch a film, we all participate in disability discourse.[8]

Film theory requires disability analysis and critique, particularly
because of its longstanding attention to spectatorship and to the gaze.
While the gaze is a form of physicality that disability studies seeks to
redirect, the mis-assumed relationship between looking and knowing is
particularly salient to film reception. In front of a screen—in an audience-
directed cinema or individually at home—lies a space for a normative
and deviant public not just to look but to *stare* at disabled figures without
censure.[9] Before the screen lies a place where many people can take an
extended look at the disabled body and live comfortably or even uncomfortably with their reactions, be they to shudder, to desire, to identify, to
pity, to turn away. While we intervene in scholarly debates about projection and the gaze by refusing to accept the filmic frame as seamless representation, we recognize the value of film analysis and movie watching.
While we challenge basic tenets of film theory, presuming to redirect
them, we also recognize that a collection of essays such as this one contributes to film theory's continued but expanded relevance to contemporary social issues, notably those involving disability.

---

7. As James I. Charlton points out, disability is "a significant part of the human condition"; knowledge about disability, he argues, is therefore knowledge about "the human condition itself" (4).

8. The very category of ubiquitous "we" becomes suspect when discussing bodies that do or do
not fit a normative ideal of health and well-being. It is therefore incumbent on each viewer to understand the consequences of such visual participation. For the duration of this essay, "we" indicates "we
two book editors."

9. The parental admonishment toward children, "Don't stare!," insistently commands both a
looking at and a looking away. For a more detailed analysis of the relationship between disability and
staring, see Rosemarie Garland-Thomson's "The Politics of Staring" and her *Staring: How We Look*.

"We Are All Handicapable"

In the 1990s, the weekly Canadian television skit show *Kids in the Hall* confronted socially problematic comedy. Unlike other male-dominated comedy troupes (such as Monty Python), dressing up as women (or other characters physically different from their own bodies) for the actors in *Kids in the Hall* is not the punch line. Indeed, representing bodies not their own (the troupe comprises five male actors) is rarely the *source* of amusement so much as are the social situations that represent such bodies within contemporary mass culture. Although *Kids in the Hall* does not deal extensively with issues of disability, the comedy troupe often focuses its humor on the representations of bodies that do not "fit" implicit normative standards, thus presenting to the viewer a full range of what we call problem bodies—awkward, medicalized, edgy bodies.[10] Their comedy helpfully prevents the viewer from falling passively into the long-available role of gawker at nature exhibited as freakish. We include an analysis of their work here not as an example of television representation but as an example of cultural criticism of the reception of cinematic portrayals of disability.

We focus here on one notable *Kids in the Hall* skit that highlights and parodies film studio and audience responses to disability-focused movies. The skit, "The Academy Awards," plays off a social situation that frequently accompanies celebratory ceremonies for and about mainstream film, a social situation whose allegorical proportions motivate this collection of essays. This skit makes fun of the "issue film" and its supporters while at the same time exposing the limits of the metaphorical language available for disabling declarations. "The Academy Awards" features four actors receiving nominations for Best Actor category at the Oscars.[11] The skit does more than offer merely another parody of the Oscars, for it also returns the viewers' attention back onto the language that des-

---

10. The term "problem body" is explicated in the next section of our introduction.

11. In the skit, *Kids in the Hall* pokes fun at the viewers who participate in what Tobin Siebers calls "disability drag":

> The modern cinema often puts the stigma of disability on display, except that films exhibit the stigma not to insiders by insiders, as is the usual case with drag, but to a general public that does not realize it is attending a drag performance. In short, when we view an able-bodied actor playing disabled, we have the same experience of exaggeration and performance as when we view a man playing a woman. (115)

The *Kids in the Hall* skit anticipates Siebers's nuanced critique of actors who "play" disabled and are then rewarded for their (overly sentimentalized, yet assumed-to-be verisimilitude) role with a shared Oscar win. In the drag films Siebers points to, audiences expect the depiction to be unmistakably exaggerated, whereas these Academy Award winners—though obviously overacting, even within the melodramatic milieu of an "issue"-focused film—are received (and hailed) as representing "true" disability experience.

ignates one kind of body as having a say over another kind. In the skit one actor is nominated for his role as Hamlet, a role that is dramatically and expertly depicted in an exceedingly short "Oscar clip." The remaining three have all played characters with disabilities. Predictably, rather than a single Oscar winner, there is a three-way tie among the able-bodied actors playing disabled characters. As one of the award presenters calls it, "Everybody but the Hamlet guy!"

Charles Riley drolly points out in his book on disability and/in media, "The safest nomination bets for Oscar gold, year after year, are disability flicks" (70). Playing on this pattern of recognition, of the three *Kids in the Hall* "victors," the first actor is nominated for his role as a Deaf activist.[12] In the clip, from a film named *Hear the Light*, he speaks to a group of anti-Deaf protestors, declaring: "I can't believe what I am lip-reading here today. Now I may not be able to hear with these [points to his ear], but you people, you can't hear with THIS! [makes a fist over his heart]." The second actor is nominated for his portrayal of a wheelchair activist, righteously struggling against the big-business company determined to install "bumps" in every road and sidewalk. The clip from his film, named *Rolling Tall*, also includes a speech: "Large bumps?! . . . Well if that's your idea of AMERICA then count me out. [points to himself] I'm not the one that's handicapped. [points to the crowd] YOU'RE the ones that are handicapped . . . IN HERE! [points to his heart]."

Breaking the mold, the third actor depicts a character with a traumatic head injury. The first two "clips" in this skit set up and remind viewers of the sentimental genre that a third such "clip" would then demolish: how will a character convincingly (even tongue-in-cheek convincingly) accuse anti-head-injury crowds that *they* are the ones with a head injury, "IN HERE! [pointing at heart]" As avid *Kids in the Hall* fans, and nascent disability scholars at the time the skit began circulating, when we two view a film or performance particularly guilty of depicting the usual suspects of disability clichés,[13] one of us invariably remarks to the other: "*I'm* not the one with a spike in my head, *you're* the one with a spike in your head, in your heart!" in effect parodying the parody. Needless to say, the *Kids in the Hall* skit does *not* present this exclamation as a well-set-up punch line: They do not project the humorous logic of their skit to its ultimate conclusion. Rather, the clip for the third actor playing a disabled character

---

12. In the various clips from the nominated films, "protestors" carry signs reading "SCREW THE DEAF" and "I LOVE BUMPS." Meanwhile, the obviously hearing actor, during his nomination clip, is shown signing (in popular idiom rather than in ASL) a single word: "OK."

13. For an extensive list of such filmic clichés, see Martin Norden's significant publication *Cinema of Isolation*, where he expands upon various disabled "types" (such as "Tragic Victim," "Noble Warrior," etc.).

opens at his birthday party. After being given a hat for his birthday, he says to his mother:

> You know I can't wear this. I've got a spike [points to spike] through my head. . . . I've accepted it. Why can't you? I've got a spike through my head, a spike through my head, spike through my head, a spike through my head, a spike through my head!"

The Oscar audience reacts as appreciatively to this film "clip" as to the other issue-focused clips. The cliché invoked and "driven" home here is the attempt by well-meaning family and friends to ignore a disabling injury and pretend the injured character is "the same" as before, or "the same" as "us," or, in the cynical reading of the initial plural evocation in our introduction, "we are all" *handicapable* (as one character in the *Kids in the Hall* skit sarcastically names it). The *Kids in the Hall*'s ending to their "Academy Awards" skit invokes issues films about disability and parodies the predictable moment in these films when a disabled character "overcomes" disability to end up "just like" everyone else.[14] The character needs to convince his mother that he will never be "the same," will never fit, will always have a spike in his head. This is a funny and useful parody; still, we prefer to think of our own ending to the skit as leading us to that narrative projection, eminently theorizable, where disability clashes uncomfortably with disability metaphors, where "having a spike in your head, in your heart" is not only an "issue" of disability but also a problem of spectatorship, meaning, and the normative gaze. That is, *we*'re not the ones with spikes in our heads, in our hearts—*you* are. In this book we collect a set of critical essays about disability in cinema that collectively identify and reimagine the spectatorship, meaning, and normative gaze that settle upon what we call "the problem body" on film, transforming the spike from our joke into what Canadians would recognize as "the last spike."[15]

Through their characters' continuing refrain that "*I'm* not the one who's disabled [blind, Deaf, injured, etc.], *society* is," we read this *Kids in the Hall* sketch allegorically as a challenge to rethink every social situ-

---

14. One Hollywood example of this plot structure is the character of Sam (Oscar-nominated Sean Penn) in *I Am Sam* who proves that he can draw on aspects of his cognitive disability to parent "just like" other parents.

15. "The last spike" is a titular element of both popular Canadian historical accounts and popular narratives about the completion of a transcontinental railroad, constructed in the name of nation building with underpaid immigrant labor across unceded indigenous lands. Just as The *Kids in the Hall*'s spike illustrates the twisted logic required to maintain patterns of disability representation, the railway's "last spike" illuminates the violent logic of nationalism.

ation that entails a response to disability that follows such sentimental logic. These comedians reveal underlying social expectations for and about the disabled body not only to successfully and invisibly function within an ableist society, but also to represent, for the general public, a moralizing symbol. This moralizing symbol acts as a commodity for viewers not only to reject particular bodies, but also to expect accumulated metaphorical weight (morally and symbolically) from those othered bodies.

For the most part, in independent cinema, representations of illness and disability *can* interrogate the various binary constructions of "healthy" versus "ill" that mainstream films have traditionally constructed around "our" bodies and the bodies of others. In most mainstream films, not only are disabled individuals relegated to marginally participating identities, but so too are groups who prefer to identify themselves as socially and politically determined, rather than as medically defined. The irony of the *Kids in the Hall* skit is that, as the "disabled" character points an accusing finger at others, the metaphor perpetuates itself as a literal and self-reflecting mirror for audience members. Ultimately, the "I'm not but you are" binary of the skit reconfigures the notion of a disabled body, judged by an ableist projection of a "healthy" attitude onto the "ailing" attitude.[16]

The Problem Body

We propose and examine the term the "problem" body which Nicole Markotić first used for critical analysis in an essay on the "coincidence" of body and texts in the Canadian feminist journal *Tessera*. We propose this term in alliance with—and juxtaposed to—other terms upon which theorists have drawn to investigate the role of the disabled body constructed within the framework of the normative body. Some examples include Rosemarie Garland-Thomson's the "extraordinary" body, G. Thomas Couser's the "recovering" body, Susan Wendell's the "rejected" body, and Michael Davidson's "defamiliar" body.[17] In our usage, the term

---

16. Disability as social metaphor has been discussed greatly by such critics as Lennard Davis, David Mitchell and Sharon Snyder, Martin Norden, and others. An obvious example of such a conflation comes in the movie *At First Sight* where Val Kilmer's character, newly sighted after growing up blind, reacts badly to his girlfriend urging him to walk quickly past a homeless man. In the subsequent scene he rants against sighted people who "don't want to see" unpleasant truths.

17. See Garland-Thomson's *Extraordinary Bodies*, Couser's *The Recovering Body*, Wendell's *The Rejected Body*, and Davidson's *Concerto for the Left Hand: Disability and the Defamiliar Body* for further elaboration.

the "problem" body[18] refers to various manifestations and representations of the Deaf body, the disabled body, the aged body, the ill body,
the obese body.[19] In presenting this term, we do not intend an emphasis
on physical disability per se but an emphasis on the transformation of
physical difference into cultural patterns of spectacle, patterns that replicate a range of pathologizing practices that oppress people.[20] We trace the
history of the phrase to Louis Althusser's term "problematic," which he
uses to indicate how a word or concept cannot be considered in isolation.
Indeed, the problematic points to the fundamental contradiction within
the capitalist apparatus. Althusser's term invokes a Marxian history of
production relationships, in order to "define the nature of a concept by
its function in the problematic" (39), but it allows us here to analyze the
problematic construction of bodies as essentialized, rather than merely
contextualized, contradictions within an ideological framework. Thus we
evoke a status that is both discursive and material.

Michel Foucault invokes the problematic in *Madness and Civilization*
less to designate cause and effect and more to scrutinize the idea of subjectivity within scientific power structures. Such science-based power
structures construct the subject based on classification rather than subjectivity. Psychiatry, for example, divides the "sane" from the "mad"; similarly, medical practice has routinely divided the normal body from the
disabled body, rendering the latter a "problem" within normative hierar-
chies and creating both the category of "normal" and of "disability." For
our purposes, the "problem" body stands for those bodily realities that—
within shifting ideologies—represent the anomalies that contradict a normative understanding of physical being. In the context of this collection
we examine the problems and possibilities of filmic representation that
classifies and thereby problematizes bodies. The essays collected herein
each take on a cinematic process of division in order to transform disability into a representative signal for a set of social problems that extend
beyond the interpretive bounds of medical practice. As Susan Crutchfield

---

18. We thank many writers and critics (especially Julia Gaunce) who helped us develop this term as
a useful marker of physical and mental difference.

19. This list expands with each revision of our essay, and with other essays we research in this field,
an expansion that we find to be reflective of the ongoing work by disability scholars in the humanities
who seek to define disability without confining it and who aim for inclusion but not dilution. We hope
that adjectives left off this list intrude conceptually through our term "problem" body, and we hope the
ever-expanding list speaks to such "problems."

20. The physicality of this process hides but does not obliterate the relevance of mental disability
to filmic representation and the pathologizing practices which oppress people. We do not separate
physical from mental disability in our work, believing the binary set up between them to be false. As
Eunjung Kim's included essay makes clear, disability in the film *Oasis* is not clearly physical *or* mental.
With that noted, we and our contributors are careful throughout to heed ways in which film projects
physical disability as though absolutely distinct from projections of mental disability.

and Marcy Epstein argue in the introduction to their collection, *Points of Contact*, "disability, like art, has no particular physical geography, though history has treated the category as something manifest, palpable, boundaried" (3), thus aligning the "category" of disability with the cultural landscape of "art" and representation. They are, they say, interested in "disability as a farrago of contradictory effects, a sideshow in which there is no outside" (9). In this collection we not only challenge looks *from* the outside but also invite critical responses to how that outside gaze refigures the body as a problem, as a sideshow in which, for many film spectators, there exists no perceptible *inside*.

The word "problem" shows up throughout disability studies to signify how lived bodies participate in a web of social relations and especially how certain lived bodies strain the threads of that ideologically delicate web. Simi Linton provides a perfect example of the role the adjective "problem" plays in disability studies: "the fact that impairment has almost always been studied from a deficit model means that we are deficient in language to describe it any other way than as a 'problem'" (140). To date, disability theorists have avoided the conceptual lens of the "problem" because it is situated outside disability studies actions and inside oppressive social structures. For example, in *Disability, Self, and Society*, Tanya Titchkosky sketches out her section, "The Problem of Disability":

> "Problem" is the definition of the situation of disability. . . . Such an understanding does not arise simply because our bodies, minds, or senses give us problems; the problem is brought to people through interaction, the environment, and through the production of knowledge. (131)

In *Reading and Writing Disability Differently*, Titchkosky hyphenates Markotić's term, "problem-body," and draws on it to evoke this sense of how disability connotes problem in a broader social sphere.

In returning to the articulations of Althusser and Foucault, our goal is to take on and expand the concept of the "problem" body to include multilayered corporeal realities and the intersections to which such realities lead. In particular, our objective is to define and reveal the "problem" body as a multiplication of lived circumstances constructed both physically *and* socially, in order to call into question the ways that certain bodies more frequently invite the label "problem" than do others. This critical strategy is in keeping with recent theoretical work in disability studies, and especially Snyder and Mitchell's concept of the cultural model of disability that imbricates the physicality of disability with the social and imagines the two always working in concert.

Cultural Locations

Through our collection we hope to shift the "either/or" structure of dis-ability studies to a "both/and" model so that disability can be under-stood as *both* physical *and* social. In narrative filmic representation dis-ability is both given and taken away, both opportunistic metaphor and phenomenological experience. In order to encourage and account for multiple readings of the disabled body on-screen, we shall also examine the "problem" body as it is projected along with gendered, homosexual, racialized, classed, and abused bodies. As Carol A. Breckenridge and Candace Vogler point out, "disability studies reminds us that feminism, sexuality, gender studies, and critical race theory meet at a point of incomprehension when faced with the corporeality of the disabled body" (350–51). We hope to shift that sectioned meeting from incomprehension to renewed interest in the multiple deviations and differences that bodies share. *The Problem Body: Projecting Disability on Film* will bolster readers' and critics' conceptualization of problematized bodies in Althusser's sense of the term "problematic." Our projection of Althusser's term into film and disability studies directs our argument that it is not that dis-abled bodies pose social "problems" so much as that disabled bodies both materialize and symbolize moments of interaction between the social and the physical, and among many other so-called identity categories.

Our *project*, then, is to examine projection (in both Freud's and Chow's sense of this notion) through the ways in which disability, gender, race, cultural otherness, and sexuality intersect. Intersection-ality has become a pivotal critical term to call attention to the need to think of difference in context. Kimberlé Crenshaw solidified the term in order to "[highlight] the need to account for multiple grounds of iden-tity when considering how the social world is constructed" (1245). Her work on race and gender reveals the need to think through *structural intersectionality* about how black women's experience of violence differs from white women's experience of violence, through *political intersec-tionality* about how identity-based politic movements have "marginal-ized" violence against women of color as a political issue, and through *representational intersectionality* about how women of color are cultur-ally constructed, specifically in popular culture (1245). We consider how projected images of disabled characters require analysis that attends to the experience of disability. Vivian M. May and Beth A. Ferris, in their analysis of Atom Egoyan's film *The Sweet Hereafter*, draw on what they call the "productive methodological practice" of intersectionality in order to adequately account for agency on the part of a young, female, newly disabled character (132). Disability theorists engage with literary and cultural theories in order to argue the necessity to account for race in critical analysis and to ground scholarly work in geographical, political, and gendered landscapes.

We wish to distinguish disability as a category of identity as well as investigate the usefulness of expanding disability's definition and challenging identity as a critical paradigm and a political strategy. Most importantly, we hope to demonstrate the importance of disability as a category of analysis even in those blurred instances where disability may not overtly preside.[21] We recognize that adding yet another adjective in front of the noun "body" (in identity discourse, critics speak of the "female" body, the "queer" body, the "racialized" body, etc.) cannot replace the critical work of designating and examining the role of bodies in scholarly criticism through simple nomenclature. Rather, we hope to open up the discussion for readers to further examine the discourse that perpetuates and challenges ongoing projections of "problem" bodies. We seek what Alexa Schriempf calls an "interactionist model" for the analysis of "problem" bodies, rather than an additive model that risks ignoring the fusion of identity categories (65). Othered bodies often reveal a self/other edge that not only marks gendered borders but also limits configurations of the physically ideal such that physicality both is and is not a problem. As Jim Overboe argues, the disabled/non-disabled binary model elevates the able-bodied argument to tout it as superior because "normalized embodiment and sensibility sets not only the parameters of 'what the problem is,' but also the limits of the discussion and the type of communication required to take part in the dialogue" (25). The body's literal edges and social roles—our focus here—discount the economy of normalized embodiment and instead demand cinematic challenges to visual conventions, to able-bodied actors, and to narrative genres.

The social contexts surrounding the physical other invite further discussion about a spectrum of physically diverse bodies. At times that spectrum threatens to become so diffuse as to render disability irrelevant or merely a subcategory competing for status, albeit marginal. Our collection draws on disability theory to provide a viable framework for examining the complicated and socially enriched process that determines the boundaries between the "normal" body and the "problem" body. We shall concentrate on bodies repeatedly left out of—or exploited by—tra-

---

21. Our argument is not simply a reframing of the claim that all bodies are ultimately, or will ultimately become, disabled. Rather, we find disability theory an effective starting place for the scrutiny of physicality, and, as such, it promises a mode of analysis that refuses the normativity of the white, male, heterosexual, fit, young, tall, athletic body.

ditional cultural and especially film criticism, and on the social problems that so-called deviant bodies confront because of normative cultural expectations. Rather than claiming the disabled body as an object that existing theories could simply reconfigure, we wish to reveal—through the visual dramatization of disability—the "problem" body as a challenging multiplication of physical and social problems. The "problem" body, then, demands a rich discourse to advance thinking beyond a focus that limits itself as either *this* body or *that* body.

Our aim is not, of course, to conflate all othered bodies into one trope but rather to suggest and examine the terminology of identity in order to better recognize ways in which disability has, historically, been assigned to the margins of the margins. By proposing our term, the "problem" body, we look critically at filmic bodies termed, rendered as, dismissed as, and rejected as "problematic." We explore the changing rubric of disability against such traditional rejections, and continued projections, and we consider the role of disabled bodies—and of other bodies configured as problems—in the emergence of public, and culturally determined, identities.

Projecting the Problem Body

"Project," both verb and noun, slices through the history of film studies to ground visual ideals and to highlight the problematic in filmic narrative. Though disability scholars discuss film frequently, especially on academic listservs and at scholarly meetings, omnibus publication about the relationship between film and disability is scant. In the following essays, this book seeks to solidify and clarify that widespread interest and dialogue. In addition to the need for more attention to what have been variably named mental/cognitive/intellectual disabilities on film, there is a continued need for further film scholarship on disability and race, sexuality, international cinemas, gender, and documentary. Essays in this volume begin the work in these areas, but we do not organize them under such headings because the articles, like the disabilities they parse, do not lend themselves to easy categorization.

In the first essay, "'The Whole Art of a Wooden Leg': King Vidor's Picturization of Laurence Stallings's 'Great Story,'" Timothy Barnard points to the interest an early Hollywood film, *The Big Parade*, takes in the portrayal of realism and the "great story" of the amputee war veteran. Thanks to King Vidor's portrayal of "absence" as high pathos to an audience just beginning to come to terms with postwar masculinity, Jim Apperson (John Gilbert) became a "triumph" of early war movies. The spectacle of Apperson as simultaneously embodied and disembodied, argues Barnard, provided a means to present "real" war and "real" war casualties. Post-WWI, then, the war vet reemerges, this time on film, as a powerful symbol—as well as a problematic sign—of both "exceptional masculinity and exceptional masculine loss." The hero's "loss" of a leg becomes also his gain of an exceptionally stiff phallus, one that he removes to sleep and puts on to run, awkwardly, toward his love and his new life.

Michael Davidson's essay, "Phantom Limbs: Film Noir and the Disabled Body," continues this investigation of the relationship between masculinity and disability in early U.S. cinema. Davidson looks closely at film noir images of gendered, queered, and disabled bodies. Such projections allow for minor, often cameo, characters to enable a non-normative narrative about the protagonist. Namely, Davidson says, "the disabled character represents a form of physical deviance necessary for marking the body's unruliness." But he argues beyond the simple narratives based on disabled characters as foil for the non-disabled. In his argument, the disabled body is a site for "social panic" about problem bodies, and the film's narrative presents such characters' stories as "phantom limbs" that would—given the time period and the Production Code—be unspeakable. Citing numerous gay icons that emerged from the film noir oeuvre, Davidson discusses the noir hero's heteromasculinity as dependent on the gay and lesbian counter-figures. He points out that the psychoanalytic gaze has relied on the act of looking as formulated through a trope of castration, thus—in contrast to Barnard's argument about *The Big Parade*—equating the missing limb with the missing phallus. For Davidson, moments of social agency in film noir undermine and relinquish the normative narratives the films endeavor to bolster.

Also focused on the psychoanalytic gaze, Johnson Cheu's essay, "Seeing Blindness On-Screen: The Blind, Female Gaze," revisits Laura Mulvey's classic argument, but in his argument the gaze is an ableist trope, signifying particular ways of seeing for sighted audience members. As the male gaze reconfigures all audience members into male voyeurs, so too does the normative gaze configure and insist upon audience members as not only assuming the identity position of non-blind, but problematically infusing audience members with the power-laden act of viewing blind (female) characters as particularly needy and disadvantaged. Presuming from the start a "disabled gaze," Cheu goes on to discuss the on-screen gaze of blind female protagonists and argues that such characters are "co-opted in order to take away the blind woman's agency." Rather than repudiating simple stereotypes, film and filmmakers co-opt a Blind gaze for the benefit of the (projected) able-bodied audience members. Relying on critical race and postcolonial theory, Cheu observes the normative gaze as defining racially dominant identity groups and the normative gaze as defining bodies as either able or not able.

Focusing on the interconnectedness of physical, cognitive, and sensory disability, Dawne McCance examines the relationships among speech, subjective autonomy, and medicalization in her essay, exploring projections of modernity in François Truffaut's *The Wild Child* (*L'enfant sauvage* [France, 1970]). This film, McCance argues, offers a speech-and-hearing model as trope for other (mental and mobility) disabilities. Such an approach allows her to investigate, via Jean Marc Gaspard Itard (chief physician at the Paris Institute for Deaf Mutes), early-nineteenth-century crises of how to define humanity, intersecting with late-twentieth-century crises of narrative representation. Positing what she calls the "theatre of mimesis," McCance places the film within the hybrid genres of "memoir, confession, family history, and political commentary," ultimately demonstrating how the director doctor projects the intertwined notions of speech and autonomous subjectivity onto the character of Victor. Throughout the film, argues McCance, Truffaut "portrays Victor's incapacity to hear-and-speak as what keeps him from crossing the human/ animal line," thus revealing the doctor's *and* the director's investment in human realization as aligned with hearing and verbal articulation.

Paul Darke's essay, "No Life Anyway: Pathologizing Disability on Film," also articulates the challenges of imagining disability as a human trait. Darke posits that the projection of an overly medicalized character and a narrative that advocates de-medicalization in *Whose Life Is It Anyway?* locates itself on the bodies of the disabled. In other words, any argument against medical intervention conflates into the argument against keeping disabled patients alive. Darke analyzes the implications of portraying disability rather than pathologization as burdensome. In doing so, he points to the demeaning technology that "unnaturally" perpetuates "sub-human" life. Such routine devaluing of the disabled body on-screen, argues Darke, becomes increasingly circular: as the film insists on the protagonist Ken's dehumanization, it must more and more depict Ken's body as inhuman. Ken himself rejects the hospital's medical intrusions; the film portrays him as refusing to consider himself as fully human. Like a "good cripple," says Darke, Ken "overcomes his abnormality by preferring death to impairment." Death, then, and a hero's choice for death, project as superior the character "trapped" inside an inferior container. Ken's "body logic," suggests Darke, best describes the default sacrifice for disabled characters that pervades the cinematic representation and construction of normalcy.

Projecting notions of illness and treatment, of terminal disease and its exacerbating "cures," Heath Diehl's essay, "'And Death—*capital D*—shall be no more—*semicolon!*': Explicating the Terminally Ill Body in Margaret Edson's *W;t*," circles around the protagonist's terminal illness and her own problematic articulation of that illness as a grammatically definable experience. The patient is in constant pain, not so much because of her illness, but because of the *treatment*. Vivian Bearing, projected as pure intellectual, becomes invested in her own ongoing analysis of the process, particularly its semantics. By examining this film through the trope of literary criticism, Diehl connects the meaning (or lack of meaning) of the body dying in pain to the representational strategy of analogy. Diehl argues that the film "voices a meta-filmic commentary on how instances of pain and suffering complicate the process of cinematic creation." Diehl argues that the role of the protagonist, Vivian Bearing, is not so much "true" confessor as "first-person narrating I." Bearing, a New Critic, attempts to render her physical experiences as readable and as "research" for other scholars, based on her training as a scholar who relies on analysis and poetics. But Diehl argues that the film's conflation of the body as a screen of pain and scrutiny relies on Bearing's textual embodiment as sentient experiment: her words, in other words, fail her.

In "'A Man, with the Same Feelings': Disability, Humanity, and Heterosexual Apparatus in *Breaking the Waves, Born on the Fourth of July, Breathing Lessons,* and *Oasis,*" Eunjung Kim argues that many cinematic representations of disabled men attempt to sexualize them, usually by means of non-disabled, usually non-white, female prostitutes. The prostitute characters pity, fall for, service, or swindle the male characters, these "once men" who must now pay to participate in their own sexuality and thereby "rehabilitate" their masculinity. She concludes her argument with a contrast to the South Korean film *Oasis*. Whereas the disabled characters in the preceding films are each presented as "a man, with the same feelings they have" (i.e., they are each offered as sexually desiring and deserving intimate attentions from non-disabled women), *Oasis* presents disabled female sexuality as a "deviant" means to a normative end. As Kim puts it, "The film plays on the belief that sexual abuse is a part of the experience of heterosexuality, yet problematically disallowed to disabled women because violent sexual attacks are regarded as "saving" them from asexual genderlessness." She argues that cinematic portrayals

of disabled sexuality rely on heteronormative apparatuses that emphasize the ways in which presumed desexual beings are resexualized into a
humanized presence.

Looking closely at the representations of gender and sexuality in
Million Dollar Baby and *Murderball*, Robert McRuer's essay, "Neoliberal
Risks: *Million Dollar Baby, Murderball*, and Anti-National Sexual Positions," argues that these films are "haunted" by a "proper sexuality"
that supposedly provides stability within a politically and economically
unstable world. Beginning with Fredric Jameson's notion of the comfort of nostalgia in film, McRuer examines how *Million Dollar Baby* positions itself as a "comfort" to millions of viewers, while at the same time
offering death as the radical solution to its recently disabled protagonist. The "currency" for such a disability story, says McRuer, circulates
throughout the film, indicating a homogenized subtext about the "confluence of market and state." Watching Hilary Swank's character, Maggie
Fitzgerald, audiences are schooled, argues McRuer, on "what it means to
be an American." McRuer furthers his argument to look at the ways that
Murderball may—and may not—function as an antithesis to *Million Dollar
Baby*. The nationalism in *Murderball* is more overt and thus also becomes
easier for audiences to challenge in the moment of the viewing. Patriotism as depicted through the disabled individual turns on the responsibility characters express toward the "common good," by remaining personally responsible for their own bodies.

Sharon Snyder and David Mitchell, in their essay, "Body Genres: An
Anatomy of Disability in Film," proceed from their notion of the "cultural location of disability" to discuss viewer identification or, as they
call it, "dis-identification" with visual disability performances. Viewership itself, Snyder and Mitchell argue, provides an opportunity for audiences to play both witness and gazing subject upon marginalized and
exoticized object. They discuss normative views and viewing practices,
critically addressing the "dynamic relationship between viewers and disabled characters." Taking up Linda Williams's argument about excessive
(female) bodies on film, they argue that disabled bodies, within the rubric
of "excess," form a critical nexus in film viewing practices. Simply put,
they point out that disabled bodies in film function as "delivery vehicles"
in order to transfer extreme sensations to audiences, positioning disabled
characters as a physical and emotional "threat" to the supposed "integrity" of the able body. The out-of-control, excessive, disabled body both
slips easily within and challenges the "shared cultural scripts" that audiences recognize as they view disabled characters on-screen. Audiences

approach these cinematic bodies with a social investment that displays disabled bodies as anomalous and incorporates all other bodies within a "masquerade of normalcy."

As a coda to the book, Anne Finger's short story, "'Blinded by the Light' OR: Where's the Rest of Me?" fictionally reassesses the value of disabled bodies as depicted on-screen and as viewers. In her narrative Finger begins with a "fictional character" who is "limping towards a movie theatre." The fictional character gains a name, a social context, and a relationship with the narrator herself. Indeed, Finger presents her character and her narrator engaged in a metafictional relationship that comments on the film viewing experience as much as on film's representations of disabled (female) characters. The narrative layers unfold through the film: the viewing of the film and the telling of that viewing come to readers through Irma's limping body. Refusing to settle on the "cause" of Irma's limp, the narrator manages to convey the importance that question has for readers (and viewers). The story asks, How does *cause* signify identity? Disability, Finger concedes, "requires a narrative." And as she gives one, that narrative grows into a commentary about going to see *Mata Hari*, about "fire-engine red" crutches, and waiting for a friend as endless well-wishers attempt to hold open doors. "Imperfectly blind," Irma's friend, Linda, needs to sit close to the front of the theatre; Irma needs to sit on the left aisle. As Finger's story winds through character development and plot development and narrative development, the plot in the story—so to speak—thickens. Mata Hari falls for a good man, the good man becomes a disabled good man, Mata Hari goes on trial for treason, and her blind lover sees nothing of her impending doom. And Irma and Linda? They fall into the film entranced, but as "THE END" appears on-screen, Linda snaps open her cane and Irma picks up her crutches: The End.

Conclusion

Many scholars who focus on representations of the body come to rely on terminology that refers to physicality as existing within a "sliding" or "floating" scale of subjectivity. The *problem* in relying on such gradation lies in definitions of disability that include, ultimately, virtually every physical signifier indicating *any* deviation for the "ideal" body. As illustrated in the preceding essay descriptions, the focus in *The Problem Body: Projecting Disability on Film* is rather an appraisal of certain focal points on that sliding scale between the normal body and the problem body that scholars here address and that we deem valuable: junctures illuminated by filmic projections that deserve critical consideration.

Does the significance of ever-expanding bodily realities on film permeate the social/political construction of marginal bodies? By analyzing bodies that cultural labels render into "problems," we have turned to disability theory's ongoing attempts to revamp the social model and re-incorporate the body into a cultural model. We look to disability studies to provide a rich methodology for critics to re-enter and re-evaluate complicated filmic narratives that do not simply exploit or resist repeated stereotypes of disability. We argue that such use of disability theory promises to strengthen film analyses, which need to take into account narrative arguments currently at risk of over-dilution and reckon with the role of the panopticon voyeur. The unpredictability of disability—its refusal to be confined within current paradigms of study—leads to a reading of the body as a projection of constantly in-process theoretical shots. In turn, readings of such films through disability theory offer a means by which to grapple anew with the role of the body in film and disability studies.

Works Cited

Althusser, Louis. *For Marx.* Translated by Ben Brewster. London: Verso, 1969.

Blake, William. "The Human Abstract." *Songs of Innocence and Experience: Showing the Two Contrary States of the Human Soul.* Paris, France: Orion Press, 1967.

Bogdan, Robert. *Freak Show: Presenting Human Oddities for Amusement and Profit.* Chicago: University of Chicago Press, 1988.

Breckenridge Carol A. and Candace Vogler. "The Critical Limits of Embodiment: Disability's Criticism." *Public Culture* 13.3 (2001): 349–57.

Charlton, James I. *Nothing about Us without Us: Disability Oppression and Empowerment.* Berkeley: University of California Press, 2000.

Chow, Rey. *Ethics after Idealism: Theory-Culture-Ethnicity-Reading.* Bloomington: Indiana University Press, 1998.

Couser, G. Thomas. *Recovering Bodies: Illness, Disability, and Life Writing.* Madison: University of Wisconsin Press, 1997.

Crenshaw, Kimberlé. "Mapping the Margins: Intersectionality, Identity Politics, and Violence against Women of Color." *Stanford Law Review* 43.6 (1991): 1241–99.

Crutchfield, Susan and Marcy Epstein, eds. *Points of Contact: Disability, Art, and Culture.* Ann Arbor: University of Michigan Press, 2000.

Davidson, Michael. *Concerto for the Left Hand: Disability and the Defamiliar Body.* Ann Arbor: University of Michigan Press, 2008.

Davis, Lennard. *Enforcing Normalcy: Disability, Deafness, and the Body*. London: Verso, 1995.

Doane, Mary Ann. *The Desire to Desire: The Woman's Film of the 1940s*. Theories of Representation and Difference. Bloomington and Indianapolis: Indiana University Press, 1987.

Foucault, Michel. *Madness and Civilization: A History of Insanity in the Age of Reason*. Translated by Richard Howard. New York: Vintage, 1973.

Freud, Anna. *The Ego and the Mechanisms of Defense* (*The Writings of Anna Freud, Volume Two, 1936*). Revised Edition. Translated by Cecil Baines. New York: International Universities Press, 1966.

Garland-Thomson, Rosemarie. *Extraordinary Bodies: Figuring Physical Disability in American Culture and Literature*. New York: Columbia University Press, 1997.

———. "The Politics of Staring: Visual Representations of Disabled People in Popular Culture." In *Disability Studies: Enabling the Humanities*. Edited by Brenda Brueggemann, Rosemarie Garland-Thomson, and Sharon Snyder. New York: MLA Press, 2002. 56–75.

———. *Staring: How We Look*. New York: Oxford University Press, 2009.

hooks, bell. *Reel to Real: Race, Sex, and Class at the Movies*. New York: Routledge, 1996.

Linton, Simi. *Claiming Disability: Knowledge and Identity*. New York: New York University Press, 1998.

Markotić, Nicole. "Coincidence of the Page." *Tessera* 27 (Winter 1999): 6–15.

May, Vivian M. and Beth A. Ferris. "'I'm a Wheelchair Girl Now'": Abjection, Intersectionality, and Subjectivity in Atom Egoyan's *The Sweet Hereafter*." *Women's Studies Quarterly* 30.1/2 (2002): 131–50.

Metz, Christian et al. *The Imaginary Signifier: Psychoanalysis and the Cinema*. Bloomington: Indiana University Press, 1982. MLA International Bibliography. EBSCO. Web. 21 Nov. 2009.

Mitchell, David and Sharon Snyder. *Narrative Prosthesis: Disability and the Dependencies of Discourse*. Ann Arbor: University of Michigan Press, 2000.

Mulvey, Laura. "Visual Pleasure and Narrative Cinema." *Screen* 16.3 (1975): 6–18.

Norden, Martin. *Cinema of Isolation: A History of Physical Disability in the Movies*. New Brunswick, NJ: Rutgers University Press, 1994.

Overboe, Jim. "'Difference in Itself': Validating Disabled People's Lived Experience." *Body & Society* 5.4 (1999): 17–29.

Riley, Charles. *Disability and the Media*. Hanover: University Press of New England, 2005.

Schriempf, Alexa. "(Re)fusing the Amputated Body: An Interactionist Bridge for Feminism and Disability." *Hypatia* 16.4 (2001): 53–79.

Siebers, Tobin. *Disability Theory*. Ann Arbor: University of Michigan Press, 2008.

Snyder, Sharon L. and David T. Mitchell. *Cultural Locations of Disability*. Chicago: University of Chicago Press, 2006.

Titchkosky, Tanya. *Disability, Self, and Society*. Toronto: University of Toronto Press, 2003.

———. *Reading and Writing Disability Differently: The Textured Life of Embodiment*.

Toronto: University of Toronto Press, 2007.

Wendell, Susan. *The Rejected Body: Feminist Philosophical Reflections on Disability.* New York: Routledge, 1996.

Williams, Linda. "Film Bodies: Gender, Genre, and Excess." *Film Genre Reader, III.* 141–59. Austin: University of Texas Press, 2003. MLA International Bibliography. EBSCO. Web. 21 Nov. 2009.

James Apperson (John Gilbert), amputee veteran. *The Big Parade.* Directed by King Vidor. MGM, 1925.

TIMOTHY BARNARD

"The Whole Art of a Wooden Leg"

King Vidor's Picturization of Laurence Stallings's "Great Story"

So in discussing the whole art of a wooden leg, let it be understood that this impedimental aid to locomotion ties one to the wooden things of life.
—Laurence Stallings, "The Whole Art of a Wooden Leg: An Essay," March 1923

I pictured Laurence Stallings the author, among the men of that platoon. He surely must [have] been there!
—Robert M. Finch, "An Overseas Veteran's Impressions of *The Big Parade*," November 1925

The picture is nothing less than a triumph for Vidor. His handling of "scenes" is great, while the "Inside" stuff that Stallings has slipped him consummates a flavoring vein ever present.
—Review of *The Big Parade*, Variety, December 2, 1925

The penultimate scene of MGM's 1925 WWI epic *The Big Parade* depicts protagonist Jim Apperson's poignant homecoming after the war. In a long shot showing Jim (John Gilbert) coming through the entryway on crutches, his family and the film audience see for the first time that one of his legs has been amputated. After a reaction shot zooms in to a close-up of his mother's anguished face, she embraces him and the audience

I presented a version of this paper at the NYU Modernism Conference, February 2002, on the panel "Modern Bodies in Crisis." Panel Chair John Honerkamp, fellow panelists Suzanne del Gizzo, Gillian White, and Nancy Nield Buchwald, and audience members all provided insightful and encouraging feedback that helped develop many of the ideas and arguments here. A number of friends and colleagues also generously shared invaluable insights and editorial suggestions. For this I would like to thank Matt Cohen, Michael Blum, Kelly Gray, Caroline Nichols, Jennifer Blanchard, Gretchen Schoel, Robert Nelson, and Magali Compan. I am also indebted to the collection editors Sally Chivers and Nicole Markotić for their editorial assistance, patience, and many helpful suggestions. Additionally, I am indebted to one of this collection's peer reviewers for insights on John Barrymore's career as not only an idealized matinee idol but also an actor who pursued performances of physically disabled masculinity.

sees (through a double-exposed mini-narrative) her memories of her son growing up with two legs. This flashback montage culminates with a medium shot of Jim's lower half showing one intact leg and what appears to be the stump of the other. The film, however, does not end on this note of high pathos. Jim and his mother withdraw to an interior room where he confesses his love for a peasant girl in France. With his mother's blessing, and fitted with a prosthetic leg, Jim returns to France where, in the film's final scene, he and the young woman, Melisande, run across fields to one another. The film ends with their climactic embrace and the closing credit. This ending would conform to melodramatic formula but for Gilbert's distinctive limp-running gait.

During the filming of *The Big Parade*, MGM head Louis B. Mayer was shocked when he heard that the studio's romantic star, John Gilbert, would be depicted as an amputee with his lower leg bound up in a harness. He insisted that the scene be reshot to depict instead a wounded but intact leg (Vidor, *King Vidor* 74). Mayer, worried about the studio's fortunes, and Gilbert, worried about his own career aspirations, both thought that images of a veteran's dismembered body might prove too disturbing for American postwar film audiences. King Vidor, the film's director, insisted on including the image of an amputated leg, and after test audiences received it enthusiastically, MGM released the film using the original homecoming sequence. *The Big Parade* went on to an unprecedented ninety-six-week run at New York's Astor Theatre and a highly lucrative road show. It grossed the highest box-office receipts of the silent era and boosted the careers of Mayer, Irving Thalberg, Vidor, and Gilbert. Mayer's MGM grossed over $19 million with the film and became a major studio, Thalberg prospered as Hollywood's production boy wonder, and Vidor became a sought-after directorial auteur gaining creative autonomy and bigger film budgets. The film also established Gilbert as a top male star of silent cinema and marked what he later called "the high point of my career" (Brownlow 187–93).

With Gilbert's performance as Jim Apperson culminating in a presentation of his body as physically less than it once was, the film creates a new kind of problematic yet appealing male star portrayed as both romantically desirable and physically disabled. Both more and less of a man, Gilbert's Apperson serves as a simultaneously realized and diminished masculine icon, as the film transforms postwar manhood into a cinematic spectacle simultaneously embodied and disembodied, both dismembered and redeemed. Audiences of the1920s received the film as unprecedentedly "real" despite the tricked representation of an ablated body serving as a key source of its claim to realism.

In *The Big Parade* the absent, as a referent to what was once present, serves as a means of representing something more convincingly "real" than the physically material. This absent presence operates on two convergent levels in the film: both in its textual properties as an immaterial shadow image of a previously present material world and in its narrative construction of a male body first presented as physically whole, -abled, and normative and then amputated, disabled, and physically diminished. As such, the film draws upon what David T. Mitchell has identified as a strategy of "narrative prosthesis" that renders disability as a means of lending "a distinctive idiosyncrasy to any characters that differentiate themselves from the anonymous background of the norm" (17). And yet while Mitchell argues that all literary narratives, in their dependency on disability, "operate out of a desire to compensate for a limitation or to reign in an excessiveness," *The Big Parade*'s film narrative appears to turn such desire on its head. "Disability inaugurates narrative," Mitchell asserts, "but narrative inevitably punishes its own prurient interests by overseeing the extermination of the object of its fascination" (20). In *The Big Parade*, however, the presentation of Jim Apperson's newly disabled body culminates rather than inaugurates the film's narrative and, as such, serves as a sign of contradictory masculine realization and a fetishized object of melodramatic fascination. Ultimately, the film's power as a cultural text resides in its projection and symbolic resolution of a convergence of perceived modern crises—of postwar manhood, of soldiers' physical mutilation and disability, and of what is "real" and right in a world shaped by both destructive and creative technological forces. The film offers a cultural response to the technological destruction of WWI by replacing it with a cinematic construction narrating change as both loss and regeneration and portraying a (dis)embodied problem body made both more and less than whole and exemplary.

Besides being a boon for MGM and its team of filmmakers, the success of *The Big Parade* also validated and valorized Laurence Stallings, the veteran amputee whose military service and wounding in the war inspired the film's narrative. As its promotional posters announce, *The Big Parade* was "King Vidor's Picturization of Laurence Stallings'[s] Great Story." In the 1920s, Stallings established himself as a prominent intellectual American veteran of WWI with powerful credentials of both cultural and masculine authenticity. As a Marine officer wounded in action, an author, a playwright, and, ultimately, a Hollywood screenwriter, Stallings achieved period fame as a producer, a reviewer, and an embodiment—both literally and figuratively—of "the real thing." Stallings's war-inflicted disability provided him with problematic cultural capital that placed him in a unique position to tell, judge, and contribute to a "great story" of the Great War deemed distinctively "real."

Stallings's contribution to the *The Big Parade*'s contradictory claims to postwar realism reflect early-twentieth-century dilemmas centering on the knotted relationship among manhood, modernity, technology, visual culture, and questions of absent presence and "the real." As Scott McQuire has observed in *Visions of Modernity*, cinema contributed to the modern dilemma of the "real" because "cinematic images not only depicted motion in new ways[;] . . . they combined 'realism' with a unique immateriality and mutability. The shift from a regime of stable, fixed or monumental images to images which are transitory, immaterial and incessantly labile, marks the fundamental threshold of modern experience" (66). Thus the power and appeal of Stallings's disabled subjectivity—capable of representing the body's status as labile and mutable—provided him with a powerful cultural agency as it intersected with the medium of Hollywood film. "Far from shoring up the real," McQuire argues, "cinema accentuates its ambiguity. Opting for neither one nor the other, cinema finally cannot choose between faking reality and the reality of its own fakes" (72).

Such problematic yet dynamically promising negotiations among the body, modernity, realism, and absent presence saturate cultural preoccupations of the post-WWI period. As Jani Scandura and Michael Thurston argue in *Modernism, Inc.*, the tomb of the unknown soldier (the dedication of which Stallings dramatizes in the conclusion of his novel *Plumes*) represents "not so much anonymous corpses as named absences—[but instead] the emptiness of the corpse as a sign and the hollowness of the image that we have buried and refuse to bury with the corpse" (3). In the case of Stallings's body, as a living but disabled body rather than a corpse, it manages to serve as an absent (yet, as the above-quoted reviewer of *The Big Parade* put it, seemingly "ever present") inspiration for a performance of these same traumas, yet one that also allows for a tacked-on fantasy of cinematic-cum-prosthetic resolution through regeneration.

In his authorship and criticism, and in his contribution to *The Big Parade*, Stallings's status as a uniquely "real" individual relied inextricably on his amputated leg—the irrefutable proof that he had served in the war and made a profound physical sacrifice for his country. Prior to his contribution to *The Big Parade*, Stallings had rendered his experience of war and wounding through literary and critical prose and through coauthorship of a Broadway play. In these earlier endeavors, his war wound proved a simultaneously powerful and problematic sign of both exceptional masculinity and exceptional masculine loss. With his contribution to *The Big Parade,* Stallings's ablated leg and prosthesis became the sources of and inspiration for a powerful new cinematic realism. In an ironic essay written for *The Smart Set* in 1923, Stallings describes his prosthesis as an "impedimental aid" and characterizes his postwar creative efforts as those of an artist in search of "The Whole Art of A Wooden Leg." This search coincides with what Scandura and Thurston call "the High Modernist aesthetic dream of wholeness in fragmentation" (3). And yet Stallings came closest to achieving such an art through the "low" modernist mass medium of Hollywood film. Just as a wooden prosthesis makes one ostensibly whole, Stallings found in Hollywood a creative medium that could magically represent him as newly whole—both physically and as a more wholly realized creative voice of postwar modernism. With this filmic agency, however, came sacrifices, compromises, and a process of absenting certain aspects of his perspective as a disabled veteran.[1]

From the Page, to the Stage, to the Silent Screen

The Problems and Promise of (Re)presenting a War Wound

In the transition from novelist and essayist to playwright and screenwriter, Stallings shifted his focus away from the details of his physical disability and toward the experiences of trench warfare in Europe. Both were unfamiliar to most Americans, yet the latter held greater appeal as an intriguingly exotic yet comfortably distant "reality." With the failure of his first and only novel, *Plumes,* based on his experiences as a disabled veteran back in the United States, Stallings discovered that the details of postwar disability could prove to be too "real" and too close to home.

With a far more damning antiwar message than *The Big Parade*'s, *Plumes* depicts a soldier's bitter re-entry into American civilian life and his frustrated efforts to fight against the social phenomenon of war. Unlike *The Big Parade,* where Jim Apperson returns home at the end of the film with his leg amputated, Stallings's novel opens back in the United States after the war and with the autobiographical protagonist Richard Plume's leg badly damaged yet still intact. The novel centers on an omni*present* wound as it haunts and tortures the protagonist from the outset. In possession of its own agency, Plume's "raging knee" (147) tortures him and

---

1. For a historical analysis of post-WWI disability that focuses on British veterans—and that has informed this essay's consideration of cultural actors and texts—see Joanna Bourke's *Dismembering the Male.*

the novel's narrative in general. Throughout the novel, Stallings portrays the wounded leg as an autonomous character that literally speaks to his protagonist and taunts him with its ability to inflict pain: "'A thousand miles walking,' it flamed up to his brain, 'couldn't make any one as tired as I can make you, old boy.' It flickered maliciously as he rolled to the floor and projected himself across the carpet with long, lunging swoops" (147). Doctors amputate the wounded leg only toward the novel's end so that its unrelenting presence—as opposed to a traumatizing absence—dominates Plume's consciousness and constitutes the novel's central narrative tension.

With his novel *Plumes*, Stallings chose not to write about life in the trenches but to focus instead on the experience of returning to the home front as a wounded veteran whom people saw as a freakish spectacle and an object of pity. Subjected to stares of horror and guilt, Plume confronts postwar America's paradoxical indifference to and awkward fascination with the situation of its disabled veterans. Critics, however, panned *Plumes* and characterized it as an artless book marred by the author's preoccupation with his disability.[2] The novel went immediately out of print, and Stallings responded to the damning critical reactions by later trying to have his own novel suppressed shortly after the publication of its first and only edition.

For his next project, Stallings co-authored the play *What Price Glory?*, a war-front drama based on his combat experiences in France that became a Broadway sensation. Like *Plumes*, *What Price* sought to intervene in romanticized portrayals of war by offering a more realistic alternative. Unlike *Plumes*, however, the play—with its depiction of the chaos and violence of the trenches together with its frank use of profanities in the soldier's dialogue—received critical acclaim as an exceptionally "realistic" portrayal of modern warfare. Whereas Stallings's novel centers on the omnipresence of a problematic war wound after the fact and does not include any depiction of the war itself, *What Price* depicts, exclusively, life in and near the trenches where the specter of getting wounded simul-

---

2. Most reviews of *Plumes*, like Robert Littell's in *The New Republic*, acknowledge a certain power in the novel while dismissing it as flawed in more general literary terms and in relation to Stallings's treatment of his disability. "If *Plumes*," Littell writes, "by reason of its narrowness, its singleness of suffering is not an interesting book, nor its characters very real, except in that core of themselves which feels and suffers really deeply, it is far harder to forget than many a more interesting book." In a note to his editor, F. Scott Fitzgerald is far less equivocal in his assessment of the novel. He condemns it as "disappointingly rotten" and describes Stallings as lacking the "genius to whine appealingly" (82). Hard-boiled novelist and critic Jim Tully dismisses Stallings as someone whose amputated leg impairs his creative abilities. "The war seems to have robbed Stallings of two things," Tully declares, "a leg and a sense of humour. His attitude toward it is still sophomoric. One would think that he and Pershing were the only men who went over the top and suffered in their country's cause" (46).

taneously haunts and tempts the play's protagonists as both a threatening and a potentially liberating possibility. Unlike *Plumes*, the war play allowed American audiences to focus on experiences clearly separated from their day-to-day lives, including the presence of disabled veterans such as Richard Plume and Stallings. The play could give its audiences a safe, imaginary entry into a distant, and thus more comfortably "real," albeit violent and nightmarish, setting. Everything about the play (its subject, setting, and presentation) remained safely apart from the lived experience of Americans on the home front. As audiences bought tickets and filled theatres to see this theatrical reenactment of distant trench warfare, *What Price* proved far more palatable than Stallings's earlier prose rendering of a disabled veteran's ongoing struggles back home.

After its release in 1925, the unprecedented success of *The Big Parade* would overshadow both Stallings's novel and his Broadway play as the most lasting and widely received representation of his war experience and postwar problem body. In attendance at the film's opening night at the Astor Theatre, the *New York Times* reviewer, Mordaunt Hall, describes its power as "an eloquent pictorial epic of the World War" that had stirred its audience to both "laughter and tears":

> This powerful photodrama . . . [has] been converted to the screen from a story by Laurence Stallings, co-author of "What Price Glory," and directed by King Vidor. It is a subject so compelling and realistic that one feels impelled to approach a review of it with all the respect it deserves, for as a motion picture it is something beyond the fondest dreams of most people.

As Hall's review illustrates: "Laurence Stallings, [as] co-author of 'What Price Glory'" proved central to the film's reception as "compelling and realistic." Thus through the medium of the silent cinema photodrama, Stallings—with the help of Vidor, Thalberg, and MGM Studios—successfully translated his wartime experience of physical mutilation into something that appealed to American audiences as it carried them "beyond [their] fondest dreams."

Kicked in the Head by Disembodied Manhood

King Vidor's Epiphany of Cinematic Realism

In an interview with Kenneth Brownlow, King Vidor describes the creative inspiration at the root of *The Big Parade:*

> Stallings had been a Marine, and had been at Belleau Wood, and had lost a leg. That's why I had Gilbert lose a leg in the picture; he copied Stallings's leg movement for the last scene. Stallings was the biggest source of inspiration about the war. (Brownlow 188)

Thalberg saw *What Price* in New York, sought out Stallings, and brought him to Hollywood to work on the film. Having offered a short summary treatment for the film, Stallings returned to New York by train accompanied Vidor. The young filmmaker later recalled a career-changing epiphany he had during that train voyage—one brought on by the violently inspirational and undeniable "realness" of Stallings's physical loss and compensating prosthesis:

> Late into the night the war reminiscing would go on. Towards morning, when I'd hear Stallings snoring above, I'd tell myself that it was time to relax and get to sleep. But the horrors and details of Chateau-Thierry and Metz had me too excited for sleep. I kept saying to myself, "This is all too fantastic and unreal. It never happened." One night, as I sat in my lower berth with eyes closed, the train started a violent swaying action. Stallings's wooden leg, hanging on a wall hook, swung in a wide arc with the motion of the train and the heavy brogue on the wooden foot kicked me hard in the chin. When I recovered from the blow, the evidence of the swaying leg with the sock and shoe still on it was all too real. I could never again say to myself that the horrors of war didn't happen; I accepted the facts. I have often wondered if this timely blow on the chin didn't contribute much to the reality and later success of the film. (Vidor, *A Tree* 74–75)

This remarkable moment suggested to Vidor the potential of a supplement or proxy to communicate truth and assert itself as an undeniably real thing. Swaying with the train's machine-generated rhythm, Stallings's disembodied prosthesis—as Vidor characterizes it—comes to life as a seemingly vengeful spirit of the technologically driven violence of the Great War. The leg (with the assistance of the train) does not allow Vidor to dismiss the destructive power that technology could wield. For him, it was not just Stallings's prosthetic leg that had kicked him in the face; it was also the hard truth about the war and all that Stallings and men like him had experienced. Vidor's epiphany—how to make a powerful narrative film—proves to be one best characterized as both literally and figuratively inspired by the phenomenon of "narrative prosthesis" in line with Mitchell's explanation of his "coinage of the phrase 'narrative prosthesis'" as a means of arguing that "disability has been used throughout history as a crutch on which literary narratives lean for their representational power, disruptive potentiality, and social critique" (17). Vidor, however, would use the inspiration of "narrative prosthesis" for a film rather than literary narrative and thus would wind up including powerful—though equivocal—visual narrative commentary on the problematic "social construction of disability itself" (17).

This "prosthetic" moment on the train with Stallings inspired Vidor as a filmmaker by providing him with the means for achieving a similar in-your-face shock using the film medium in a way that could counteract audience's efforts to dismiss it as fiction, just as he had tried to dismiss Stallings's war stories as "too fantastic and unreal." Getting kicked by Stallings's prosthetic leg made Vidor realize that (to draw upon Mitchell's characterization of disability's role in narrative constructions), "disability [could] serve as the 'hard kernel' or recalcitrant corporeal matter that cannot be deconstructed away" (17). As Vidor tells his story, the proxy for Stallings's missing leg struck him with the realization of how to create a cinematic realism that could also be a powerful proxy for the real. Stallings's wooden leg simultaneously communicated masculine loss and a regenerative new potency as a kind of ideal phallus that remains eternally rigid, even while Stallings sleeps.

Having had the inspiration for how to make *The Big Parade* a powerfully real war epic kicked into his head by Stallings's disembodied prosthesis, Vidor went on to construct recurring images of the protagonist's legs performing as if they had an agency of their own. Through close-ups, framing, and clever manipulation of the mise-en-scène, Jim Apperson's legs practically become autonomous characters in the film. The focus on Jim's two legs in scene after scene sets the stage for the film's melodramatic climax which depicts only one leg and the other's disturbing partial absence. At the film's outset, Jim's two feet (and the goading of "the girl next door") get him into the war. When the "Big Parade" of recruitment passes through his hometown, the marching band's marshal beat appeals to Jim's feet. In close-ups crosscut with medium shots of his torso, we see his feet tapping in rhythm with the drumming, seemingly of their own volition. These same feet carry Jim into the parade to join his friends on their way to enlist.

Jim's legs really come into their own once he arrives in France and initiates his courtship of Melisande. In a patently Chaplinesque instance of slapstick, for example, Jim first meets Melisande as he stumbles through the streets of her village with a barrel over his head. Harking back to silent cinema's roots, such physical humor punctuates *The Big Parade*'s first half. In the second half, a physical gravitas of wounding and mutila-

tion replaces this physical humor. The barrel-over-the-head gag also contributes to the film's disembodied leg motif, for, with the barrel coming
down to his waist, Melisande first meets Jim's legs on their own. At their
second meeting, she identifies him from the unraveling leg puttee he
unwittingly drags through the mud. In a flirtatious exchange, Melisande
volunteers to rewrap the puttee, and this leads to a charged intimate contact with her fondling his muddied leg. In both this scene and the film's
promotional poster, Jim's leg serves as a suggestively phallic allusion to
the sexual tension between the French peasant woman and the American
doughboy.

As the lovers' courtship develops, the film draws attention to Jim's legs
so frequently that Melisande seems to have a relationship with them on
their own. Close-ups feature Jim's legs and feet again and again. One scene
includes close-ups of him polishing his boots before a date; in another
sequence his legs hang from a hay wagon as Melisande talks to them and
then shakes them to attention while the rest of Jim's body remains off-
screen. The lovers' poignant farewell amid the evacuation of Jim's battalion
to the front culminates with Melisande clinging to Jim's leg. Once again,
the framing cuts off the rest of his body as he climbs up into a truck. As the
truck pulls away, Jim throws one of his boots to Melisande as a last sou-
venir. She holds it up triumphantly and then falls to the ground clutching
it to her breast. The film's first half ends with a long shot of Melisande
alone on an empty road as she holds Jim's boot. With this shot, Vidor ends
the film's first half with a desolate image serving as a counterpoint to the
frenzy of the evacuation sequence. As he later described it, "Where minutes
before had been frantic confusion, there was now lonely solitude. In the
roadway crouched the girl alone with the boot. Nothing marred the stillness as the scene slowly faded out" (*A Tree* 78). This visual transition from
a frenetic and cluttered mise-en-scène to one of "lonely solitude" and still
desolation prefigures the climax of the film's second half that also moves
from fullness to absence with the tense stillness of Jim's homecoming following a visual crescendo of chaotic battle sequences. For the film's final
scene, however, Vidor added a redemptive coda—a cinematic prosthesis
coinciding with Jim's prosthetic leg—that depicts a romantic union and a
happy return to seeming wholeness.

Jim Apperson's Jazzy New Gait

The Contrapuntal Rhythm of Disability

The film's famous evacuation sequence exemplifies what Vidor describes as his experimentation with creating cinematic "silent music." Attuned to how movement before the camera and the later act of editing could create "distinctive rhythms . . . blended into a total symphonic effect," Vidor sought to exploit such rhythms and effects as a means of contributing to the dramatic power of his film narratives. In the case of *The Big Parade*'s evacuation sequence, he uses this silent music "to achieve a powerful surge of emotion just before the theatre lights went up for intermission." He describes another example of this technique in a battle scene with men slowly marching through a grove of pine trees meant to replicate the U.S. Marine's offensive at Belleau Wood. In preparing for this sequence, Vidor studied "almost [one] hundred reels of documentary film made during World War I" by the U.S. Army's Signal Corps (some of which were later integrated into *The Big Parade*'s battle sequences). Viewing this footage provided him with a promising inspiration for creating his visual silent music:

> One day . . . I was struck by the fact that a company of men were passing the camera at a cadence decidedly different from the usual ones. It was a rhythm of suspended animation and their movement suggested an ominous event. There was no sound track, but the whole pattern spelled death. Then a flag-draped coffin came into view on top of a horse drawn caisson. The men were in a funeral cortege. The thought struck me that if I could duplicate this slow, measured cadence as my American troops approached the front line, I could illustrate the proximity of death with a telling and powerful effect. I was in the realm of my favourite obsession, experimenting with the possibilities of "silent music." (*A Tree* 76)

Using "a metronome and a drummer with a bass drum [who] amplified the metronomic ticks," Vidor instructed all actors and extras "that each step must be taken on a drum beat, each turn of the head, lift of a rifle, pull of a trigger, in short, every physical move must occur on the beat of a drum." Later reflecting on one British extra's complaint that he felt he was performing "some bloody ballet," Vidor explains, "I did not say so at the time, but that is exactly what it was—a bloody ballet, a ballet of death" (76–78). In orchestrating his "bloody ballet of death," Vidor adds a visually rhythmic component to his film's antiwar message: Soldiers who march in metronomic time march to a militaristic and mechanical rhythm linked to the unprecedented death and technological destruction of WWI. Thus the film implicitly critiques the standardized physical movements of a military march that require men to move their bodies in a uniform cadence and, as such, contribute to a militaristic display of a normative masculine body. Having carefully orchestrated images of controlled and standardized body movement, Vidor then replaces it with images of an individually distinctive physical movement inspired by Stallings's disabled body and its gait. In short, Stallings's body provides the film with a rhythmic counterpoint for its conclusion.

As Vidor explains, Stallings's distinctive gait inspired the culminating instance of the film's visual "silent music": "That's why I had Gilbert lose a leg in the picture; he copied Stallings's leg movement for the last scene" (*King Vidor* 58). This movement results in a closing counterpoint to the earlier rhythm of the death march. Where the metronomic march through the woods had been Vidor's "bloody . . . ballet of death," the film's final sequence—with Jim hobbling to Melisande in "a cadence decidedly different from the usual"—represents a visual equivalent of a modern, syncopated jazz solo—music of a U.S. postwar era characterized by improvisation and the irregular accenting of downbeats. The ending of the film represents a visual American musical counterpoint to the earlier visual symphony of death in a European theatre of war. Having depicted images of the war's death and carnage using carefully synchronized visual rhythms that Vidor associates with European musical forms such as the symphony and the ballet, he then ends the film using a jazz-like syncopated gait of disability that aligns the film's redemptive conclusion with the national optimism of the U.S. postwar Jazz Age. Jim Apperson, a wounded survivor of the war's European death marches, leaves the drumbeat of The Big Parade behind and, as a new man fitted with a wooden leg, jerks his new body to an independent new rhythm of international love and healing. Just as Vidor's bloody ballet of death prefigures the counterpoint of Jim's jazzy postwar gait of disability, so too does Vidor's visual motif of Jim's disembodied legs precondition the final revelation of his missing leg and its ultimate replacement with a prosthesis. The normative soldier's body linked to the death and destruction of the war enables the counterpoint for a veteran's disabled body tied to new postwar hopes represented as individualistic, transcendentally different, and ultimately redeemed.

The Big Parade's New Leading Man

Crossing the Romantic Heartthrob with the Tortured Freak

Using MGM's romantic star property John Gilbert and Laurence Stallings's body as an inspiration, Vidor made the actor's body deliver a new kind of physical, fallible, and more "realistic" star performance. Vidor describes altering Gilbert's "personal style of make-up and dress" for the film and explains, "I decided that in his new character of down-to-earth doughboy, he would use no make-up, and wear an ill-fitting uniform. Dirty finger-nails and a sweaty, begrimed face were to take the place of perfectly made-up skin texture" (*A Tree* 75). In addition to changes in make-up, hygiene, and skin texture, Vidor also manipulated Gilbert's body by using a harness to conceal the lower half of one of his legs. With amputation representing one of the most irrefutable signs of service and sacrifice in the war, Vidor concealed part of Gilbert's leg as a means of linking physical absence with "realism" in his construction of the "character of down-to-earth doughboy." As Stallings's irreverent self-description put it—making an ironic reference to the prosthesis he used—his status as an amputee made him someone uniquely "tied to the wooden things of life."

In emphasizing (and constructing) Gilbert's body as fallible, Vidor risked de-emphasizing the idealized handsome face that, up to that point, had been the key to his star status. In the end, Gilbert's portrayal of the physically disabled Jim Apperson succeeded as a groundbreaking performance of postwar manhood. The performance, however, was not entirely unprecedented as a cinematic depiction of injured masculinity. It was, rather, an innovative crossing of Gilbert's romantically desirable star qualities with those of an alternative, yet highly influential, star persona: the silent-film phenomenon Lon Chaney whose portrayals of physically tortured characters had established his unique stardom beginning with his lead role in the 1920 film *The Penalty*.

In playing the romantic, handsome male lead who appealed (and was marketed) to female audiences in the 1920s, Gilbert had to compete with other, more established matinee idols, including, among others, Douglas Fairbanks, John Barrymore, and Rudolph Valentino. Gaylyn Studlar has compared these men's star personae to that of Lon Chaney, whose silent-era stardom marked a radical departure from their brand of physically idealized masculinity. As Studlar points out, Chaney, one of the silent era's biggest box-office draws, played an entirely different kind of male lead that "embodied a startling rejection of [their] character-building, cult-of-the-body norms" (201). Where stars such as Fairbanks, Barrymore, and Valentino (and Gilbert) performed images of virility and physical perfection, Chaney portrayed "the grotesque body and the male body in pain" (8). In *The Big Parade*, elements of Chaney's alternative star persona combined with Gilbert's standing as a romantic male lead and, together, resulted in a contradictory new postwar masculine type.

Chaney achieved his stardom playing mentally and emotionally tortured characters who also had physical disabilities—most famously in *The Hunchback of Notre Dame* (1923) and *The Phantom of the Opera* (1925). The marketing of Chaney's pictures, Studlar explains, targeted male audiences, and his depiction of tortured and mutable physicality could not have been further from the physically idealized and sexually objectified star bodies of actors cast as matinee heartthrobs for female moviegoers. Studlar reads Chaney's unique and overlooked significance as an alternative male star of the silent era in connection with the cultural legacy of the freak show: "Chaney's variations on the grotesque male body create a radical contrast with the beautiful male body foregrounded for the audience's specular consumption of Barrymore, Valentino, and, albeit in less explicitly sexual ways, of Fairbanks" (201). In *The Big Parade*, Gilbert's role as Jim Apperson portrays a male body that manages to be simultaneously grotesque and romantically desirable. With his homecoming as a wounded veteran, the film portrays Jim as someone who loses a leg but "gets the girl." The film's remarkable success (which brought unprecedented numbers of men and women to the box office) can be attributed in part to Vidor's decision to cast Gilbert, an idealized heartthrob, in a role that borrowed elements from Chaney's physically tortured "freak" persona.[3]

Vidor later acknowledges Chaney as the inspiration for creating the illusion of physical mutilation in *The Big Parade*. "I had seen Lon Chaney in *The Penalty*," he explained, "with both of his legs strapped up and we figured that if Chaney could do it, Gilbert could do it. We worked out some sort of harness" (*King Vidor* 58). In an earlier MGM film, *He Who Got Slapped* (1924), Gilbert plays opposite Chaney in a romantic supporting role that serves as a counterpoint to Chaney's lead role as a masochistic clown. With *The Big Parade*, the earlier, contrasting star performances melded into one romantically freakish character.[4] As a result, much of Studlar's description of Chaney's alternative male stardom fits *The Big Parade*'s Jim Apperson:

> Chaney's roles offered a revelation . . . of masculinity allowed to be failed and freakish. The masculine self exposed in Chaney's films was in the freak show mold of the Other constructed in contradictory terms: stigmatized and yet aggrandized, grotesque and yet still romantically capable of suffering for love. This male suffering is totally unlike that of the Barrymore hero. (210)

---

3. For a discussion of how a similar "enfreaking" of "war-injured bodies" played out contemporaneously in propaganda and modernist literature of the 1920s, see Thomas Fahy's "Enfreaking War-Injured Bodies," 529–63.

4. For a detailed theoretical and historical analysis of the social construction of freaks that seeks to "develop an understanding of past practices and changing conceptions of human variation," see Robert Bogdan's article in Rosemarie Garland-Thomson (ed.), *Freakery: Cultural Spectacles of the Extraordinary Body* (23).

Gilbert's role in *The Big Parade* combines in one character what Studlar characterizes as oppositional male types "totally unlike" one another. The portrayal of Jim Apperson demonstrates how much more contradictory postwar masculine performance becomes when portrayed as a simultaneously stigmatized, aggrandized, and romanticized grotesque capable of suffering physically and for love and ultimately uniting with his female love interest. By drawing upon Laurence Stallings's actual veteran's body and employing the cinematic tricks of Lon Chaney's performance of freakish masculinity, *The Big Parade* presented a new kind of male star spectacle that was both romantically desirable and physically disabled in a way that appealed to audiences of both men and women as an unprecedentedly "real" instance of postwar manhood.[5]

Conclusion
Hollywood Film as Prosthesis—
Stallings's "WholeArt of a Wooden Leg"

In his 1923 essay, "The Whole Art of a Wooden Leg," Stallings irreverently describes living in New York City facing the frustrations, embarrassments, and exhilarating perils he experienced as a amputee veteran—"one of those soldiers who shed a leg or two for the cause of liberty bonds" (107).

---

5. Rudolph Valentino's sadomasochistic performance in *The Son of Sheik* (1926)—a departure from his earlier roles—and Charles Farrell's role as a wounded veteran in Frank Borzage's *Seventh Heaven* (1927) both illustrate the groundbreaking influence of Gilbert's role in *The Big Parade*. Both these highly successful silent film performances followed in the years just after *The Big Parade*. Furthermore, John Barrymore developed his early cinematic roles of the 1920s—which Studlar characterizes as a "woman-made object" of eroticized desire for a young, perfect, soft-focus male body (93–102)—toward more tormented characters, and characters depicting a variety of physical body types and movements. Barrymore's career in fact reveals one harbinger of the kind of marriage of a Chaneyesque freak with the dominant idealized matinee idol achieved by *The Big Parade*: Barrymore's cinematic breakthrough role in *Dr. Jekyll and Mr. Hyde* (1920). Barrymore's "younger and more attractive" (Studlar 129) variation on Stevenson's original Dr. Jekyll is accompanied by a physically gruesome counterpart in his performance of Hyde. The latter, however, is ultimately eliminated and expunged from that ideal young body as what Studlar characterizes as a "eugenicist's nightmare of masculinity" (130). While the Jekyll/Hyde narrative reinforces the clear antithesis between an ideal masculine body and its excessively freakish counterpart, Gilbert's performance as a physically disabled matinee idol concludes *The Big Parade* by leaving the two types as one new version of desirable, disabled, postwar masculinity. In the wake of that precedent, Barrymore went on to play the hunchback Richard III in a cinematic reprise of his earlier theatrical performance, as well as Herman Melville's peg-legged Ahab twice, in *The Sea Beast* (1926) and *Moby Dick* (1930). For a more detailed discussion of Barrymore's film career shaped by "Hollywood's objectification of masculinity for female spectators in the 1920s," see Studlar (95). For another theoretical discussion of female spectatorship and Hollywood masculinity during the silent era and, in particular, the sadomasochistic turn in Valentino's later films, see Miriam Hansen, *Babel and Babylon*, 287–94; on Farrell and Borzage and a reading of Farrell's performance of wounded masculinity in *Seventh Heaven*, see Pat Kirkham, "Loving Men," 94–112.

Stallings explains frankly to whom his tongue-in-cheek essay is directed: "I address myself primarily to my public, that army of men and women who eye me suspiciously in the church, the theatre, and the busy marts of trade; to those who are highly curious about this unsatisfactory adjunct to locomotion." Aware of the spectacle he and his prosthesis make in the streets and public venues of Manhattan, Stallings reacts with the prescribed authorial tone of the day: a modernist's balance of irony and pity. The essay reaches its painfully comic climax at the theatre where Stallings finds himself unable to escape into the easy anonymous role of the spectator as his wooden leg, once again, takes on a problematic life of its own:

> I became absorbed in a drama unfolding itself upon the stage and paid scant heed to the erring foot. The hero of the play was kissing his sweetheart in fond farewell, while offstage the drums of his gallant regiment were thumping martially. The drum beats evoked memories, and while its owner became stirred by them the ubiquitous extremity crept forward and nestled companionably among the feet of the woman ahead. I was first made aware of this highly objectionable familiarity, impersonal though it certainly was, by the woman's mother who turned and glared for a moment before denouncing me in firm, well heard tones. The experienced uniped theatre-goer should learn to park his badge of patriotism in the aisle.

Upon leaving New York for Hollywood and working with Vidor and Thalberg at MGM, Stallings gained access to another place where he could safely place "his badge of patriotism" which was so prone to turning into an uncontrollable, unwanted sign of potent yet problematic masculinity: onto the silent silver screen. Through the regenerative magic of the Hollywood narrative, Stallings contributed to the displacement of (or at least an alternative to) the romanticized military pap performed in the theatres he attended as a critic. By working with Stallings, Vidor—who could draw on the vast resources and filmmaking apparatus of the burgeoning Hollywood studio system—took the veteran's story and disabled body and successfully "picturized" them (as the film's poster proclaims) as a means of crafting a new form of cinematic "realism."

While making *The Big Parade*, Vidor saw himself as working in conjunction with Stallings on a powerful antiwar statement "from the realistic GI viewpoint" and in a way that "cut out all the bunk, all the fantasies and insincerities about the war [because it] happened to be the way we both wrote" (*King Vidor* 73). Years later Vidor came to view the film more critically and in a 1974 interview declares, "I don't encourage people to see [it]" (Baxter 21). Vidor's later dismissal of a film he had previously characterized as groundbreakingly realistic indicates a hindsight acknowledgment of the film's melodramatic elements and "realistic" shortcomings. Indeed, the film's melodrama, as much as its realism, shaped its depiction of war as one designed to help Americans make sense of, rationalize, and accept the historical trauma of a deeply irrational mass destruction.

In his novel *Plumes*, Stallings renders a far more bitter narrative about the experience of returning from war as a painfully wounded and physically disabled veteran. Through an ironic and debunking use of overblown diction and euphemistic clichés, *Plumes* challenges comfortable melodramas and romantic depictions of wounded warriors who fling "wide their caparisoned banners" and return "to some close chimney side to lick their wounds awhile and adjust their bodies to the gentler arts of peace." With his novel Stallings attempted to rewrite the happy story of men who lose legs to "the stroke of the merciful knife" and "amputating iron" and then "hobble home to [their wives'] arms" (71). *Plumes*, however, failed in the cultural marketplace of the 1920s, and Stallings went on to contribute both his body and his writing as source texts for a film that blended melodramatic narrative formulas with more groundbreaking cinematic representations in a contradictory portrayal of masculinity that comes to a happy resolution with an amputee limping on a prosthetic leg into his lover's arms.

Drawing on a combination of melodrama and attempts at cinematic "realism" inspired by physical disability, *The Big Parade* translates Laurence Stallings's postwar problem body into an exemplary and powerful portrayal of postwar masculinity. As a veteran, an author, and an inspirational body, Stallings served as the realistic key to what became a widely appealing and influential cinematic spectacle of war, wounding, love, and recovery. With *The Big Parade*, Stallings engaged with a medium commensurate with his contradictory postwar subjectivity and the simultaneously problematic and promising "reality" of a veteran's disabled body.[6] Ultimately, Stallings's leg and its prosthetic

---

6. A comparison of the cinematic portrayals of postwar masculine disability in *The Big Parade* and in the post-WWII film *The Best Years of Our Lives* (1946) offers an illuminating contrast that I do not have the space to fully explore in this essay. In the later post-WWII film the fictional role of a veteran who has lost his hands is played by the actor Harold Russell, who actually did lose his hands in the war. For an insightful exegesis of this film and the complicated role that Russell's disability plays in its cinematic narrative significations, see Kaja Silverman, *Male Subjectivity*, 52–90. While this later postwar epic has many compelling parallels to *The Big Parade*, it also has at least two significant and

replacement—one conspicuous in its absence, the other equally conspicuous in its hard, wooden presence—together served as two powerfully contradictory signs of authentic postwar manhood that helped to create a new cinematic "whole art of a wooden leg."

---

revealing differences. First, *The Best Years of Our Lives* focuses on the painful experience of a veteran's adjustment to postwar life on the home front—something Stallings tried to render in his novel *Plumes* that was rejected by critics and readers in the 1920s. Second, *The Best Years of Our Lives* includes the actual body of an amputee veteran within the profilmic text itself. Silverman explains that although "Harold Russell's double amputation does not 'make the movie spill over into the real world'[,] . . . it does situate the image of Homer Parish's arms on a different level of representation than the rest of the film" (73). This results in what Silverman calls "a strong referential pull, seeming to point beyond the text and Russell's acting to his body and the traces left there by the war." With *The Big Parade*, Stallings's body remained entirely "beyond the text" as nothing more than an implied absence and yet still managed to inspire a fictional depiction of amputation with a uniquely "strong referential pull."

Works Cited

Anderson, Maxwell and Lawrence Stallings. *What Price Glory?* 1924 stage play. Published 1926 in *The American Plays*. Edited by Maxwell Anderson. New York: Harcourt, Brace, Jovanovich.

Baxter, John. *King Vidor.* New York: Monarch Press, 1976.

Bogdan, Robert. "The Social Construction of Freaks." In *Freakery: Cultural Spectacles of the Extraordinary Body.* Edited by Rosemarie Garland-Thomson. New York: New York University Press, 1996. 23.

Bourke, Joanna. *Dismembering the Male: Men's Bodies, Britain, and the Great War.* Chicago: University of Chicago Press, 1996.

Brownlow, Kenneth. *The War, The West, and The Wilderness.* New York: Knopf, 1979.

Fahy, Thomas. "Enfreaking War-Injured Bodies: Fallen Soldiers in Propaganda and American Literature of the 1920s." *Prospects,* Vol. 25. Cambridge: Cambridge University Press, 2000. 529–63.

Finch, Robert M. "An Overseas Veteran's Impressions of *The Big Parade.*" *The Director* (November 1925).

Fitzgerald, F. Scott. *F. Scott Fitzgerald: A Life in Letters.* Edited by Matthew Bruccoli. New York: Scribner's, 1994.

Garland-Thomson, Rosemarie ed. *Freakery: Cultural Spectacles of the Extraordinary Body.* New York: New York University Press, 1996.

Hall, Mordaunt. "A Superlative War Picture." Review of *The Big Parade. New York Times* (November 20, 1925): 18.

Hansen, Miriam. *Babel and Babylon: Spectatorship in American Silent Film.* Cambridge, MA: Harvard University Press, 1991.

Kirkham, Pat. "Loving Men: Frank Borzage, Charles Farrell and the Reconstruction of Masculinity in 1920s Hollywood Cinema." In *Me Jane: Masculinities, Movies, and Women.* Edited by Pat Kirkham and Janet Thumim. New York: St. Martin's Press, 1995. 94–112.

Littell, Robert. Review of *Plumes. The New Republic* (August 27, 1924): 394–95.

McQuire, Scott. *Visions of Modernity: Representation, Memory, Time and Space in the Age of the Camera.* London: Sage Publications, 1997.

Mitchell, David T. "Narrative Prosthesis and the Materiality of Metaphor." In *Disability Studies: Enabling Humanities.* Edited by Sharon L. Snyder, Brenda Jo Brueggemann, and Rosemarie Garland-Thomson. New York: The Modern Language Association of America, 2002. 15–30.

Review of *The Big Parade. Variety* (December 2, 1925).

Scandura, Jani and Michael Thurston. "Introduction: America and the Phantom Modern." In *Modernism Inc.: Body, Memory, Capital.* Edited by Scandura and Thurston. New York: New York University Press, 2001. 1–18.

Silverman, Kaja. *Male Subjectivity at the Margins.* New York: Routledge, 1992.

Stallings, Laurence. *Plumes.* New York: Harcourt, Brace and Co., 1924.

———. "The Whole Art of a Wooden Leg: An Essay." *The Smart Set: A Magazine of Cleverness 70* (March 1923): 107–11.

Studlar, Gaylyn. *This Mad Masquerade: Stardom and Masculinity in the Jazz Age.* New York: Columbia University Press, 1996.

Tully, Jim. "King Vidor: The Fourth in a Series of Twelve Interviews with Motion Picture Directors." *Vanity Fair* (New York, June 1926): 46, 100.

Vidor, King. *King Vidor: A Director's Guild of America Oral History.* Interviewed by Nancy Dowd and David Shepard. Metuchen, NJ: Scarecrow Press, 1988.

———. *A Tree Is a Tree.* London: Longman, 1954.

Opening credits superimposed over the figure of a man with crutches who moves menacingly toward the audience until his shadowy form covers the entire screen. *Double Indemnity.* Directed by Billy Wilder. Paramount Pictures, 1944.

MICHAEL DAVIDSON

❀

Phantom Limbs

Film Noir and the Disabled Body

Specular Distractions

In Jacques Tourneur's film *Out of the Past* (1947), a deaf boy (Dickie Moore) protects Jeff Bailey (Robert Mitchum) from police and gangsters who, for differing reasons, are pursuing him for his role in a murder. Jeff is subsequently killed by the femme fatale, Kathy (Greer Garson), when she discovers that he is handing her over to the police as the killer. When Jeff's current girlfriend, Ann (Virginia Huston), asks the deaf boy whether Bailey had intended to return to Kathy, the boy nods affirmatively, telling a lie that frees her from her emotional dependence on the hero and permits her to marry a local policeman. In *Fallen Sparrow* (1943), Kit (John Garfield), having been tortured in prison during the Spanish Civil War, is haunted by one of his tormentors, a "man who limps," who has followed him back to the United States. The sound of the man's foot being dragged reduces the shell-shocked Kit to shuddering hysteria until, faced with evidence that his pursuer is a Nazi spy, the hero confronts him in a final shootout. In *The Blue Dahlia* (1946) Johnny Morrison (Alan Ladd) has returned from WWII to find that his wife has been unfaithful. After an argument the wife is killed, and suspicion points to Ladd, but more particularly to Ladd's wartime buddy, Buzz (William Bendix), who has been injured in the war and suffers from what we would now call "post-traumatic stress syndrome." His mental disability, although not visible all the time, causes him to become violent whenever he hears certain kinds of loud music.[1]

---

1. The music that sets Buzz off is referred to as "jungle music," clearly a reference to jazz and black music in general. The movie implies that Buzz's music-induced violence is due not only to his combat

These examples could be expanded to include numerous films in which a person with a disability plays a supporting role, serving as a marker for larger narratives about normalcy and legitimacy.[2] The deaf boy in *Out of the Past* mirrors Jeff Bailey's flawed yet stoical integrity, providing a silent riposte to the flashy glamour and tough-guy patter between the other males in the film. The limping tormenter in *Fallen Sparrow* is also a Nazi spy, permitting the director, Richard Wallace, to use disability to shift Kit's problematic leftist involvement in Republican Spain to WWII patriotism. Buzz's mental disability in *Blue Dahlia* annexes the era's concern about soldiers psychologically damaged in the war. In most cases disabled figures—at least in the noir films that I discuss—play cameo roles, much the way that Hollywood uses Black, Latino, or Asian figures to provide a racialized counter-narrative to the hero's existential malaise. In Eric Lott's terms, the proximity of a racially marked character assists in "darkening" the white hero, linking him to more subversive or morally suspect forces within the society at large (81–83). A similar troping of able-bodied disability appears in films based around a male who, although internally wounded, must nevertheless be physically able to walk down the mean streets of Cold War America.[3]

experiences but also to his participation in an integrated, mixed-race Army, for which black music serves as a troublesome reminder.

2. In addition to the films that I discuss in this essay, a brief survey of disabled figures in noir films would include the following: In *Kiss of Death* (1947) a deranged Richard Widmark pushes a woman in a wheelchair down a flight of stairs. In *The Spiral Staircase* (1945) Dorothy McGuire plays a mute servant in a small town where a number of disabled people are murdered. In *The Big Sleep* (1946) Humphrey Bogart, as Raymond Chandler's detective, Marlowe, works for Colonel Sternwood who is confined to a wheelchair; Sternwood's daughter, Carmen, suffers from some undiagnosed mental condition and drug addiction. Another Chandler film, *The Brasher Doubloon* (1947), features Marlowe in a blackmail scheme involving a secretary who is mentally disturbed. In *Sorry, Wrong Number* (1948) Barbara Stanwyck plays a bedridden woman who overhears a phone conversation plot to kill her. In *Thieves Highway* (1949) Nick Garcos (Richard Conte) returns from the war to find his father crippled due to a truck accident. In *Rear Window* (1954) Jimmy Stewart, injured by an accident and recovering in a wheelchair while wearing a full leg cast, observes what he thinks is a murder plot in a neighboring building. In *Ministry of Fear* (1944) the spy who pursues Stephen Neale (Ray Milland) is blind. In *They Live By Night* (1949) Howard Da Silva plays a one-eyed demented robber and sadist. In *The Big Heat* (1953) Glen Ford gets crucial information on a crime from a crippled secretary; in the same movie Gloria Graham is scalded with boiling coffee by her boyfriend (Lee Marvin), thus "ruining her looks." In *The Manchurian Candidate* (1962) Laurence Harvey is a brainwashed Korean War veteran who is programmed to be an assassin. In *The Big Combo* (1955) Brian Donleavy plays a tough crime boss's enforcer who is deaf and who tortures his victims by forcing them to listen to loud music through his hearing aid. In *Ride the Pink Horse* (1947) a mob figure, Mr. Hugo, is deaf and uses a primitive cochlear implant attached to his ear. In every case, disability is a sign of weakness or, more often, evil, but the disability often serves as a metonymic reflection on the noir hero's own internal flaws. Although cognitive disorders and mental illness exist in a separate category of disability, they form the backbone of many noir films, including a number of Alfred Hitchcock's films such as *Spellbound* (1945), *Strangers on a Train* (1951), *Vertigo* (1958), and *Psycho* (1960).

3. Although some films of this period—*Sorry, Wrong Number; The Spiral Staircase;* and *Rear Window*—feature a main character who is disabled, it is usually the bit character whose deafness or

This phenomenon can be partially explained by what David Mitchell and Sharon Snyder call "narrative prosthesis," the use of **dis**-ability to **en**-able a story. The disabled body serves as a "crutch upon which literary narratives lean for their representational power, disruptive potentiality, and analytical insight" (49). If narrative closure depends on restoration of the able-bodied individual (to health, society, normalcy), the disabled character represents a form of physical deviance necessary for marking the body's unruliness. But, as I hope to show, disability may often facilitate other narratives not so easily represented. Moreover, it may utilize the disabled body as a site for social panics about unruly bodies in general, diverting the gaze from one stigmatized identity onto another. Hence the title of my essay, "Phantom Limbs," refers to the residual sensation of narratives that the film cannot represent or reconstitute. We might say that the phantom limb phenomenon is the affective response to narrative prosthesis, the way that trauma is experienced after the limb has been surgically removed and therapy undergone.[4]

The phantom limb phenomenon is especially prevalent in film noir, a genre that emerged during a period of Cold War consensus when the maintenance of normalcy and national health coincided with geopolitical imperatives at large. Cultural representations of sexual or personal excess, from Elvis's gyrating hips to Beat bohemians and motorcycle outlaws, were dismissed by consensus intellectuals, on the one hand, or were heavily monitored by congressional investigating committees and the Motion Picture Production Code on the other.[5] Film noir sometimes supported those national goals by celebrating returning war heroes or crooks who go straight, yet many of them (often made by black- or gray-listed directors) achieved their ends by presenting dystopic views of marginal social types—the criminal, the disgraced detective, the wrongly accused fugitive. The noir hero is a tough loner who is flawed but who has integ-

---

limp marks the hero's psychic wounds.

4. The first description of the "phantom limb" phenomenon was provided by Ambroise Pare in the mid-sixteenth century when he wrote of patients who "imagine they have their members yet entire, and yet due complaine thereof" (qtd. in Gorman 30). Silas Weir Mitchell provided the fullest early discussion of the phenomenon in the late nineteenth-century. He noted that among his patients who had lost organs or limbs, almost all experienced the phantom limb phenomenon. Although the phrase usually applies to amputated arms or legs, according to Weir Mitchell it was experienced with loss of eyes, internal organs, or rectum, and in cases involving hysterectomy. Perhaps most interesting, given our topic, is the fact that it was reported in cases of a missing penis. Mitchell was the inventor of the famous "rest" cure for women suffering from nervous disorders. On phantom limb and body image see Warren Gorman, *Body Image,* and Elizabeth Grosz's *Volatile Bodies.*

5. The Motion Picture Production Code was begun in 1930 by the Motion Picture Producers and Distributors of America under the administration of Will Hays. As Vito Russo points out, "the Code survived under different names until the late Sixties, often taking the name of its current administrator. Thus, at various times it was called the Johnston Office, the Hays Office and the Breen Office." Russo, *The Celluloid Closet,* 31.

rity in a corrupt world. He fights on his own terms, even though he is haunted by a dark past. Although noir films usually present him as prey to the femme fatale, his non-domestic status and bachelorhood mark him as a sexually indeterminate figure. His phantom relationship to the dominant culture is assisted by a range of cinematic techniques that destabilize the viewing experience. Expressionist camera angles, high-contrast lighting, disjunctive scores, and the use of voice-over and flashback stylistically reinforce psychological states of anxiety. Lost in an anonymous bureaucratic system or suffering from traumatic events incurred during the war, the noir hero must discover a code of honor based on contingent necessity rather than sanctioned authority.

One way to historicize the phantom limb phenomenon with regard to Cold War culture is to look at the ways that physical disability served as a marker of gender trouble. Critics usually describe film noir as a masculine genre, marked by its literary origins in the hard-boiled detective novel, but it is often characterized by anxiety over the stability and definition of gender roles. Although the Production Code severely limited what directors could show of "deviant" passions, noir films created unforgettable gay icons—the butch masseuse in *In a Lonely Place* (1950); the effeminate drama critic, Waldo Lydecker, in *Laura* (1944); the fussy, effeminate Joe Cairo in *The Maltese Falcon* (1941); and the psychopathic Bruno Antony in *Strangers on a Train* (1951)—who have made film noir a highly prized genre within queer culture. These thinly veiled figures of gay and lesbian identity serve to show that although the noir hero is often conflicted sexually, his heteromasculinity is never in serious question. In Richard Dyer's terms, such sexually marginal figures "remind us of how far [the noir hero is] removed from that sort of thing" (69).

"That sort of thing" may help shore up a normative sexuality, but it also provides a conflicted specular site that complicates the viewing of film noir generally. Robert Corber notes that in Otto Preminger's film *Laura*, Clifton Webb's portrayal of the homosexual theatre critic, Lydecker, is a "transgressive form of visual pleasure film noir offered spectators." According to Corber,

> Webb's willingness to make a spectacle of his homosexuality hindered the spectator's absorption in the diegesis, which was one of the primary goals of the classical system. It encouraged a mobile and ambulatory gaze that was easily distracted by the surface of the image. (56)

Although Lydecker is not disabled, he occupies a place of specular "distraction" often occupied by such figures. When, for example, he conducts an interview with the detective, Mark McPherson [Dana Andrews] in a bathtub, it disrupts the latter's sexual obsession with Laura and redirects it onto the naked male body. The fact that the body is that of an effemininate drama critic helps to reinforce the theatrical character of such distractions throughout the film. I am adapting Corber's terms about homosexuality to speak of the ways that the disabled body in film noir turns performance into spectacle, diverting a gaze between viewer and unruly body to one between viewer and queer bodies elsewhere in the film.

In numerous noir films a physical or cognitive disability marks a sexual inscrutability, otherwise unspeakable within terms of 1940s and 1950s Production Code directives. Film theory has focused extensively on the mantis-like features of the femme fatale, but less has been said about her husband, a man whose physical disability serves as a camera obscura upon the noir hero's existential wounds.[6] In *Double Indemnity* (1944) Mrs. Dietrichson's husband is on crutches; in *The Lady from Shanghai* (1948) Elsa Bannister's husband wears braces and uses a cane; in *Walk on the Wild Side* (1962) Jo's husband's legs have been amputated, and he pulls himself around on a dolly. In all three cases the husband's crippled condition contrasts with the noir hero's phallic potency, but it also produces a visual spectacle around the body in excess of the narrative's ability to contain it. The presence of a disabled figure complicates the triangular gaze between viewer, noir hero, and femme fatale and provides a conduit for representing perversity that cannot be solved by reference to the film's diegesis.

The presence of a cinematic "phantom limb" provides a diversion for a more subtle subplot about same-sex alliances. Walter Neff's (Fred MacMurray's) appropriation of Mr. Dieterichson's crutches diverts attention away from the affectionate relationship between Neff and his insurance coworker, Barton Keyes (Edward G. Robinson). Arthur Bannister's (Everett Sloane's) crutches, braces, and exaggerated pelvic thrust

---

6. By speaking of the femme fatale's husband, I am speaking somewhat metaphorically about a figure, male or female, whose disability thwarts the smooth functioning of a heterosexual gaze. Because psychoanalytic "gaze" theory has been based largely around a specifically Oedipalized dyad, it has not been able to address the ways that other subjectivities are constructed and contested through acts of looking. In Robert Aldrich's 1963 film, *Whatever Happened to Baby Jane*, for example, Bette Davis plays a former child star forgotten by Hollywood while her disabled sister, Blanche (Joan Crawford), is still remembered, despite being a paraplegic. In the film's visual rhetoric, Blanche is the stoical, "beautiful" former actress who is now "tragically" crippled, while Jane is the able-bodied but mentally deranged, alcoholic shell of her former self. Much of the film's drama centers on the ways that Jane's heterosexual gaze is mediated by a Hollywood studio system that promotes ideals of youthful beauty against aging and physical decay. Jane fantasizes that she is still Baby Jane until she looks into the mirror and sees her decrepit, older self. She then looks into the "mirror" of her disabled sister and sees the success that she never had. Both gazes intensify her growing dementia. The film is thus about the ways that heterosexual desire is constructed through institutional contexts that disability makes strange.

mediate his queer relationship with his law partner, George Thirsby (Glenn Anders). Jo's (Barbara Stanwyck's) husband's amputated condition frames her erotic desire for the female lead (Capucine). Each of these examples illustrates the way that the disabled body reinforces a normative heterosexuality embodied by the noir hero, while at the same time it allows another sexuality to "pass" before the eyes of the Breen Office censors. Filmic passing is performed by containing homosexual content through the period's "compulsory homosociality" in which male same-sex alliances and power are reinforced by excluding women, in which the threat of genitalized contact is replaced by official forms of male bonding.[7] Such formations become important in a society in which certain types of homosocial association (Neff's and Keyes's loyalty to the insurance firm, Bannister's and Grisby's participation in the law) are essential to the perpetuation of capitalist hegemony. When women get together, as in *Walk on the Wild Side*, such homosocial bonds, instead of providing a socially (and economically) redemptive community, are signs of lesbian attachments and prostitution.[8]

Although it would be reductive to see the disabled figure in film noir as a surrogate for queer identities, it is safe to say that these films build on a well-established connection between discourses of disability and sexuality that can be found in cultural texts from *Richard III* (1955) to *Fight Club* (1999). Representations of a king, "rudely stamped," or a man with dissociative identity disorder (DID) manifest themselves through narratives about non-normative sexuality; perceived "weakness" of (in these cases) masculine power seems impossible to express outside of sexual difference. Robert McRuer defines the phenomenon as follows:

> [T]he system of compulsory able-bodiedness that produces disability is
> thoroughly interwoven with the system of compulsory heterosexuality

---

7. I have discussed this phenomenon in relation to Cold War literary communities in "Compulsory Homosociality," 197–216.

8. Another example of this double vector of sexualities and disabilities is Andrew Niccol's 1997 noirish film *Gattaca*, in which the genetically "invalid" but physically able-bodied main character, Vincent (Ethan Hawke), must appropriate the genetically "pure" DNA of the paraplegic, Jerome (Jude Law), in order to participate in a specialized space program. The fact that the relationship between the two men is thematized as queer—a condition reinforced by their sharing of bodily fluids, spaces, and identities—reinforces the close link between narratives of genetic perfection and sexual pollution. Jerome's self-immolation at the end of the film provides an all-too-typical Hollywood denouement for both queers and disabled figures. Here, Vincent's crippled condition is the prosthesis that supplements the film's allegory of physical "normalness": his queerness supplements the film's allegory of heterosexual normalcy, figured in the main character. Although the film was made in 1997, its cinematic techniques and themes of alienation and social control refer to many aspects of film noir. I am grateful to Liberty Smith for her own (as yet unpublished) work on the intersection of queer and disabilities issues in *Gattaca*. For an excellent disabilities reading of the film, see Mark Jeffreys, "Dr. Daedalus and His Minotaur," 137–52.

that produces queerness, that—in fact—compulsory heterosexuality is contingent on compulsory able-bodiedness and vice versa. (89)

Finding the historical specifics of compulsory able-bodiedness is an important task for disabilities and queer studies, but such scholarship is often hamstrung by residual medical and psychoanalytic models that generalize the connection of bodies and sexualities around narratives of loss and lack. What, then, is the body of theory that the phantom limb remembers—and makes strange?

Disabling Theory

"Midge, do you suppose many men wear corsets?"
—Jimmy Stewart in *Vertigo* (1958)

Before looking more closely at my filmic examples, I want to frame my readings by considering feminist psychoanalytic film theory for which film noir is often a test case for how subjects are enlisted in dominant structures of desire. Such theories have been important for understanding the ways in which cinema structures acts of looking through gendered spectacles. In the process such theory has disabled the disability narrative of many films by treating acts of looking and gazing as defined by castration. For Slavoj Žižek the fantasy object creates an "immobilising, crippling effect" upon the subject who must transform his "impotence into power by means of the gaze" (126). And Claire Johnston, speaking of *Double Indemnity*, notes that the film's title sequence, showing a man on crutches, places the movie "under the sign of castration" (90). By equating visibility and acts of looking with castration, by equating feminine "lack" with physical difference, the missing limb always becomes a missing phallus. Whether one agrees or argues with this reading of visual pleasure, psychoanalytical theory defines this reading by invoking an Oedipus whose blindness must always be a fatal loss, whose insight must be purchased through self-mutilation. Since much film noir criticism is indebted to this tradition, it serves as a kind of theoretical gaze itself, creating the terms by which films suture the "incomplete" body onto the "incomplete" woman.

As we know from Laura Mulvey's influential 1975 article, "Visual Pleasure and Narrative Cinema," phallocentrism "depends on the image of the castrated woman to give order and meaning to its world" (361). Classical narrative cinema embodies this Freudian truism where the camera adopts the position of the male protagonist as active viewer of a passive female subject. The male's "looking" or scopophilia seeks to gain erotic control of that which he finds threatening. Fear of castration drives the male protagonist, often a detective or police inspector, to establish his authority by fixing her actions through voyeurism and fetishization. Film noir's extensive use of flashback/voice-over to interpret the diegetic material of the film reinforces such male control by framing threatening (libidinal) events from the past in the voice of authority who may provide a "rational" and "truthful" narrative.[9]

For Mulvey the films of Alfred Hitchcock embody this fetishized gaze *in extremis* since they invariably center on a wounded protagonist's anxiety about the reality of the female object of his desire. In *Rear Window* (1954) Jeff (Jimmy Stewart) has been disabled by an accident and his entire left leg is in a cast. While sitting in his wheelchair, he compensates for his inactivity by speculating on the lives of his neighbors from the vantage of his window. His detection of a crime in an adjacent apartment is furthered by his role as a photographer, but it is equally enhanced by the participation of his girlfriend, Lisa (Grace Kelly), whose erotic interest for Jeff increases when she becomes involved in the detection process. Once she moves—quite literally—into Jeff's line of vision by entering the apartment of the crime perpetrator, Jeff's scopophilic desire increases and he begins to regard her as a possible companion and sexual partner. In terms made familiar by Mulvey, Jeff overcomes his physical limitations—his castrated position in a wheelchair—by being able to orchestrate his gaze toward solving a crime; his impotence as a disabled male is thus transformed by his controlling Lisa's actions in his line of sight.[10] Although Lisa had presented herself to Jeff's (and the viewer's) view in a variety of extravagant outfits in her professional role as a high-fashion model, it is only when she participates in Jeff's fantasy of murder and marital intrigue across the backyard that her performance of femininity achieves the required erotic element.

In Mulvey's second example, *Vertigo* (1958), ex–police detective Scottie Ferguson (Jimmy Stewart) is disabled by a paralyzing fear of heights. He agrees to help an old friend, Gavin Elster (Tom Helmore),

---

9. A variation on this use of flashback/voice-over occurs in *Mildred Pierce* where the title character, played by Joan Crawford, narrates "her" story of domestic trials while raising an ungrateful daughter and running a restaurant. But since her voice-over narration is told to a police inspector who suspects her of killing her husband, it is still contained within the figure of the masculine Law, although it offers, as Pam Cook observes, a corrective version of the noir crime frame. On *Mildred Pierce* and voice-over see Pam Cook, "Duplicity in *Mildred Pierce*," 69–80.

10. The fact that Lisa initiates the decision to assume a more active role in Jeff's fantasy is irrelevant, given the all-consuming nature of the male gaze. "He" structures the terms of agency that "she" exerts.

whose wife, Madeleine (Kim Novak), has become obsessed with a long-dead female relative, Carlotta Valdez. It turns out that Madeleine is not Elster's wife but his mistress whom he has made over to resemble his wife as part of a murder plot. Scottie follows Madeleine around the streets of San Francisco, becoming gradually obsessed with her—and, more significantly, with her obsession with a dead ancestor. She leads him finally to a church tower at a mission south of the city from which Madeleine, under the pretense of being possessed by Carlotta, leaps to her death. The woman whom Scottie sees falling from the tower is not the woman pretending to be Madeleine but Elster's actual wife. Elster had planned on Scottie's being unable to climb the stairs to save her, due to his vertigo, and thus can witness what looks like a suicide but is actually a murder. In despair over the loss of (and inability to save) his beloved, Scottie meets another woman, Judy Barton, who resembles Madeleine whom he, like Elster, makes over into his lost Madeleine. It turns out that Judy *is* the actress who played Madeleine, and she seizes the opportunity of Scottie's reappearance in her life to rekindle their lost romance. But her hopes are doomed since Scottie actually loves the dead Madeleine, for whom the working-class Judy can only be a simulacrum. In the climactic scene, Scottie takes Judy, now dressed as Madeleine, back to the mission bell tower for a reenactment of the original deception. There, after Scottie confronts her about her role in deceiving him, Judy falls to her death.

As Mulvey notes, Scottie's obsessive pursuit of Madeleine and his equally obsessive desire to recreate her in Judy become "our" point of view; there is no room for Judy's perspective. "Apart from one flashback from Judy's point of view, the narrative is woven around what Scottie sees or fails to see" (371). Scottie's fear of heights is transferred onto his ability to control the image of Madeleine, and viewers become complicit in this act of coercion. In both films Hitchcock represents the attempt of a male to overcome a disability, coded as impotence, by recreating the woman into his own fantasy. Lisa must move from being object of society's desire as a fashion model into object of his binocular gaze; in *Vertigo* the working-class Judy must be made over into the wealthy, aristocratic Madeleine.

Mulvey's article launched a significant body of critical response that continues to attempt to develop a theory of female spectatorship. The work of Tania Modelski, Linda Williams, Teresa de Lauretis, Karen Hollinger, and others has retrieved a feminine gaze from Mulvey's scopophilia.[11] Modelski, for example, notes that Scottie's former girlfriend,

---

11. See Teresa de Lauretis, *Alice Doesn't*; Karen Hollinger, "The Look," 18–27; Tania Modleski, *The Women Who Knew Too Much*; and Linda Williams, "When the Woman Looks," 561–77.

Midge, possesses important knowledge that Scottie lacks, her spectacles bespeaking clear insight of the constructed nature of gender against Scottie's mystified vision. Modelski also criticizes Mulvey's failure to consider one crucial scene in *Vertigo* in which Judy does gaze back at the camera, a moment that expresses her recognition of her own complicity in Scottie's fantasy. Here, the female protagonist acknowledges the camera's presence, thereby placing viewers in command of knowledge that Scottie is unable to see (87).[12]

What is disturbing about both Mulvey's and her critics' responses to Hitchcock and noir films generally is the ease with which castration remains unchallenged as a definition of the disabled protagonist's relation to women. Rather than call into question Freud's theory of castration anxiety—which is a theory of sexual differentiation after all—critics redirect their focus from the Lacanian Symbolic, the realm of language and law, to the Imaginary, the child's pre-Oedipal ties to the Mother. The heterosexual relationship between protagonist and femme fatale is not altered; power dynamics are merely readjusted between genders. And this has implications for my reading of the disabled figure in film noir since it fails to recognize his links to female characters in the films. Although such links are often pathologized (Norman Bates in *Psycho* [1960] is the obvious version), they are nevertheless complicating factors in any treatment of gender. When Scottie asks Midge if many men wear corsets, he is also asking about the role he must assume when wearing clothing usually identified with women—and by extension when he is placed in a culturally disabled position vis-à-vis normative bodies. To see Scottie at this point as representing his castrated state in relation to a maternal figure seems beside the point. To see him recognizing the ways that disability in a compulsorily heterosexual (and ableist) world is figured as feminine helps explain his obsessiveness over Madeleine. Midge, as a designer of women's underwear, knows something about male fantasies as well as about the construction of bodies according to male designs (she claims that the brassiere she is drawing in this scene was designed by an aircraft engineer). Scottie's inability to live within his "darned fear of heights" is also his inability to live in a world that expects certain actions to comply with gender expectations. And vertigo is equally a fear of gender uncertainty when the normative body is no longer "normal."

---

12. On the epistemological implications of feminist film criticism, see Susan White, "*Vertigo* and Problems of Knowledge," 279–98.

Noir Bodies

"You know, a dame with a rod is like a guy with a knitting needle."
—Fisher in *Out of the Past* (1947)

In shifting my focus to film noir, I would like to build on Mulvey's important idea that cinema constructs its viewers through the gaze but add that the viewer is neither unitary nor necessarily a heterosexual male. Furthermore, the "gaze" in film noir is not so simply a reincarnation of some primal scene—the male child witnessing his parents *in flagrante delicto*, the mother revealed as castrated. The gaze occurs in highly specific historical contexts that frame what the act of seeing means. In the period during which noir films were being made, specularity often implied acts of surveillance and political scrutiny that had specific geopolitical implications for national security.[13] For Mulvey, the invariable object of the protagonist's gaze is a woman, but what happens when the protagonist is himself the object of scrutiny—when his or her crippled body is no less a spectacle than that of the femme fatale? Such is the case with Billy Wilder's *Double Indemnity*.

Most theorists of film noir regard *Double Indemnity*, based on James M. Cain's thriller, as the *ur*-noir film that invented many of the terms for the cycle. The opening credits foreground the importance of disability in the film by superimposing titles over a man with crutches who moves menacingly toward the audience until his shadowy form covers the entire screen. Given the film's setting within an insurance company, the credits announce not only the physical but also the economic impact of that menace.[14] The film opens with Walter Neff driving erratically through the early morning Los Angeles streets, arriving at the Pacific All-Risk Insurance building and staggering to the office of his coworker, Barton Keyes. There, he starts a Dictaphone and confesses his role in an insurance scam. Neff's confession—which becomes the voice-over for the entire movie—begins by identifying himself through the rhetoric of an insurance affidavit: "Walter Neff,

---

13. As Jennifer Nelson, Timothy Melley, Robert Corber, and others have pointed out, acts of looking during the Cold War were often underwritten by a surveillance ideology that placed communists and queers as the inevitable objects of a national gaze. See Jennifer Nelson, *Pursuing Privacy in Cold War America;* Timothy Melley, *Empire of Conspiracy;* and Robert Corber, *Homosexuality in Cold War America.*

14. As Paul Starr notes, the defeat of a national health insurance plan during the 1930s (and opposed by the AMA) led to the expansion of private health insurance companies during the postwar years. Defined as "socialized medicine," the idea of a national plan could now be perpetually demonized during the anti-communist decades. See Paul Starr, *The Social Transformation of American Medicine,* 280–89. It is worth pointing out that Wilder returned to the image of the vast, impersonal insurance company in his 1960 film, *The Apartment,* in which Fred MacMurray appears again, this time as the head of the office.

insurance agent, 35 years old, unmarried, no visible scars . . . [he glances down at his wounded shoulder] . . . until a little while ago" (Wilder 11). The visible scar refers to the bullet wound recently inflicted by Phyllis Dietrich-son, but it also refers to the film's thematics of visibility and invisibility in which the couple has had to maintain the appearance of normalcy ("no visible scars") in order to conceal their role in a crime.

Neff is erotically attracted to Phyllis Dietrichson when he first encounters her in her Los Feliz home, but his ardor diminishes once he becomes inveigled into her plot to kill her husband and collect on an insurance policy. The couple becomes edgy and short-tempered, their meetings more fugitive. The erotic charge that prompted Walter to collude with Phyllis in a murder plot transfers to his associate, Keyes, an investigator whose relentless pursuit of insurance malfeasance is inspired by what he calls a "little man" inside him. His belief in actuarial odds leads him to suspect that the insurance claim filed by Mrs. Dietrichson is a fraud and that she has colluded with a shadowy lover to murder the husband and make it look like an accident. Keyes's accuracy in pinpointing the fraud earns Neff's respect and establishes the terms of male competitiveness and camaraderie that drive the movie, a bonding reinforced by witty repartee shared by the two men. At one point, after Keyes lights Neff's cigarette, Walter says, "I love you, too," a remark repeated at the end of the movie but given emotional force by the fact that Neff is now dying of a bullet wound. While Keyes comforts him, Neff says, "[you] know why you didn't figure this one, Keyes? Let me tell you. The guy you were looking for was too close. He was right across the desk from you," to which Keyes replies, "[closer] than that, Walter." "I love you too," Neff says, in his final line before dying (Wilder 119). This final scene of male consolation is a good deal more intimate than most of the scenes between Neff and Phyllis, leading some critics to suspect that Neff's voice-over is more of a lover's confession than a report.[15]

The film frames homosocial desire between the two men in terms of professional respect against the brittle ambition of the female lead. But unlike the homosocial triad diagnosed by Eve Sedgwick, in which males form alliances *through* the female, there is a second triad in which Neff and Keyes's relationship is bound to the husband (1–5). Mr. Dietrichson, who has become disabled in a construction site accident, is scheduled to attend his homecoming football game by traveling on a train. On his way

---

15. Claire Johnston reinforces the idea that the relationship between Neff and Keyes is to some extent determined by the compulsorily homosocial nature of the insurance company for which they work, a business in which women are distrusted: "Women represent the possibility of social excess which the insurance business seeks to contain" (91).

to the station, Neff murders him while Phyllis drives the car (in Cain's novel they strangle Dietrichson with his own crutches). Neff impersonates the husband by adopting his crutches and catching the train for which Dietrichson had bought tickets. The plan is for Neff to fake falling from the back of the train, whereupon the previously murdered husband would be placed on the tracks, making the murder seem like an accident. Here, Neff's prosthetic legs join him to a male who is both literally and symbolically disabled: literally through an accident and symbolically through his relationship to a scheming wife. But such filmic depictions are less about persons with disabilities and more about the role such persons play in a corporate world dependent on defining and restricting plausible forms of injury. When Billy Wilder changed the name of Cain's insurance company, from "Fidelity" to "All Risk," he pointed to the instability of bodies that must be "covered" by actuarial odds. But he pointed to other, sexual risks that occur when the domestic frame is broken and the wife begins to take out her own policies. Wilder makes pointed reference to Keyes being "married" to his job and to the idea that by being unmarried, he may have more time to pursue his passion for work. Neff, too, is unmarried, spending his bachelor hours in bars and bowling alleys, and while one might see both as examples of the corporate-driven, other-directed individual diagnosed by sociologists of the period, they are also figures whose indefinite sexuality is covered by (and aligned with) a pair of crutches.

The film highlights links between wounded husband and lover in the opening credits sequence in which a shadowy person on crutches could be either man. The links are reinforced by the fact that once they have completed the murder, Neff assumes a paternal role in relation to Dietrichson's daughter from a former marriage. This role places him in direct conflict with Phyllis and replicates the exact circumstance of the Dietrichson family romance. And just as she schemed to get rid of her husband, so too does Phyllis intend to kill Neff once he becomes squeamish about the insurance fraud aspect of the crime. Finally, Phyllis literally "cripples" Neff at the end of the film, and his bullet wound continues to bleed into the fabric of his coat as he recites his confession to Keyes. Thus the "visible scars" that mark Neff's fatal attraction for Mrs. Dietrichson link him to her disabled husband in ways that ultimately prove fatal.

A variation on triangulation between lover, disabled husband, and femme fatale occurs in Orson Welles's *The Lady from Shanghai*, between Elsa Bannister (Rita Hayworth), her husband, Arthur, and a tough Irish sailor, Michael O'Hara, played by Welles. Elsa involves Michael in a scheme to murder her husband, but the plot goes awry, and Arthur Bannister's partner, Grisby, is killed, with Michael set up as the fall guy. Much of the movie involves establishing the erotic relationship between Elsa and Michael, but there is a second, queer connection between Arthur and Grisby that has never been discussed. Although he is Bannister's law partner, Grisby is also inexplicably included in a yacht trip from New York to San Francisco, suggesting more than professional connections with the family.

Arthur Bannister walks with crutches and braces, a sign, for any viewer of the 1940s, of the virulent poliomyelitis epidemic that affected thousands of people in the postwar era and that was ameliorated by development of the Salk vaccine in the mid-1950s. Although Bannister is not disabled in the novel upon which the movie is based (Sherwood King's *If I Die Before I Wake*), Welles made him a polio survivor presumably in order to link him with a virus associated in the public mind with impotence and physical wastage. Polio was seldom fatal, but it disfigured the limbs and limited physical activities severely. Daniel Wilson notes that the disease had a profound impact on young men in the highly masculinized postwar period, creating "an infant-like dependency: temporary loss of control over bladder and bowel and of sexual function, confinement to bed and dependency on others for the most basic necessities" (9).[16] The disease was initially called "infantile paralysis," but even when the name was changed, polio continued to be associated with childhood diseases and childlike conditions.[17] Fred Davis's 1963 sociological study of polio victims and their families points out that in the United States, "crippling not only signifies a relative loss of physical mobility but also suggests social abnormality, isolation, and in the eyes of some, visible manifestation of inherent malevolence" (qtd. in Gould 219). By displaying Bannister's crutches and braces, Welles built upon several layers of 1940s social stigma: fear of contagion, often identified with immigrants who first manifested the disease in the early part of the century; anxiety about physical emaciation and wastage in a productivist economy; and paternalist philanthropic responses to the disease, manifested by the March of Dimes fund-raising effort. All these associations figure Bannister as an "unfit" husband for Elsa, but they also blend into his effeminate manner and theatrical courtroom gestures.

One scene that points up the queer connections among characters occurs at a fiesta that Bannister has arranged. While sailing up the coast of Mexico, the ship's passengers and crew go ashore. Bannister and Grisby carry on a drunken conversation that mocks Michael's macho toughness

---

16. On polio in general see Tony Gould, *A Summer Plague*.

17. It is precisely such infantalizing images of polio that drove FDR to hide all signs of his disability throughout his three terms as president.

and Elsa's seductiveness while establishing a personal collusion between them. Many of their references to Michael's heterosexual prowess are coded in terms of disability. Bannister says that if Michael wants to compete in their verbal sparring, he'll need a "handicap" (earlier, at the seaman's hiring hall, Bannister asks Michael if he is "able-bodied"). Responding to the news that Michael might be quitting the ship, Bannister retorts to his wife that "George likes to have [Michael] around, Lover; Michael's so big and strong—makes a good body guard for you . . . a big strong body guard with an Irish brogue." The bitchy repartee between Bannister and George Grisby over Michael's body sets up a speech by the latter about sharks that devour each other, a remark that applies to the Bannisters and their moneyed idleness but also to the partners' homoerotic interchange. Elsa is the focal point of the interchange—her beauty and youth counter-poised to Michael's strength and virility. She is shot in soft lighting and gauzy filters, gazing upward at Michael, in sharp contrast to Grisby and Bannister who are shot in harsh, low-key light and unflattering close-ups showing their sweaty faces and grotesque grimaces.

Grisby's presence in this and other scenes is one of generalized sexual threat. He leers at Elsa in a bathing suit, attempts to seduce Michael into a complicated insurance scam, and whines in a sycophantic way at Bannister. Although his threat is not overtly homosexual, Grisby's effeminate manner and unspecified links to both Bannisters create narrative ambiguities that have plagued most readings of the film. While critics have attempted to resolve these ambiguities by focusing on the triangle of the Bannisters and O'Hara as primary players in a heterosexual drama of sexual intrigue, they have ignored Grisby's odd presence as O'Hara's provocateur and nemesis.[18] Furthermore, Grisby's ambiguous sexuality combines with his right-wing political allegiances (he served on a pro-Franco committee in contrast to O'Hara's participation in the Lincoln Brigade) and Cold War paranoia. He is obsessed with the threat of nuclear annihilation and wants to escape to a desert island where he will be safe. In these scenes Welles wears his leftist sympathies broadly on his sleeve while demonizing the idle, right-wing rich.

The telescope that he carries with him to spy (for no apparent reason) on various members of the yachting entourage embodies Grisby's nuclear paranoia. He uses the telescope to capture Elsa in a bathing suit, sitting on a rock in a perfect imitation of a *Photoplay* magazine pinup. He later trains his optic on Bannister lurching up the beach with his braces while

---

18. On the Oedipal triangle between Michael and the Bannisters, see Ann West, "A Textual Analysis of *Lady from Shanghai*."

others carry heavy hampers around him. The first shot reminds us of the camera's specular potential within the Hollywood "star" system—Rita Hayworth as well-known "bombshell" and sex goddess, made famous from her role in *Gilda*. Welles critiques this system broadly in this film by showing Hayworth in pinup poses and then cutting to a close-up of Grisby, sweating and grinning, while holding his telescope. But just as Welles participates in the system by fetishizing Hayworth's pose, so he uses her physical perfection in contrast to Bannister's disability in these matching shots. Both "good" and "bad" bodies are viewed through the optic of the sexually (and politically) tainted Grisby. The message is about contagion, Elsa's physical perfection tainted by her proximity to a camera lens and crippled husband. The fact that Welles and Hayworth were themselves going through a difficult divorce at the time of the filming adds yet another layer to the film's thematics of specular control.

Bannister's disability performs several functions in the film. As I have said, on a historical level, it reminds viewers of the pervasive impact of polio during the postwar period. On another level, prosthetic signs of Bannister's polio metaphorize his sexual inadequacy as a husband in relation to the macho Michael O'Hara. He uses his rolling gait and halting movements as part of his courtroom manner to gain dramatic effect, alternately gaining sympathy from the jury for his disability and creating comic moments as a "helpless" lawyer forced to take the stand in his own defense. Welles reinforces the importance of his disability in several scenes by focusing on Bannister's crutches first and then panning away to show his entire body—as though the crutches are a synecdoche for the entire man. These theatrical representations of physical weakness combine with his racialized Jewishness (in contrast to O'Hara's Irishness and Elsa's Nordic blondness) to create a figure of ambiguous racial and physical threat.[19] Finally, Bannister's prosthetic and theatrical elements reference his unspoken homoerotic attachment to Grisby and, ultimately, to O'Hara.

All these elements come together in the famous shootout in the mirror room of the funhouse that concludes the movie. Bannister is first represented by his crutches as he enters the mirror maze and then by a full image of him, cane in one hand, gun in another, his image juxtaposed to head shots of Elsa. His ensuing speech to his wife attempts to unravel the various plot threads, but Welles's violent montage and crosscutting undermine visually what the speech tries to resolve thematically. Ban-

---

19. Bannister is also ethnically typecast as a "clever Jewish lawyer" in distinct contrast to O'Hara's honest Irishness (complete with brogue). Although this fact is never explicitly stated, it can be supported by the fact that the actor who plays Bannister, Everett Sloane, portrayed Bernstein, the lawyer in *Citizen Kane* (1941), whose Jewishness is central to his characterization.

nister admits to Elsa that "killing you is killing myself. It's the same thing, but you know I'm pretty tired of both of us." The shootout that follows is verification of these remarks: husband and wife blast away at each other, destroying one illusion while creating another. This final scene is a spectacular send-up of the film's metaphorics of illusion and reality, but it is also a destruction of both sexual and medical threats in an act of mutual self-immolation, permitting the hero to walk out at the end, wounded but wiser. Disability and sexual transgression are eliminated within mirrors that, rather than confirm identity, replicate it in an infinite regression of partial identities.

My earlier reference to compulsory homosociality in the first two films undergoes a change in the case of Edward Dmytryk's *Walk on the Wild Side*, a film in which same-sex alliances are among women. In his autobiography Dmytryk refers to the film as "a woman's picture," made as such by transforming the Depression-era hobo camps and slum shacks of Nelson Algren's novel into a Mexican café and a brothel, both presided over by women.[20] The film was made in 1962, placing it slightly outside the noir cycle, but it deploys many noir stylistic stocks-in-trade: a dislocated, lonely drifter; a tragic femme fatale; a dark, underworld milieu; and occasionally cinematic effects involving odd camera angles, low-key lighting, and a violent conclusion. Its more overt depiction of (thwarted) lesbian desire shows how the authority of Code censorship had diminished. Dmytryk changed Nelson Algren's original novel considerably, adding Jo's lesbianism and transforming one of her customers, Schmidt, into her husband. In the novel Schmidt is a former freak-show and carnival giant, whose physical prowess is brought to an abrupt end when he loses his legs in a train accident. In the film Jo and Schmidt are married in order to link two kinds of freaks, sexual and physical, to preside over a dysfunctional family of wayward girls in a brothel called "The Doll's House."

The hero is Dove Linkhorn (Laurence Harvey), a Texas drifter searching for his lost girlfriend, Hallie (Capucine). He discovers her working in a New Orleans brothel, whose madam, Jo, is clearly in love with Hallie and who does everything in her power to prevent Dove from intervening. Jo's husband, Schmidt, is an amputee, his lost limbs providing a convenient metaphor for male subordination and weakness against Dove's and Jo's desires for Hallie. The husband moves around the brothel on a wheeled dolly, his proximity to the ground enhanced by director Edward Dymytryk's camera which hovers over Jo's shoulder as she looks down upon him.

---

20. Edward Dmytryk, *It's a Hell of a Life*, 246.

In one scene this filmic perspective heightens the links between the husband's disability and Jo's problematic sexuality. Schmidt has just learned that Dove intends to take Hallie away from the brothel, thus eliminating the sexual barrier in their marriage that has been created by the distracting younger woman. "Will things be different?" he asks Jo. "No, things will be the same," she responds, to which he adds,

> [T]hat's what you said after the accident—the one that took away my legs—Are things the same? Am I still your husband? Let her go. I know what's going on inside him. I know what it's like, loving somebody and not being able to do anything about it.

But Jo dashes his hopes and repudiates the husband's declaration of affection:

> Love! Can any man love a woman for herself without wanting her body for his own pleasure? Love is understanding and sharing and enjoying the beauty of life without the reek of lust. Don't talk to me about love. What do you know? What does any man know?

As an expression of Jo's sexuality, this speech is unusually explicit for its time, yet it trades in a stereotype that, as Vito Russo observes, "attempts to explain—but not excuse—her man-hating lesbianism" (144). Love of life "without the reek of lust" may sound odd coming from the proprietress of a whorehouse, but it is what she *must* say to reinforce lesbian stereotypes and enlist the viewer's sympathy in her marital plight with a crippled husband. The fact that, as the husband admits, "everything changed" between him and his wife as a result of his accident recycles a disability stereotype in which the castrated male produces the phallic female, a transference of sexuality across phantom limbs.

To reinforce this transfer, the scene that follows displays the husband taking revenge on both wife and heterosexual hero by butting his head into Dove's groin while the latter is held by the brothel's bouncers. The scene between husband and wife heightens the film's linkage of disability and emasculation, but it also stresses Jo's butch authority over a world of women. Capucine's weary femme posture and Dove's attitude of resignation stand in stark contrast to Jo's drive and determination as well as her command of a mock-domestic household. As with *The Lady from Shanghai,* deviant sexuality is punished in a final shootout that leaves Hallie dead and Jo criminally indicted for running a whorehouse, while the heterosexual hero remains alive to continue his lonely odyssey.

Volatile Bodies

What can scholars learn from this (admittedly slight) evidence for a crossing of medical and sexual closets during the early Cold War? For one thing, I observe the close intersection of the two that always attends representations of the non-normative body. What is Tod Browning's *Freaks* if not a film that exploits "extraordinary" bodies by imagining them as sexual? In Elizabeth Grosz's terms, such bodies are "volatile" in their challenge to models of physical "wholeness" and heterosexuality. But they are volatile because they make visible the field of sexuality itself, not as a set of drives toward an object but as a multifaceted field of positions, desires, acts, and practices. The disabled figure in film noir is a phantom haunting Cold War society, never given star billing, yet necessary for assisting the narrative of sexual containment embodied in the noir hero.

Whereas discussions of the phantom limb usually involve nostalgia for a prior "whole" body ("a libidinal memorial to the lost limb" as Grosz says [41]), based on Freudian lack I would posit a cultural phantom limb that imagines bodies still under construction.[21] In a society that figured the struggle between superpowers as one between "healthy" Protestant capitalism and "invalid" or diseased Communism, such bodies played a vital role in representing national insecurity. George Kennan, in his famous "Long Telegram" of 1946, begins a tradition of identifying Soviet expansion as a form of disease. Soviet leaders put forth a dogma that presents the outside world as "bearing within itself germs of creeping disease and destined to be wracked with growing internal convulsions until it is given a final *coup de grace* by [the] rising power of socialism that yields to [a] new and better world." And later in the document Kennan inverts his disease metaphor, stating that future world stability depends on the "health and vigor of our own society. World communism is like [a] malignant parasite which feeds only on diseased tissue." The fact that

---

21. Lennard Davis speaks about the way that volatile bodies arrest the gaze in an essay that links the Venus de Milo, epitome of classical beauty, and the disabled body, site of fragmentation. Davis notes that accounts by art historians of the Venus de Milo, such as those of Kenneth Clark, attempt to replace the missing limbs of the classical sculpture with the ideal "normal" body it displaces, "an act of re-formation of the visual field, a sanitizing of the disruption in perception." Davis concludes that the "mutilated Venus and the disabled person in general . . . will become in fantasy a visual echo of the primal fragmented body—a signifier of castration and lack of wholeness." Although I am unsatisfied with the castration definition, I recognize that Davis is trying to link the disabled body with a pervasive condition of fragmentation that occurs prior to the stage of self-objectification that Lacan figures as the mirror stage. For Davis, the disabled body, "far from being the body of some small group of victims, is an entity from the earliest of childhood instincts." In this sense disability is a social and cultural construction, the encounter with which provides an uncanny memory of pre-Oedipal condition. See Lennard Davis, "Nude Venuses, Medusa's Body, and Phantom Limbs," 57, 61.

he issued this foundational document of Cold War containment while recovering in a sick bed in Vienna is a significant fact in the metaphor of contamination that he uses.[22]

By studying a cycle of films created in the shadow of such documents, where the discourses of national health and economic stability are geopolitical imperatives, I see some fraying in the fabric of national consensus. The sexual content that was to be kept out of films through Production Code censorship could be introduced through other doors. I also see how a cycle of films usually described in terms of expressionist mood utilize those features to legitimate an ableist gaze. Orson Welles's spectacular mirror-room shootout may dash perspectives on reality, but it permits the "real" Welles (actor, director, heterosexual, able-bodied) to walk out into the sunlight at the end. Finally, by speaking of the phantom limb of Cold War sexuality, I point to how a moment of (albeit repressed) social agency for queer men and women, many of whom had formed homosocial communities during the war effort, was being formed through film. Films of this era—*Johnny Belinda, Gilda, Laura, Rebecca, Johnny Guitar, The Maltese Falcon, Mildred Pierce, The Manchurian Candidate,* and their retro versions in the 1980s and 1990s—show that noir style is more than a set of surface features; it is also a venue for representing otherness in a culture of the same.

---

22. George Kennan, "Moscow Embassy Telegram #511," 54, 63. On Kennan's own health, see Anders Stephanson, *Kennan and the Art of Foreign Policy,* 44–45.

Works Cited

Cain, James M. *Double Indemnity.* 1936. From Murder Mystery Monthly, no. 16, 1943.

Cook, Pam. *"Duplicity in Mildred Pierce."* In *Women in Film Noir.* 2nd edition. Edited by E. Ann Kaplan. London: British Film Institute, 1998.

Corber, Robert. *Homosexuality in Cold War America: Resistance and the Crisis of Masculinity.* Durham: Duke University Press, 1997.

Davidson, Michael. "Compulsory Homosociality: Charles Olson, Jack Spicer, and the Gender of Poetics." In *Cruising the Performative: Interventions into the Representation of Ethnicity, Nationality, and Sexuality.* Edited by Sue Ellen Case and Phillip Brett. Bloomington: University of Indiana Press, 1995. 197–216.

Davis, Lennard. "Nude Venuses, Medusa's Body, and Phantom Limbs: Disability and Visuality." In *The Body and Physical Difference: Discourses of Disability.* Edited by David T. Mitchell and Sharon L. Snyder. Ann Arbor: University of Michigan Press, 1997. 57, 61.

de Lauretis, Teresa. *Alice Doesn't: Feminism, Semiotics, Cinema.* Bloomington: Indiana University Press, 1984.

Dmytryk, Edward. *It's a Hell of a Life But Not a Bad Living.* New York: Times Books, 1978. 246.

Dyer, Richard. "Homosexuality and Film Noir." In *The Matter of Images: Essays on Representations.* New York: Routledge, 1993.

Gorman, Warren. *Body Image and the Image of the Brain.* St. Louis: Warren H. Green, 1969.

Gould, Tony. *A Summer Plague: Polio and Its Survivors.* New Haven: Yale University Press, 1995.

Grosz, Elizabeth. *Volatile Bodies: Toward a Corporeal Feminism.* Bloomington: Indiana University Press, 1994.

Hollinger, Karen. "The Look, Narrativity, and the Female Spectator in *Vertigo.*" *Journal of Film and Video* 39.4 (Fall 1987).

Jeffreys, Mark. "Dr. Daedalus and His Minotaur: Mythic Warnings about Genetic Engineering from J. B. S. Haldane, François Jacob, and Andrew Niccol's *Gattaca.*" *Journal of Medical Humanities* 22.2 (2001): 137–52.

Johnston, Claire. *"Double Indemnity."* In *Women in Film Noir.* 2nd edition. Edited by E. Ann Kaplan. London: British Film Institute, 1998.

Kennan, George. "Moscow Embassy Telegram #511, Feb. 22, 1946." In *Containment: Documents on American Policy and Strategy, 1945–1950.* Edited by Thomas H. Etzold and John Lewis Gaddis. New York: Columbia University Press, 1978. 54, 63.

King, Sherwood. *If I Die Before I Wake.* New York: Simon & Schuster, 1938.

Lott, Eric. "The Whiteness of Film Noir." In *Whiteness: A Critical Reader.* Edited by Michael Hill. New York: New York University Press, 1997. 81–101.

McRuer, Robert. "Compulsory Able-Bodiedness and Queer/Disabled Existence." In *Disabilities Studies: Enabling the Humanities.* Editedy by Brenda Jo Brueggemann, Rosemarie Garland-Thomson, and Sharon L. Snyder. New York: Modern Language Association, 2003.

Melley, Timothy. *Empire of Conspiracy: The Culture of Paranoia in Postwar America.* Ithaca: Cornell University Press, 2000.

Mitchell, David T. and Sharon L. Snyder. *Narrative Prosthesis: Disability and the Dependencies of Discourse.* Ann Arbor: University of Michigan Press, 2000.

Mitchell, Silas Weir. "Phantom Limbs." *Lippincott's Magazine of Popular Literature & Science* 8 (1871): 563–69.

Modelski, Tania. *The Women Who Knew Too Much: Hitchcock and Feminist Theory.* New York: Methuen, 1988.

Mulvey, Laura. "Visual Pleasure and Narrative Cinema." *Screen* 16.3 (1975): 6–18; reprinted in *Art After Modernism: Rethinking Representation.* Edited by Brian Wallis. Boston: David R. Godine, 1994.

Nelson, Jennifer *Pursuing Privacy in Cold War America.* New York: Columbia University Press, 2002.

Russo, Vito. *The Celluloid Closet: Homosexuality in the Movies.* New York: Harper and Row, 1981.

Sedgwick, Eve. *Between Men: English Literature and Male Homosocial Desire.* New York: Columbia University Press, 1985.

Starr, Paul. *The Social Transformation of American Medicine: The Rise of a Sovereign Profession and the Making of a Vast Industry.* New York: Basic Books, 1982. 280–89.

Stephanson, Anders. *Kennan and the Art of Foreign Policy.* Cambridge: Harvard University Press, 1989. 44–45.

West, Ann. "A Textual Analysis of *Lady from Shanghai.*" *Enclitic* 5.2 (1982).

White, Susan. "*Vertigo* and Problems of Knowledge in Feminist Film Theory." In *Alfred Hitchcock: Centenary Essays.* Edited by Richard Allen and S. Ishi Gonzales. London: British Film Institute, 1999. 279–98.

Wilder, Billy. With an Introduction by Jeffrey Meyers. *Double Indemnity.* Berkeley: University of California Press, 2000

Williams, Linda. "When the Woman Looks." In *Film Theory and Criticism.* Edited by Gerald Mast et al. New York: Oxford University Press, 1992.

Wilson, Daniel J. "Crippled Manhood: Infantile Paralysis and the Construction of Masculinity." *Medical Humanities Review* (Fall 1999).

Žižek, Slavoj. "The Hitchcockian Blot." In *Alfred Hitchcock: Centenary Essays.* Edited by Richard Allen and S. Ishii-Gonzales. London: British Film Institute, 1999.

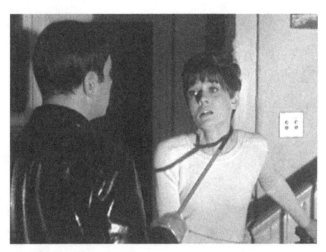

Susy (Audrey Hepburn) tries to put out the light. *Wait Until Dark.* Directed by Terence Young. Warner Bros., 1967.

JOHNSON CHEU

Seeing Blindness On-Screen

The Blind, Female Gaze

Examining 1940s women's films, Mary Anne Doane in *The Desire to Desire* asserts, "Disease and the woman have something in common—they are both socially devalued or undesirable, marginalized elements which constantly threaten to contaminate or infiltrate that which is more central, health and masculinity" (38). By making the comparison between disease and woman, Doane negates the existence of disabled women. As Rosemarie Garland-Thomson asserts in *Extraordinary Bodies:*

> The normative female body, then, occupies a dual and paradoxical cultural role: it is the negative term opposing the male body, but it is also the privileged term opposing the abnormalized female body. . . . So the simple dichotomy of objectified feminine body and masculine subject is complicated by other oppositions. Indeed, the unfeminine, unbeautiful body defines and is defined by the ideal feminine body. This aberrant figure of woman has been identified variously in history and discourse as black, fat, lesbian, sexually voracious, disabled or ugly. (28)

While Doane sees both diseased bodies and female bodies posited as oppositions to healthy bodies and masculine bodies, she fails to recognize a third marginalized category: the disabled woman.[1] To be disabled or

---

An earlier version of this article appeared in *The Journal of Popular Culture* 42.3 (2009) under the title "Seeing Blindness on Screen: The Cinematic Gaze of Blind Female Protagonists."

1. For my purposes I make the following distinctions between "disability," "disease," and "health": Disease is something that a healthy body can get, such as polio or AIDS. Disability, though it may be acquired via, for example, medical malfunction or accidents, is not disease. Blindness, for example, can have many causes such as diabetes, glaucoma, brain injury, or the loss of an eye. While diabetes and glaucoma are diseases, getting one's eye poked out is not a disease. Blindness is impair-

diseased as well as female then is to be doubly marginalized.[2]

North American films increasingly value strong women and repudiate gender stereotypes; however, many filmic stereotypes about disability—that we are unsightly, ugly, sexually undesirable—remain. In the 1930s film *Dark Victory* (1939), upon learning that her blindness has returned and is incurable, Bette Davis's Judith Traherne bids goodbye to her doctor and romantic love interest and sends away both her friend Anne and the maid. She then retreats into her bedroom to die alone. Judith's attractiveness, so inextricably tied to her gender, becomes a moot point when complicated by disability, her blindness. In keeping with the conventions of melodrama, she decides that it is best to die alone rather than as a "burden" to others. Her deathbed scene showcases a recognizable stereotype of disability in cinema, in a scene typical of what film theorist Martin Norden has termed "the cinema of isolation."[3]

Film studies scholars have long proposed and examined "the gaze" as a way of making meaning, particularly the gaze at women in feminist film studies and its relevance to gender stereotyping. An examination of the gaze at and of the disabled, however, and its role in perpetuating disability stereotyping has not yet taken place. What, for instance, is the meaning of Judith's Blind gaze, and what does it say about cultural stereotypes of the blind? While I presume a Disabled gaze, in this essay I shall discuss the gaze of blind female protagonists and theorize how the gazes of blind female characters are co-opted in order to take away the blind woman's agency. I argue that these films dehumanize Blind women[4] and perpetuate stereotypes within a broader social context.

Film studies has been enamored with examining the Male gaze, and

---

ment, not a disease, although a disease can cause blindness. "Health" is a generic term; it includes everything from a scraped knee, to AIDS, to baby care, to open-heart surgery. In this way a "diseased" and/or "disabled" body can be considered "healthy." For example, HIV-positive athlete Greg Louganis is thought of as healthy. Of importance here, though, is that both the "diseased" body and the "disabled" body, however delineated, are constructed as socially devalued and undesirable.

2. The terms "disabled/able-bodied people" historically allude to the idea of impairment. The terms "disabled/non-disabled people" are gaining parlance in disability studies to signify cultural identity. By utilizing the term "able-bodied," I am attempting to serve the dual purpose of referencing the historical use of the "disabled/abled" paradigm—that is, impairment—while simultaneously recognizing the reclamation of naming as part of the process of claiming a disability identity. I use the term "Able-bodied gaze" as the polar opposite of the "Disabled gaze" (see note 4 for an explanation of the capitalized forms) when I intend to reference literally physically embodied difference. In this way I examine a doubly marginalized, "othered" group, namely, characters who are both female and blind. Since both these groups are subject to dominant ways of looking, the term "normative" better encompasses the dominant power structure in play.

3. For further discussions of disability stereotypes see Martin Norden's *The Cinema of Isolation* and Paul K. Longmore's "Screening Stereotypes," 131–46.

4. My capitalization of "Disabled" and "Blind" invokes the claiming of an identity and community. Other times, my non-capitalization refers to the more common usage of these terms as either medical impairment or societal label.

critics within feminist and queer studies have responded by articulating a female gaze and a queer gaze. However, in works such as Judith Mayne's *Cinema and Spectatorship,* and in edited collections such *How Do I Look?* edited by Bad-Object Choices, these theorists do not articulate a normative gaze as a means of understanding how a film operates to perpetuate stereotypes of gender or sexuality. Laura Mulvey writes of the Male gaze:

> The man controls the film phantasy and also emerges as the representative of power in a further sense: as the bearer of the look of the spectator, transferring it behind the screen to neutralise the extra-diegetic tendencies represented by woman as spectacle. (20)

While Mulvey's first essay on the topic articulates a Male gaze as both the dominant and default gaze in cinema, later studies of the gaze further her theory. E. Ann Kaplan in her essay "Is the Gaze Male?" writes, "To begin with, men do not simply look; their gaze carries with it the power of action and possession that is lacking in the female gaze. Women receive and return a gaze but cannot act upon it" (121). Like Mulvey, Kaplan draws on psychoanalysis to arrive at the following conclusion: "We have arrived at the point where we must question the necessity for the dominance-submission structure. The gaze is not necessarily male (literally), but to own and activate the gaze . . . is to be in the masculine position" (130). She moves theories of the gaze from Mulvey's more literal question of who is doing the looking to a more thorough questioning of what those positions—the bearer and the receiver of the look—signify.

The concept of an able-bodied position and a disabled position that are markedly different—while explored in terms of disability stereotypes by theorists Martin Norden, Paul K. Longmore, and others—remains largely unexplored in terms of the gaze. My goal, then, is not only to articulate the presence of a Disabled gaze or, more specifically, a Blind gaze, but also to explore how that gaze interacts with a normative gaze in film and how it functions on a dominant-submissive structure of able-bodied and disabled characters in film. I am interested not only in how disabled characters are represented in film but also in what such representation means and/or what happens when a disabled character does the looking. As I will argue, although many theorists and filmmakers often presume that the Blind gaze is nonexistent, they also draw on the Blind gaze to remind viewers that blind characters are different, "othered" from the "normal" able-bodied characters in film.

Rosemarie Garland-Thomson posits the term "normate" in her book *Extraordinary Bodies.* This term articulates the type of normativity pivotal to my own argument. Thomson writes:

> In this economy of visual difference, those bodies deemed inferior become spectacles of otherness while the unmarked are sheltered in the neutral space of normalcy. Invested with meanings that far outstrip their biological basis, figures such as the cripple, the quadroon, the queer, the outsider, the whore are taxonomical, ideological products marked by socially determined stigmata, defined through representation, and excluded from social power and status. . . . Normate, then, is the constructed identity of those who, by way of the bodily configurations and cultural capital they assume, can step into a position of authority and wield the power it grants them. (8)

Thomson's "normate" is not specific to disability but rather serves as the overarching polemical term against which all identities and bodies marked "other" may be measured. As I will discuss shortly, the normative gaze often co-opts the Blind gaze in film as a means of upholding stereotypes of dependency, isolation, and infantilization in relation to disability.[5]

Co-optation as I use it here has to do with power relations between groups.[6] I borrow the term "co-optation" from black studies. Scholars following Frantz Fanon have employed the term co-optation to discuss the process by which the dominant group must keep the social order and the existing power structures stable by imbuing the colonized group with an inferiority complex.[7] Fanon writes:

> Quite simply, there are instances in which the educated Negro suddenly discovers that he is rejected by a civilization, which he has nonetheless assimilated. So that the conclusion would come to this: To the extent to which M. Mannoni's real typical Malagasy takes on "dependent behavior," all is for the best; if however he forgets his place, if he takes it into his head to be the equal of the European, then the said European is indignant and casts out the upstart—who, in such circumstances, in this "exceptional case" pays for his own rejection of dependency with an inferiority complex. (93)

---

5. Though I focus on stereotypes of helplessness and dependency as related to Blind women, disability studies scholars such as Longmore, Norden, and others have long claimed these stereotypes as applicable to the Disability community as a whole. Further, Moshe Barashe's examination of the image of "the blind beggar" in early Western Europe points to how deeply entrenched notions of the blind as helpless and dependent are in Western culture (116–20).

6. Depending on the text, co-optation sometimes appears without the hyphen as cooptation.

7. Fanon in *Black Skin, White Masks* does not use the term "co-optation" specifically, although he does examine the phenomenon.

Fanon suggests that as long as a minority group assimilates, yet assumes a subservient position relative to the dominant European culture, stability is maintained. Co-optation occurs when the minority community threatens the dominant power structure. Thus the dominant culture must develop ways to make the minority feel inferior. As Diana Fuss suggests in *Identification Papers*, "It therefore becomes necessary for the colonizer to subject the colonial other to a double command: be like me, don't be like me; be mimetically identical, be totally other. The colonial other is situated somewhere between difference and similitude, at the vanishing point of subjectivity" (146).

In my examination of the Blind gaze, I am interested in how the normative gaze of able-bodied sighted characters or the gaze of the camera itself constructs the gaze of the blind female character so as to convey stereotypes of her helplessness and dependency. In other words, this essay examines how the Blind gaze is co-opted in order to privilege the sighted normative gaze of the able-bodied characters, thereby imbuing the Blind with an inferiority complex. In the film *Wait Until Dark* (1967), for instance, I consider how Susy's (Audrey Hepburn's) Blind gaze is co-opted by the dominant normative gaze to keep Susy helpless and dependent. In other words, Susy, as the colonized other, is situated between difference and similitude. The co-optation of her gaze is the vanishing point of her subjectivity.

Co-optation is a means to but distinct from appropriation. In other words, the process of co-optation of the Blind gaze results in the able-bodied appropriating it to further their own sense of dominance. I suggest that films about the blind often appropriate the visual experience of blindness through absence of vision (complete darkness) or through blurred vision. I argue in the section "Directing the Blind Gaze" that cinematic techniques such as a darkening of the screen or fuzzy camera shots, can in fact be co-optations of the Blind gaze meant to reinforce the dominant power that sight embodies. My argument, though, extends beyond such cinematic visual appropriations to include an examination of the gazes exchanged between sighted and blind characters as a way of understanding how the blind are stereotyped as inferior. In these scenes, such as Gloria and Susy's information exchange in *Wait Until Dark* (1967), it is the privileging of the sighted gaze itself over the blind character's gaze, not the filmic simulation of blindness as darkness or blurred vision, which is itself the co-optation of the marginalized group by the dominant group.

Many scholars who have discussed the gaze—Mulvey and the Male gaze, hooks and the Black Female gaze, queer theorists and the heterosexual gaze upon gays and lesbians—presume the particular gaze of their minority group as the "other" against the dominant group.[8] Within this structure, for instance, male characters would be the normate and their gaze "normative." All the above-mentioned groups critique a dominant spectatorial position (the male, the heterosexual, etc.) and interrogate that dominant position by examining other subjectivities. In other words, all these identities share a presumption of the dominant gaze as "the norm" and the gaze of the marginalized group as the minority gaze. In the term "normative gaze," I assume a white, male, straight, heterosexual, able-bodied cinematic gaze. I discuss such a gaze in terms of able-bodied characters and the spectacle of bodies co-opted by the able-bodied characters' normative looking.[9]

My distinction invokes dominant/minority binary oppositions that play into normative assumptions about disabled characters. Teresa de Lauretis in *Alice Doesn't* writes, "The look of the camera (at the profilmic), the look of the spectator (at the film projected on the screen), and the intradiegetic look of each character (at other characters, objects, etc.) intersect, join, and relay one another in a complex system which structures vision and meaning and defines what Aberti would call the 'visible things' of cinema" (138). For this essay my emphasis on the particular film gaze of blind characters at other characters—that is, the intradiegetic gaze of the disabled character at the able-bodied characters within the film—reveals how the Blind gaze perpetuates stereotypes of Blind people, such as dependency. My examination of the look of the camera in relation to the blind characters reveals another ableist assumption about the Blind gaze: how and what the Blind see, namely, blurred images or utter darkness. Taken together, these looks highlight the marginalized and dependent status of the blind in cinema, thus reifying ableist assumptions about blindness. The normative gaze constructs stereotypes of dependency, isolation, and infantilization of blind characters. While the Blind gaze should repudiate such simple constructions, instead, filmmakers often make present such a gaze for the benefit of the otherwise able-bodied characters and presumed able-bodied audience.

---

8. See Mulvey; hooks; and Teresa de Lauretis's "Film and the Visible," 225–76.

9. The question of audience spectatorship that includes a distinct viewpoint of Disabled spectators different from the able-bodied is a valid one and should be examined. However, it is not central to the argument about the Disabled gaze *within* film that I am advancing here.

Seeing Blindness On-Screen

Georgina Kleege in her essay "Blind Nightmares" chronicles blindness in film. She writes, "The movie blind . . . are timid, morose, cranky, resentful, socially awkward, and prone to despair. Actors represent blindness with an unblinking zombie-like stare, directing their gazes upward to give the face a supplicating look of helplessness" (45). Film theory has not recognized that blind characters have their own distinct gaze, but film critics do mention blindness, as in Linda Williams's essay, "When the Woman Looks." In the essay Williams considers blindness as simply a sensory lack, the inability to see. Thus, when she theorizes, "to see is to desire" and thus "[b]lindness . . . signifies a perfect absence of desire" (561), she assumes that Blind women, because they cannot "see," cannot desire. Within this configuration Judith Traherne assumes in *Dark Victory* that her incurable blindness takes away her ability both to desire and to be desired and that, therefore, she'd be better off dead.

However, Williams and other feminist film critics have recognized changes in female representations in film. Molly Haskell, in *From Reverence to Rape*, suggests that the typical female character of 1960s and 1970s films is "a mail-order cover girl: regular featured, [with an] inability to convey any emotion beyond shock or embarrassment and an inarticulateness that was meant to prove her 'sincerity'" (329). Given how 1960s and 1970s films portray women, the supposedly desireless and dependent blind female characters in films such as *A Patch of Blue* (1965), *Ice Castles* (1978), and *Wait Until Dark* may not seem that far afield from non-disabled female characters in cinema. There was, however, a cultural shift in the portrayal of woman in mainstream cinema in the late 1970s to "strong," liberated women such as independent divorcée Meryl Streep in *Kramer vs. Kramer*, union-organizing Sally Field in *Norma Rae*, and Sigourney Weaver in the original *Alien* standing alone after all the human males and the alien have (supposedly) perished. However, *Ice Castles*, released the same year as *Kramer vs. Kramer*, *Norma Rae*, and *Alien* (1979), represents its main character, the "tragically blinded" ice-skater, Lexi, as a dependent character who resembles 1940s and 1950s screen women more than 1970s and 1980s female protagonists.

In the final scene Lexi has supposedly adapted to her blindness enough to pass as a sighted competitive ice-skater. Although viewers see a simulation of her blurred view of the rink before her routine, she completes the routine flawlessly. At the routine's end, however, instead of skating approximately to the exit, she trips on the roses strewn on the ice. Prior to this scene the film audience may believe that she has learned how to successfully pass as sighted, yet she does something completely uncharacteristic of someone who knows how to pass—and of most competitive skaters: she attempts to pick up the roses. This scene reveals the insufficiency of Lexi's Blind gaze as she trips on the roses. Rather than present her blurred gaze as at the beginning of her routine, the camera focuses on the stumble by shooting her from overhead, assuming the normative sighted gaze of the rinkside audience, peering down at her, shocked. The normative gaze co-opts Lexi's Blind gaze, constructed as sufficient, if not powerful, at the beginning of her routine, rendering her helpless and dependent. The film ultimately conveys her blindness as a liability. "Don't leave me," she pleads to love interest Nick as he helps her to her feet at center ice. Of course Nick doesn't, assuring both Lexi and the film audience that he will always be her eyes, that she can depend on his gaze to negotiate the world. This stereotypical portrayal of disabled characters' dependency contrasts the depictions of able-bodied female characters that challenge filmic stereotypes, and it invites my examination of the normative gaze as a trajectory of the Male gaze.

I suggest that cinematic representations of blindness perpetuate ableist notions of the primacy of the physical act of seeing. Audiences presume that Blind characters are not able to possess the ability to gaze, or to gaze well enough, and still remain the object of the dominant gaze. Two levels of seeing operate here. Literally, legal definitions of blindness encompass both people who see "nothing" and people with low vision.[10] Figuratively, I argue, the film blind do possess their own gaze. Examining Descartes's theory of the mechanism of vision, Alenka Zupančič writes in his essay "Philosopher, Blind Man's Bluff," "For Descartes, the 'blind man' does not function as the opposite of those who see. As a (blind) *man* he perceives in his own way everything that others do" (32; italics in original). Further, "Descartes's point is not simply that the blind, in some way, 'see' as we do. . . . It is not the blind who are compared to 'us' (who see), it is 'we' who have to be compared to the blind in order to be able to

---

10. In *Ice Castles* (1979) and later films such as *Blink* (1994), blurred camera shots showcase the blind character's presumed gaze. This depiction of the blind character's gaze departs from that in earlier films such as *Dark Victory* (1939), *Magnificent Obsession* (1954), and *A Patch of Blue* (1965) where no such shots of the blind character's gaze exists. In a poignant scene, in *Blue*, in which blind Selina D'Arcy ventures out alone and attempts to cross the street herself, the camera shoots skateboarders whizzing by as Selina presses herself against a storefront turning her head frantically in response to the barrage of noises. As she crosses the street, the camera shoots close-ups of jostled body parts and, in an overhead shot, shows Selina being bumped and shoved along in the crowd. "You shouldn't be out alone," a man claims, assisting her. The film presents this entire sequence *in clear focus* showing viewers what Selina *would* see if she *could* see anything at all. Whether the Blind gaze is presented as blurred or nonexistent, the stereotype of the blind character as helpless and dependent remains intact.

understand what happens when we see" (33). Descartes, Zupančič claims, believes that the blind have their own distinct gaze and way of interpreting what they see. But like Fanon and Fuss, Descartes and Zupančič recognize that here, again, the colonizer uses the gaze of the colonized for his/her own benefit.

Similarly, bell hooks claims for black women a distinct minority community. She asserts that the genre of Black films "came into being in part as a response to the failure of white-dominated cinema to represent blackness in a manner that did not reinforce white supremacy" (200). Her contention of a minority viewpoint distinct from the dominant (white male) one in terms of mainstream filmic representation, spectatorship, and criticism is important to the argument I am advocating of a distinct Disabled gaze that exists in mainstream film representation, a gaze different from the able-bodied gaze. Just as the gaze of the black female character in white-dominated cinema is used to reinforce "dominant cinematic practices"—that is, white privilege, as hooks suggests—the Blind gaze is often co-opted by the able-bodied characters and their normative gaze. Because, as I suggested earlier, the trajectory of cinematic representations of blindness has remained relatively stable, an examination of an older film, *Wait Until Dark*, remains pertinent to larger questions within disability studies and film studies.

Trespassing and Transgressing
Susy's World in Wait Until Dark

Wait Until Dark, directed by Terance Young, stars Audrey Hepburn as Susy Hendrix, a woman recently blind who is unwittingly caught up in a drug plot because she has a doll someone has filled with heroin. Two major stereotypes dominate: Susy as determined overcomer intent on being "the world's champion blind lady" and Susy as helpless victim who will fail to achieve that championship status. Although she outsmarts the henchmen and ultimately reunites with her husband, like Lexi's gaze in *Ice Castles*, Susy's gaze is, in the end, co-opted by the gaze of the sighted partner on whom she will depend. It is the second stereotype, her configuration as isolated, powerless victim, that I shall examine.

Throughout many of the stalking scenes, the film presents Susy as literally isolated. Young uses the visual metaphor of a prison, filming her, for instance, behind a banister after she learns her phone line has been severed. It is precisely her blindness, her perceived inability to "gaze," which keeps her isolated and helpless, and her helplessness drives the film.

Susy depends on a seven-year-old girl named Gloria for her connection to the world while her husband Sam is absent. Gloria, a neighboring child who brings Susy groceries, takes on a significant role. Helping Susy determine the identity of men who claim to be the police, Gloria peers out Susy's kitchen window and informs Susy that there is no police car outside, only a truck. After the henchman, Mike, leaves her apartment, Susy signals for Gloria (who has by this time left) to return to the apartment by tapping on the water pipes in her kitchen. Gloria arrives and Susy gives her a set of instructions about calling the police and meeting Sam, telling Gloria to bring him back to the apartment. Often directors depict such a scene with the adult instructing the child. Not here, however. In a wide-angle shot, viewers see a standing Gloria towering over a seated Susy, holding her hands. Although Susy instructs Gloria, the camera zooms in on Gloria's face as she peers down at Susy. Through employing Gloria's normative gaze, transference occurs. In essence, Susy becomes the child and Gloria the adult in this reversal of roles and power. The audience knows this because Susy's gaze is directed upward, signifying her helplessness. At the precise moment when Susy should be empowered through her Blind gaze, instead Gloria's normative gaze takes over the power of the scene and re-establishes Susy as a pitiful object who needs help.

The climactic scene further compounds Susy's infantile and powerless status. As she prepares for the confrontation with Roat, the head henchman, a series of shots depict Susy unscrewing and breaking light bulbs. This preparation scene is her transgression. That is, the only way for Susy to win her battle with Roat is to fight it on her terms—to disable him by "blinding" him, causing him to enter "her" world. Roat is supposedly the one dis-abled in this scene. Indeed, much of the fight scene occurs in the dark with only Susy's screams as a guide.[11]

At the beginning of the confrontation, Roat has the upper hand as he pours gasoline around the apartment. This scene is shot entirely from Roat's point of view as Susy implores, "What are you doing?" and then sniffs and exclaims, "Gasoline!" As Kaplan's theory suggests, Roat's Male gaze carries with it "the power of action" while Susy remains powerless. This scene depicts the supposed transfer of power from Roat to Susy when she asks, "Mr. Roat, are you looking at me?" He answers, "Yes,"

---

11. The DVD version notes that in the original theatrical release, audiences were forewarned that during the last eight minutes of the film (the climactic confrontation between Susy and Roat) theatres "will be darkened to the legal limit . . . to heighten the suspense." Although I do not discuss audience spectatorship, such a move raises interesting questions about disability simulation and its relationship to audience spectatorship and empathy.

affirming his gaze and position, and reminding her—and the audience— of "powers" he has that she no longer does. Then she throws the acid she has already put in the table vase on his face, "disabling" him, using his "gaze" against him. Power supposedly transfers here, but Susy still depends on Roat's affirmation to act. He is the one who, to use Kaplan's phrase, "owns and activates" the gaze. Therefore he remains in the "masculine/dominant" position. Susy's gaze still largely depends on his affirmation for her to act. Instead, her reliance on his verbal cue, coupled with her blind stare, ultimately reminds viewers of the power of sight and of both her powerlessness and her stigmatized status as other.

Were this scene shot in wide-angle, framing both their faces in the shot, if she appeared to have been maintaining eye contact with him, one could read her action of throwing the acid as a typical woman's self-defensive gesture, for her blindness would be a non-issue. But Susy is not a typical woman; she is a blind woman. As such, her position is continually disempowered in relation to the sighted. This sequence works to reinforce existing power dynamics because it is predicated on her blindness, on her supposed inability to act independently, a fact of which the able-bodied viewer is continually reminded.

Susy's role as disempowered continues throughout the sequence. Susy does not rely only on her own senses to tell her Roat's position in the room—that he is close, where his head is, and so on. Her throwing the acid does immobilize him, but acid coming into contact with any part of Roat's body would do so. In fact, seconds after she asks him whether he is looking at her, she throws the acid in his general direction doing just that. Susy's insistence on knowing whether he is looking at her is neither logical nor necessary for her to act. But the question of whether he is "looking at her" is not about her independence, her ability. It is about Roat's power over Susy.

In the climactic confrontation she physically struggles with Roat. Although she is able to gain possession of Roat's knife and douse him with gasoline, she tells him to tap her white cane (he does), so she can sense where he is. Instead of relying on her own senses—listening to his footsteps, his labored breathing from their struggle—she depends on Roat's actions and his compliance.

As the confrontation continues, the film depicts her dragging herself away from Roat, screaming. Viewers can assume that she stabs and kills Roat while the screen is darkened. The privileging of her gaze over Roat's in the fleeing moment of the darkened screen is short-lived. When Sam and Gloria come to save her, viewers see a weak and fearful figure, not a strong and capable heroine. Her back to the audience, Susy is wedged between the refrigerator door and the wall, fearful and whimpering. As Susy flies into Sam's embrace, viewers are led to believe, just as in the ending of *Ice Castles*, that the normative gaze of the sighted partner will protect her.

Directing the Blind Gaze

My discussion has so far centered on the co-optation of the Blind gaze by other characters in the film: Lexi by Nick, Susy by Gloria, and even Judith by her partner. In each of these films there are moments and scenes where the Blind gaze is directed not at another character but through the camera at the audience. In Susy's fight scene with Roat, for example, she keeps lighting the match as Roat taps toward her. As a blind woman, there is no need for her to continue to light the match; it does her no good. She lights the match for the benefit of the audience and proceeds to stare out at the camera with a "zombie-like stare" denoting her supposed lack of gaze. During Lexi's routine the camera frames her so that she stares not at the audience in the rink but at the audience in the theatre. She stares straight ahead at the moviegoing audience while her skating audience in the film is behind her or at her sides. Lexi's "zombie-like stare" does little more than match an ableist assumption that all blind characters possess a "zombie-like stare," an ableist assumption about what and how blind people "see."

Ice Castles addresses this ableist assumption about the "zombie-like stare" of the blind through schooling blind people about eye contact. As Georgina Kleege writes about eye contact in her essay "Here's Looking at You":

> I shift my eyes back, centering my eyes on his, or where I know them to be. I hit my mark—bull's eye—but I see and feel nothing. Still, nine out of ten people sitting across the table from me would call this eye contact. At the precise instant I see them least, they believe me to be involved in the most significant visual exchange. (124–25)

In this passage Kleege details a way that she is "passing as sighted," a phenomenon that Tanya Titchkosky, the sighted partner of a Blind person, discusses in her book *Disability, Self, and Society*. Titchkosky writes, "Passing means knowing how to do things with eyes, and knowing what to do that looks sighted when one is unsure what to do because one cannot see"

(70). Prior to Lexi's "zombie-like stare" at film's end, she is schooled in how to pass as sighted and how to make appropriate eye contact. In this scene Lexi walks backstage linked arm-in-arm between her coach and Nick. As her friend who does not know that Lexi is blind approaches, Lexi whispers, "Now?" and they tell her "not yet." As Lexi and her friend are about to pass each other side-by-side, Nick says "Now" and Lexi turns her head toward her friend and says, "Hi." The camera's pan shot encompasses the whole scene. Never does the camera shoot Lexi's face directly in this scene: she does not possess that zombie-like stare here; she passes as sighted.

Yet at the end, when the film once again constructs Lexi as helpless (when she trips over the roses), Lexi has a brief moment where she once again stares out at nothing. Likewise, when Audrey Hepburn's Susy interacts with Gloria, running around the apartment and staring out the window, the camera films her from the side while in motion. It is only when viewers are supposed to remember that the blind are helpless that passing as sighted and lessons in eye contact are forgotten in favor of the close-up shot that displays the co-opted Blind gaze as the gaze of unfocused zombie-like eyes staring at nothingness.[12]

Conclusion
Patterns and Polarities

I began this essay with Mary Anne Doane's idea that both disease and woman form threats to the dominant paradigm of masculinity. I have taken the idea of double marginalization, embodied in the filmic figure of the blind woman, and have examined how this double threat is manifested via the mechanism of the Blind gaze and its co-optation. In so doing, I hope to further discussions of disability representation in cinema through an examination of *how* representations are manifested by the gaze and to further discussions of marginalized minority-group gazes through herding all such gazes together under the term "normative." The larger issue of power dynamics and binarism that mark the relationship of the dominant gaze to the marginalized are common to my argument regardless of grouping. Referring to masculine and feminine polarities in

---

12. This is not a question of apparatus theory, that is, how the film camera is supposed to film a "Blind" gaze. The camera films no differently from how it films the gaze of the sighted person, unless the director wishes to highlight the stereotype that blind people see nothing (which is not true; most blind people have some level of residual sight).

film, Kaplan states, "Our culture is deeply committed to clearly demarcated sex differences, called masculine and feminine, that revolve on first, a complex gaze-apparatus; and second, dominance-submission patterns" (129). I take that hypothesis and apply it to disability and then consider the presence of a Disabled gaze in film: how it operates, and the dominant-submissive patterns between the able-bodied and the disabled. The construction of blind women, indeed of disabled persons generally, as both helpless and dependent reveals, I suggest, ableist fears about disability, about the possibility of becoming disabled, and about the loss of power such acquired disability supposedly brings.

Works Cited

Bad Object-Choices, eds. *How Do I Look?* Seattle: Bay Press, 1991.
Barashe, Moshe. *Blindness: The History of Mental Image in Western Thought.* New York: Routledge, 2001.
de Lauretis, Teresa. *Alice Doesn't: Feminism, Semiotics, Cinema.* Bloomington: Indiana University Press, 1984
———. "Film and the Visible." In *How Do I Look?* Edited by Bad Object-Choices. Seattle: Bay Press, 1991. 223–76.
Doane, Mary Ann. *The Desire to Desire: The Woman's Film of the 1940s.* Bloomington: Indiana University Press, 1987.
Fanon, Frantz. *Black Skin, White Masks.* Translated by Charles Lam Markmann. New York: Grove, 1967.
Fuss, Diana. *Identification Papers.* New York: Routledge, 1995.
Garland-Thomson, Rosemarie. *Extraordinary Bodies: Figuring Physical Disability in American Culture and Literature.* New York: Columbia University Press, 1997.
Haskell, Molly. *From Reverence to Rape: The Treatment of Women in the Movies.* New York: Holt, 1974.
hooks, bell. "the oppositional gaze: black female spectators." In *Reel to Reel: Race, Class, and Sex at the Movies.* New York: Routledge, 1996. 197–213.
Kaplan, E. Ann. "Is the Gaze Male?" In *Feminism and Film.* Edited by E. Ann Kaplan. Oxford: Oxford University Press, 2000. 119–38.
———, ed. *Feminism and Film.* Oxford: Oxford University Press, 2000.
Kleege, Georgina. "Blind Nightmares." In *Sight Unseen.* New Haven: Yale University Press, 1999. 43–66.
———. "Here's Looking at You." In *Sight Unseen.* New Haven: Yale University Press, 1999. 122–38.
Longmore, Paul K. "Screening Stereotypes: Images of Disabled People in Television and Motion Pictures." In *Why I Burned My Book and Other Essays on Disability.* Philadelphia: Temple University Press, 2003. 131–46.
Mast, Gerald, Marshall Cohen et al., eds. *Film Theory and Criticism: Introductory*

Readings. 4th edition. New York: Oxford University Press, 1992.

Mayne, Judith. *Cinema and Spectatorship*. New York: Routledge, 1993.

Mulvey, Laura. "Visual Pleasure and Narrative Cinema." In *Film Theory and Criticism: Introductory Readings*. 4th edition. Edited by Mast, Cohen et al. New York: Oxford University Press, 1992. 746–57.

Norden, Martin F. *The Cinema of Isolation: A History of Physical Disability in the Movies*. New Brunswick, NJ: Rutgers University Press, 1994.

Pothier, Dianne and Richard Devlin, eds. *Critical Disability Theory: Essays in Philosophy, Politics, Policy and Law*. Vancouver: University of British Columbia Press, 2004.

Saleci, Renata and Slavoj Žižek, eds. *The Gaze and Voice as Love Objects*. Durham: Duke University Press, 1996.

Titchkosky, Tanya. *Disability, Self, and Society*. Toronto: University of Toronto Press, 2003.

Williams, Linda. "When the Woman Looks." In *Film Theory and Criticism: Introductory Readings*. 4th edition. Edited by Mast, Cohen et al. New York: Oxford University Press, 1992. 561–77.

Zupančič, Alenka. "Philosopher, Blind Man's Bluff." In *The Gaze and Voice as Love Objects*. Edited by Renata Saleci and Slavoj Žižek. Durham: Duke University Press, 1996. 32–58.

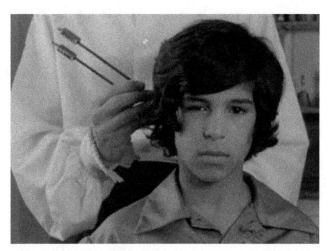

Le Dr Jean Itard (François Truffaut) tests the hearing of wild child Victor (Jean-Pierre Cargol). *L'enfant sauvage (The Wild Child)*. Directed by François Truffaut. Les Films du Carrosse, 1969. United Artists, 1970.

DAWNE McCANCE

The Wild Child

In what follows I approach François Truffaut's *The Wild Child* not as a "true story" based on scientific case reports, but as a creative undercutting of the claim to referential truth and of the binaries on which the claim builds. I argue that, with Truffaut himself in the role of the doctor, Jean Marc Gaspard Itard, *The Wild Child* portrays the physician (mentor-metaphysician) as caught in the *differend* between inside and outside: on the inside, Enlightenment science (mastery, sobriety, rationality, the economy of the hearth); on the outside, the stuff of myth (gesticulating man-animal monsters without language or ideas, the savage, the exotic, the deviant). Although the film deals with only one of Itard's case studies, his experiment with a hearing mute child, the so-called "wild child" of Aveyron, at the opening of the nineteenth century, I am interested in the fact that, by way of another of his celebrated patients, Itard reaches to the end of the century as well—and to the Paris Hôpital Salpêtrière of Jean-Martin Charcot and his favored student and amanuensis, Georges Albert Édouard Brutus Gilles de la Tourette. In making my claim as to Truffaut's contesting of referentiality, I will extend his role-playing to the character of Charcot and read his critique of "documentation" as applicable to Salpêtrière freeze-frame photography, an important forerunner of motion pictures. From Truffaut in 1970, then, I will move back to the beginning—and end—of the nineteenth century, in search of something that, in Georges Didi-Huberman's terminology, "besmirches" realist accounts, films and photographs (66). Walter Benjamin linked this something, this *differend*, to an "optical unconscious." I think there may be an acoustical counterpart. At the center of this story is the hearing mute child, Victor, whose treatment by doctors established his role as developmentally disabled.

Chirurgien Aide-Major

Truffaut's *L'enfant sauvage* (France 1970), translated as *The Wild Child* (U.S.) and *The Wild Boy* (U.K.), provides a motion-picture rendering of the case of a so-called feral child who was discovered in the forest of southern France near the end of 1799 when he was about twelve years of age; after escape and recapture, the child was brought to Paris in September of 1800 for assessment and institutional placement. It was at the National Institute for Deaf Mutes that Itard first encountered the child, who was mute, and for a time considered also to be deaf. Along with Philippe Pinel, Charcot's predecessor at the Salpêtrière, Itard examined the child, discovering some indicators of auditory awareness but a complete indifference to "civilized" sound, including the all-important sound of human speech. Mute and impassive, the child was quickly consigned to less-than-human status. In Harlan Lane's account, Pinel "considered the wild boy practically incapable of auditory attention, and took this as one more symptom of the boy's hopeless idiocy" (111). Itard alone did not concur with this bleak assessment, so much so that he sought permission to "adopt" the child he christened "Victor" and to experiment on his potential for advancement toward the "human" state. Itard's task, as he stated it, was to solve the following problem of metaphysics: "to determine what would be the degree of intelligence and the nature of the ideas of an adolescent, who, deprived from his childhood of all education, had lived entirely separated from individuals of his own species" (7).

Solution of the problem—that is, assessment of the child's rational capacity—would consist in exhibiting the extent to which Victor could assume an upright gait, attune his hearing to phonetic language, and utter articulate (what Descartes called "real") speech. If Victor remained deaf to civilization, capable of hearing only animal noise, the case would be lost—an outcome that seemed unthinkable to Itard, given his confidence in the power of Enlightenment science and given his opinion that the boy, likely abandoned by his parents, was not necessarily a member of the species *Homo ferus*, classified by Linnaeus in his 1735 *System of Nature*, but rather a *human* suffering only from years of isolation and deprivation, a child developmentally disabled.

In some ways Itard is an unlikely linchpin for this story, as he was a banker by profession before being called into military service in Revolutionary France. While in the army and without any medical education behind him, he received "on the job" training as a surgeon's assistant—acquiring his skills by imitation. Only at the conclusion of his military service did he embark on medical studies, taking up duties as a surgical intern, *chirurgien aide-major,* in 1796 at the Paris Hôpital Val de Grâce, a few blocks down the Faubourg Saint-Jacques from the National Institute for Deaf Mutes. By 1800, he had moved to the institute as its resident physician, just in time for the arrival of the "wild child." Itard had an obvious interest in otology, even before science of the ear had become a medical specialization, and he was inclined to think that hearing, as well as speech, was something one could be taught. His optimism about the potential of pedagogy was clearly at odds with the view of his senior, the father-figure Pinel, who judged the child to be "quite inferior to some of our domestic animals" and certainly "incurable."[1]

Nor was Itard's optimism shared by institute officials, particularly when, despite gradual improvements in hearing, the boy remained mute (Lane 112). Indeed, to read Itard's descriptions of the "feral" child during the period after his capture—and even five years later—is to recognize that, by the doctor's own account, the pedagogical challenge he faced was daunting. For example, Itard's first report recalls, on capture, a "disgustingly dirty child affected with spasmodic movements and often convulsions who swayed back and forth ceaselessly like certain animals in the menagerie" (Itard 4). Victor's locomotion "was extraordinary," Itard writes, even after he was made to wear shoes, "always remarkable because of his difficulty in adjusting himself to our sober and measured gait, and because of his constant tendency to trot and gallop." As do animals, the child "had an obstinate habit of smelling at everything that was given to him." And "his mastication was equally astonishing, executed as it was solely by the sudden action of the incisors, which because of its similarity to that of certain rodents was a sufficient indication that our savage, like these animals, most commonly lived on vegetable products."

On each point Itard's initial observations suggest that the case might represent a breaching of the human/animal divide—a disability stereotype that prevailed long into the twentieth century. "A dead canary was given to him and in an instant the bird was stripped of its feathers big and little, opened with his nail, sniffed at and thrown away" (8). In his second report, written five years later (November 1806) for the Minister of the Interior, Itard refers to the newly captured boy as a "man-animal" whose physical and mental faculties ranked him "not only in the lowest grade of his species but even at the lowest stage of the animals" (53–54). Invariably, Itard relates the child's perceived animality to the fact that,

---

1. In his report, government commissioner Constans-Saint-Estève took the child to be close to the state of wild animals, and it was with "wild animals" that the child was most often compared, especially soon after his capture, when he was discovered to be mute. Linnaeus, of course, listed *mutus* as the second attribute of *homo ferus* (Itard 5).

especially early out of the forest, "he made no sort of sound" (9). Even if Victor's habit of "running on all fours" could be overcome, and even if the feral creature could be taught to eat like a human rather than "like a monkey" (Lane 10), to cure his depravity Itard would still have to lead Victor to speech *by mimesis*, that is, "lead him to the use of speech by inducing the exercise of imitation through the imperious law of necessity" (Itard 10–11). The first step, however, would be to make him hear, "to awaken the ears of our savage from their long torpor" (55).

Itard recorded such observations as these in two detailed case reports, *Rapports et mémoires sur le sauvage de l'Aveyron*. The title gives away another crossing that, for posterity, distinguishes this case and that, along with human/animal breaching, is in my view the subject of Truffaut's film: Itard's recorded observations of Victor are at once paradigms of detailed scientific documentation and poetico-autobiographical memoirs. Truffaut bases his film on these clinical case histories—the would-be scientific *tableau* that not only acknowledges its reliance on mimesis, and thus dramaturgy, as a pedagogical and diagnostic tool, but also indulges in a hybrid genre of autobiography, one that includes, among other things, memoir, confession, family history, and political commentary. In short, diagnostic "science" is here based on anything but "pure fact." Of particular interest to Truffaut is the folding that these case histories enact of *logos* into *mythos*, such that Itard's clinical-pedagogical case studies (exercises in "metaphysics"), as these become voice-over for the film, have more to do with myth (and its imagined "monsters") than with referential medicine; more to do with destabilizing than with sustaining the core myth of rationality (the curative power of Enlightenment science, the human/animal hierarchy).

Theatre of Mimesis

More often than not, Truffaut's *L'enfant sauvage* is promoted as belonging to a realist genre, based as it is on the "true life" account of Victor taken from Itard's clinical tracts. Truffaut shot the film in "documentary" black and white, and, as if to accent its adherence to clinical details of the actual case, he used Itard's case reports to script the film's voice-over narrative. "Truffaut decided to make a 'barely fictionalized' historical film," Roger Shattuck writes. "By choosing to shoot in black and white instead of in color and to use little-known actors rather than stars, he kept the action soberly focused on the events as Itard told them" (209). Julie Codell makes a similar point, suggesting that "Truffaut's cool voice-over offers a conventional view of the Enlightenment itself as scientific, objective, and detached" (104). In support of the film's realism, critics cite Truffaut himself, who claimed that *L'enfant sauvage* "has a quite strong savor of authenticity, because it is a true story scarcely at all fictionalized [. . .] From the day I decided to play Itard the film took on for me a truly complete and definitive *raison d'être*. From this experience I don't retain the impression of having played a role, but simply of having directed the film 'in front of' the camera and not 'behind' as usual" (qtd. in Codell 103). Seemingly, the fact that Truffaut plays Itard encourages critics to define the film as realist representation: "His documentary style is enhanced by his impersonation of the rationalist Itard" (104).

Granted, Codell puts the film's realism into question, acknowledging the entanglement of autobiography in Truffaut's quasiscientific documentary. With Truffaut in the role of Itard, the film becomes as much an account of the director's personal life and his New Wave philosophy and filmography as a realist rendering of Itard and the Aveyron feral child case. Codell suggests that Truffaut as Itard (as Truffaut) may also be playing André Bazin, Truffaut's mentor: "Truffaut as Itard plays Bazin and himself as a mentoring adult" (103). As well as mentoring adult, critics have noted, Truffaut may also be acting out, through Victor, his own troubled childhood and his adolescent experience as outsider to the same system that could not assimilate the "wild boy." The mimetic possibilities are endless, with stories and selves folding into the film's so-called documentary realism: Truffaut as Itard as Truffaut as Bazin as Truffaut—and, why not add: as Charcot, the doctor-as-performer, lover of theatre and of play, positioning himself onstage with his patient in front of the camera as well as behind it?

I am drawn to this connection: Truffaut as Itard as Charcot and all the realists' promise the latter brought to late-nineteenth-century medical science. For one thing, Itard does provide, through one of his patients, a direct link to Charcot's "theatre of hysteria" at the Salpêtrière. The patient in question was the Marquise de Dampierre, whose history Itard documented in his 1801 report: a member of the Parisian aristocracy, Madame de D. was given to unseemly shouting, cursing, uttering of obscenities, and sexually explicit display. While this patient, with her speech-and-gait disorder, marked yet another failed cure for Itard, the Marquise nonetheless provided, some sixty years later, a case from which Georges Gilles de la Tourette, working at the time under Charcot at the Salpêtrière, defined the syndrome that bears his name. In his 1885 "Study of a Neurologic Condition" Gilles de la Tourette outlined Madame de D.'s abnormal movements, which "spread" to involve her voice and speech, such that the more uncontrolled her gestures became, the more inarticulate were her uttered sounds. Not even marriage and maternity could bring stability to the Marquise, Gilles de la Tourette reported (basing his information entirely on Itard's documentation of the case): "Professor Charcot saw this patient on several occasions and personally witnessed her movements and vocalizations." Gilles de la Tourette went on to note that "in 1884, the newspapers published her obituary and some of them included for their readers a list of the obscene words that she had sadly pronounced, in particular, '*merde*' and '*foutu cochon*' ('shit' and 'dirty pig')" (Gilles de la Tourette 3).

Gilles de la Tourette never met or examined the Madame de D., and he relied on Itard's 1825 report in defining a before-the-fact case of Tourette syndrome (for a time considered to be a form of hysteria, which in turn, with its "wandering womb," conjured up a number of "animal" associations[2]). These details add to the "besmirching" that interests me here. All the more provocative, then, is the link from Itard, through Gilles de la Tourette, to Charcot who, following Pinel, took up his place at center stage of the great anatomy theatre, indeed *amphitheatre*, of the Salpêtrière, aspiring there to a full and exact science of the speech-and-gait disorder called "hysteria." Didi-Huberman notes that when Charcot entered this *citta dolorosa* in 1863, hysteria had not yet been "invented," or at least, as Freud put it in his 1893 Charcot obituary, it had not yet been "rediscovered" (18–19). Charcot set out to give hysteria scientific-medical legitimacy, to achieve absolute knowledge, and so absolute mastery, of it by using the camera to organize its myriad and fleeting symptoms into a comprehensive and coherent nosological grid. Charcot wanted to provide for movement-disorder medicine what Linnaeus had for natural science; he wanted to configure hysteria into a purely referential classificatory *tableau*:

> For a long time, medicine was circling around a fantasy of a *language-tableau*—its own language: integrating the successive nature, and, in particular, the temporal dissemination of the "case" into a two-dimensional space of simultaneity and tabulation, into an outline against a ground of

2. These associations go back a long way, Didi-Huberman notes. Hysteria, he writes, "was the symptom, to put it crudely, *of being a woman*. And everyone still knows it. *Ustéra*: that which is all the way back, at the limit: the womb. The word 'hysteria' appears for the first time in Hippocrates' thirty-fifth aphorism, where it is said: 'When a woman suffers from hysteria or difficult labor an attack of sneezing is beneficial.' This means that sneezing puts the uterus in place, in its true place. This means that the uterus is endowed with the capacity of movement. This means that the woman's sort of 'member' is an animal" (68)—that is, "something that moves on its own" (71).

Cartesian coordinates. This tabulation would then be an exact "portrait" of "the" illness, to the extent that it could lay out, in a very visible way, just what the history of an illness (with its concurrent or percurrrent causes) tended to conceal. (24–25)

At the same time, however, this lover of power and truth, this "Sun King and Caesar" of the Paris medical profession who first "elevated the figure of the doctor into the Chief" (15, 17), drew on a "dramaturgical passion" that was equal to his "passion for measurement" (227, 179). Charcot's Tuesday lessons were thus memorable theatrical scenes—better theatre than Freud could find anywhere else in Paris. Indeed, as Ulrich Baer suggests, where hysterical symptoms were concerned, Charcot, lover of the circus, often succeeded in outperforming his patients, who were in turn regularly suspected of feigning symptoms the physician wanted them to betray (43). "Did they really suffer, or were they putting him on? Indeed, is it not the doctor who suffers the hysterics' charades—suffers them as a threat to his authority, his mastery, his grasp of truth?" (31). In the circularity of this Salpêtrière theatre of mimesis, where the doctor imitates the patient imitating the doctor simulating symptoms, Baer locates the referential crisis that plagues psychoanalysis from the start and that thwarts the anatomist-clinician's claim to conscious mastery—even as it brings to light what Benjamin called an "optical unconscious" (51).[3] I am suggesting that the same crisis plagues the diagnosis and labeling of the hearing mute Victor.

With Charcot the slippage of reference found its way into what was to have been hysteria's most advanced tableau, the *Nouvelle iconographie de la Salpêtrière*, the first volume of which appeared in 1888. The journal was supposed to be a study in exactitude, a representation, an iconography, of hysteria through pages and pages of photographic notation, many of the images "freeze-frame" portraits of female inmates of the Salpêtrière. Through the *facies* of his patients, with the sixteen-year-old Augustine as his much-preferred subject (photographed object), Charcot, the "clinical director (*metteur en scène*)," aimed to find his own version of Cartesian certitude; it seems that the director, "a bit of a performer or even an imposter" (Goetz et al. 53) did not expect to be outdone by Augustine's theatricality. While the camera may have arrested Augustine's incoherent babble, it did not so much freeze the hysteric's histrionics as make visible her mimicry, including her miming of the photographic apparatus itself (Baer 56).

---

3. Baer's reference here is to Benjamin's "A Small History of Photography."

In many ways Charcot's photographic studies of female faces are akin to the gait and locomotion photo-grids that Muybridge was developing at the same time in Pennsylvania. In the Salpêtrière footprint laboratory, Gilles de la Tourette was doing much the same thing, using white paper rather than photographic film, to record the footprint pattern of patients whose feet had been coated in red powder. Publishing the results of this study in 1886 as *Études cliniques et physiologiques sur la marche*, dedicated to "mon très Honoré Maitre: M. J.-M. Charcot," Gilles de la Tourette speculated that deviations from a normal gait could be used to diagnose neurological disease. No doubt, Gilles de la Tourette himself practiced these deviant gaits, for he was an adept mimic who even betrayed symptoms of the syndrome he named,[4] yet he may not have been a match for Charcot, who "was known to imitate various gaits with uncanny accuracy by expertly breaking down complex movements into their components and sequentially coalescing them again into the final behavior" (Goetz et al.143–44). Here is the paradox: the analytical method—breaking a footprint down into angle of inclination, length of step, lateral swerve, and so on—is both a dramaturgical method and the key to Cartesian certitude. The analytical method represents both the "loss of gesture" (Agamben 48) to positivist science and the gesture's proliferation among physicians-metaphysicians such as Charcot, for whom imitation becomes crucial to diagnostic truth.

Does the Savage Speak?

Trufffaut's *The Wild Child* is all about this theatricality of "science," where Truffaut as Itard plays (like Charcot) before and behind the camera and where Itard's would-be education of Victor—his experiment in metaphysics—depends entirely on mimicry. The pedagogical props that Itard mentions in his casebooks thus become crucial to the film and to its foregrounding of the reliance of science on game. One example is the shell game that the film returns to a number of times, a game in which Itard (Truffaut) turns silver cups upside down on a table, placing a chestnut under one of them. As outlined in Itard's journal and as shown in the

---

4. Historians and biographers (see, for example, H. Lees Krämer and C. Daniels, "Pioneers of Movement Disorders," 691–701) never fail to point out that Gilles de la Tourette was subject to vocal aberrations: a voice unusually rough and hoarse, increasingly worn-out yet disarmingly loud, particularly when he would suddenly explode into passion and shout, and as if in imitation of his patients' *maladie des tics*; he was also known for his "strange ataxic gait" and his inclination to "abrupt gestures." A. J. Lees, "Georges Gilles de la Tourette," 811, 816.

film, Victor quickly masters the game, winning the chestnut as his reward. Itard then introduces more complications—changing the order of the cups, placing nuts under two or three cups at once, replacing the chestnut with an object that cannot be eaten—but in each instance the boy performs equally well. Itard concludes in his report that what attracted Victor to the game in the first place was only his appetite for food, so that success in the shell game provides but a measure of the child's "animal attention" (21). Significantly, the film picks up on this observation and on the transition Itard then makes to games more appropriate for measurement of *human* discernment—such as drawing objects (e.g., scissors, key, hammer) on the chalkboard and having Victor hang each object on a nail beneath its corresponding image. The film is careful to depict Victor's success in such shape-recognition games, portraying the child as, if anything, bored by the repeated routines the games entail, but anxious to win his master's approval. It is where the games move into speech (progression from the game of colors and shapes to the game of alphabet letters to that of spelling the word *lait*) that Victor begins to falter. Though able to recognize (memorize) shapes and letters, Victor proves to be incapable of speech. In the end, having acquired but four words, he remains all but mute—for the reason that, Itard concedes, his hearing cannot be "awakened."

Since for Itard "of all the senses hearing is the one which contributes most particularly to the development of our intellectual faculties"—since, in other words, the mind/body, civilized/savage binary rests on this sense more than on any other—his reports stress the importance of putting "all imaginable resources into play in order to awaken the ears of our savage" (55). To "awaken" means "to lead to speech." In order to bring this phonocentrism to the fore, and to reveal it to be a sustaining myth for Enlightenment science, Truffaut introduces some changes to Itard's account of the Aveyron case. One of these changes is evident from the very opening of the film, where Victor is shown prior to his capture, running through the woods on all fours, foraging in the forest floor, drinking in animal fashion from a stream, and swiftly climbing to the top of a tall tree. In the iris shot that closes this scene, and that opens the film, we see Victor rocking back and forth in the high reaches of the tree, an unmistakable framing of his animality, as if to announce that the civilization/wilderness binary will be the subject of this film. To foreground the binary from the outset, Truffaut changed Victor's fear of heights, reported by Itard, to a fear of confinement. When "Truffaut decided to change acrophobia to claustrophobia in the later shock-therapy scene, he sacrificed authenticity at the wrong point," Shattuck contends (212). Perhaps not:

for the alteration introduced by the first iris shot critically focuses the impassible human/animal boundary that Itard's science puts into place.

Based on the Itard reports, when the "man-animal" was dragged out of the forest, "It was found that the sound of a cracking walnut or other favorite eatable never failed to make him turn round" (Itard 15). Early in the film Truffaut changes this clinical detail into village gossip. The boy has been brought to the Institute for Deaf Mutes at this point and is being examined by Itard and Pinel, while the old peasant Rémy sits to one side of the room. When Victor appears not to hear a door that is slammed behind him by Pinel, the physicians venture that "he might be deaf and dumb." Rémy then interjects with the walnut story, which he offers as hearsay that is circulating in the village, where some people in the crowd that had gathered around the feral creature claimed to have seen him wheel round at the crack of a nut. In case we might consider the village to be an appropriate site for such audio testing, Truffaut shows us the melee, with the crowd wildly taunting the captured child. What Itard records in his reports as scientific evidence of the difference between a civilized and a savage ear Truffaut thus transforms into unreliable prejudice—that is yet seized upon by institute doctors as providing the binary they need.

Although Itard's mentoring of Victor took place at the Paris Institute for Deaf Mutes, Truffaut recasts the setting altogether, having the doctor remove the child to his own country home, where, "free from the restraints and cruelties of an urban institution" (Codell 104) he might enjoy the nurturing affection of Madame Guérin. This makes for a major change to the clinical account, especially with the introduction of a family scene, what Shattuck nostalgically refers to as "the remarkable family unit of Victor, Itard, and Madame Guérin" (210). Portrayal of this idealized family, a "family" free of *eros* (there is no sexual relation shown between Itard and Guérin, and Itard's account of Victor's sexual awakening is left out of the film), accentuates the disparity (Itard's boundary) between civilized domesticity and the wilderness out of which Victor comes.

Truffaut often uses a window to frame this boundary, the separation of home-hearth from the forest beyond it; or, conversely, he uses a window to mediate between inside and outside. When they visit Itard's friends, Victor peers through the window at the domestic scene inside. When Victor returns from an attempted escape, he appears at Itard's window, again looking from the outside in. To an extent, the window is a detail Truffaut takes from Itard, who remarks that "the window was Victor's favorite place." But it is Truffaut who uses the window to call up the civilization/savage hierarchy. Codell describes one scene where "Itard is at a blackboard at the far left, with Victor as far away as possible, in front of the window on the far right of the scene, an expression of the now-hostile dichotomy between civilization (the impervious blackboard) and nature (through the window). While Itard writes on the board, Victor sneaks away, making a temporary escape that foreshadows his longer one at the end of the film" (115–16). In another scene, shot at night under a full moon, Itard stands inside the house at a window, gazing down at Victor, who has escaped from his bedroom and is rollicking on all fours in the yard. Here, again, the window frames the binary constructed by the Itard reports, the boundary between educated gentility and an animality that the doctor cannot tame.

Throughout *The Wild Child*, Truffaut portrays Victor's incapacity to hear-and-speak as what keeps him from crossing the human/animal line. Some of the framing devices he uses to this end are quite remarkable. In the institute sequences, for example, where Itard and Pinel examine the newly arrived child, two large anatomical charts—one of the ear, the other of the organs of speech—frame the diagnostic scene, marking the story as phonocentric from the start. This scene modulates into another where Victor stands before a mirror but does not recognize himself in it; thus he is incapable, in Jacques Lacan's terms, of crossing the threshold into speech and autonomous subjectivity. Truffaut frames this "mirror-stage" scene so as to capture the images of Itard and Pinel in the looking glass, standing behind the child, the two physicians framed in turn by the speech and hearing anatomical charts. The looking glass ("mirror stage") scene sets up the failure with which the film, like the Itard reports, ends: Victor's incapacity to progress from image (*imitatio*, mimesis) to speech (the measure of human rationality, the benchmark of Enlightenment science). The film's closing iris fade-out captures this binary, the boundary that the hearing mute Victor cannot cross.

Works Cited

Agamben, Giorgio. *Means Without End: Notes on Politics.* Translated by Vincenzo Binetti and Cesare Casarino. Minneapolis: University of Minnesota Press, 2000.

Baer, Ulrich. *Spectral Evidence: The Photography of Trauma.* Cambridge: MIT Press, 2002.

Benjamin, Walter. "A Small History of Photography." (1931). In *One Way Street.* Translated by Edmund Jephcott and Kingsley Shorter. London: New Left Books, 1979. 240–57.

Codell, Julie F. "Playing Doctor: François Truffaut's *L'enfant sauvage* and the Auteur/Autobiographer as Impersonator." *Biography* 29.1 (Winter): 101–22.

Didi-Huberman, Georges. *Invention of Hysteria: Charcot and the Photographic Iconography of the Saltpêtrière.* Translated by Alisa Hartz. Cambridge: MIT Press, 2003.

Freud, Sigmund. "Charcot." (1893). In *The Standard Edition of the Complete Psychological Works of Sigmund Freud. Vol. III.* Translated and edited by James Strachey. London: Hogarth Press and the Institute of Psycho-Analysis, 1962. 11–23.

Gilles de la Tourette, Georges. *Études cliniques et physiologiques sur la marche.* Paris: Aux Bureaux Du Progrés/A. Delahaye et Lecrosnier, 1886.

———. "Study of a Neurologic Condition Characterized by Motor Incoordination Accompanied by Echolalia and Corprolalia." (1885). Translated by C. G. Goetz and H. L. Klawans. In *Advances in Neurology.* Edited by Arnold Friedhof and Thomas Chase. 1982.

Goetz, Christopher G., Michel Bonduelle, and Toby Gelfand. *Charcot: Constructing Neurology.* New York: Oxford University Press, 1995. 1–16.

Itard, Jean Marc Gaspard. *The Wild Boy of Aveyron. Rapports et mémoires sur le sauvage de l'Aveyron.* (1801). Translated by George Humphrey and Muriel Humphrey. New York and London: The Century Co., 1932.

Krämer, H. Lees and C. Daniels. "Pioneers of Movement Disorders: Georges Gilles de la Tourette." *Journal of Neural Transmission* 111 (2004): 691–701.

Lane, Harlan. *The Wild Boy of Aveyron.* Cambridge: Harvard University Press, 1976.

Lees, A. J. "Georges Gilles de la Tourette: The Man and His Times." *Review of Neurology* 142.2 (1986): 811, 816.

Shattuck, Roger. *The Forbidden Experiment: The Story of the Wild Boy of Aveyron.* New York: Kodansha International, 1994.

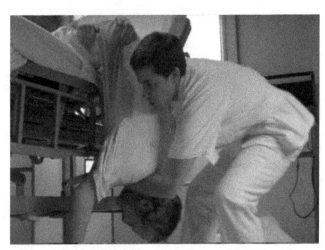

Ken (Richard Dreyfuss) reacts uncontrollably to the hospital's medical treatment. *Whose Life Is It Anyway?* Directed by John Badham. MGM Films, 1981.

PAUL DARKE

No Life Anyway

Pathologizing Disability on Film

"Deformed bodies depress me."
—Nicholas Van Ryan in *Dragonwyck*, 1946

Many films represent the problem of disability as caused by impairment rather than as socially oriented or constructed. Thus the medical model of disability has almost total hegemony over the modern definition of disability on film: placing "disability" within the individual's own body as its impairment. For the medical model (of disease and deformity), the body is a machine with a physiological norm to which the body either does or does not conform; if it does not fit the norm, all subsequent problems are due to its corporeal deviance, not to the social perception of deformity and disease. Thus, despite social change, the archetypal and stereotypical persist.

The film *Whose Life Is It Anyway?* (1981) focuses on the fictional character Ken Harrison, who sustains irreversible quadriplegia in a car accident, necessitating, in the logic of the film, lifelong hospitalization. The hospital doctors, nurses, and technicians impose every possible act of objectification and surveillance—medicalization—upon Ken to keep him alive. The film is a critique of medicalization—it even advocates demedicalization—but it bases its critique on people with impairments. The film dehumanizes and pathologizes the impaired as a burden, out of a desire to demean the technology that keeps *them* alive. The film argues that modern medicine unnaturally keeps certain people alive and that those people have to be portrayed as less than human in order to demean medicalization. The way the film ascribes certain culturally unacceptable and filmically constructed characteristics to the body of Ken Harrison makes

97

him—and his type—inhuman and other. Thus medicalization comes across as "bad" because it keeps the negative, subhuman disabled body alive. The body that becomes disabled in films is routinely devalued and degraded (Barnes) by the creation, intimation, or presentation of a glorious past or alternative normality seen in parallel with an abject present (Norden). A similar narrative process of negation for an impaired character appears in almost all films about disease, impairment, and disability, whatever date, diversity of style, genre, and production base (Norden). *Whose Life*—the epitome of its genre—achieves this process of negation by including before-the-accident and after-the-accident components.

Whose Life dehumanizes Ken by having him articulate his inhumanness himself in a particularly human way: he shows his humanness through his ability to be a thoughtful, rational, and intelligent person. The film then turns to Ken's body to render him inhuman by depicting him as dependent and impotent, as well as characterizing him as "feminine." Keeping Ken alive thwarts the ideal of independent living through the mise-en-scène implication that medicalization is essential. The film's antimedicalization argument first appears in a scene when Dr. Emmerson calls into his office a psychiatrist and Dr. Scott. Emmerson explains to the psychiatrist that he wants Ken committed on the premise that Ken's desire to have the right to die is irrational. At this point the psychiatrist immediately agrees to carry out committal proceedings without having met Ken. Significantly, the psychiatrist overly values a medical doctor's opinion over a clinical evaluation of Ken (thereby further reinforcing the excesses of medicalization). The scene takes place in Dr. Emmerson's office, an office lined with television monitors of the ICU patients. As Dr. Scott starts her speech against such a process, she strides to the monitors and points at them. She argues:

> [D]oes he look crazy to you? Look at him lying there. I mean, Christ, he's got no privacy at all, he's got no sense of dignity. I tell you, if that happened to me I don't know if I'd have the courage to live either. Would you like to live like that?

Significantly, it is a generalized argument: she is speaking not merely about Ken but about all ICU patients and, ironically, about all nondisabled people who cannot conceive of living with impairment. The validity of Dr. Scott's perspective is clearly established in this scene and by her prior and subsequent character development. For example, in this scene, Dr. Scott, a stereotypical WASP, walks into the light as she speaks her lines and is touched by the natural light coming through the office windows. Her adversary, which is what Dr. Emmerson becomes, is in the shade and, significantly, has a much darker ethnic appearance. This additional stereotype element of ethnic representation also plays into imagery that constructs certain ethnicities as evil. Further, it reveals how most stereotypes—especially, though not exclusively, gendered ones—are often interdependent and/or work interdependently (Norden 315). Since Emmerson has just ordered a psychiatrist to commit a man established in the film as highly rational and perhaps even illuminated by intellect, the lighting and mise-en-scène contrast—literally and metaphorically—with the light in which the audience sees Emmerson. Emmerson is also smoking—allowing himself (with legal consent) to self-destruct, yet he is the one who decides whether to "allow" Ken a similar right.

The monitors in Emmerson's office appear as screen representations of what Foucault calls the clinical gaze, a gaze that is on the individual at all times and in all places (*The Birth* ix–x). Dr. Scott herself states that for Ken, privacy and dignity are nonexistent. Some writers (e.g., Armstrong 8) argue that the modern hospital is a panopticon writ large (following Foucault, *Discipline and Punish*): Emmerson's hospital signifies the epitome of such a hospital. The name "Emmerson" itself is ironic because it conjures the philosophy of nineteenth-century transcendentalist poet Ralph Waldo Emerson. The film problematically uses disability as the perspective through which to examine medicalization; further, it practices in its discourse an extreme form of normalization by demeaning the successes of medical advances. The film conflates the technological benefits of medicine with the excessive potential for dehumanizing. *Whose Life*'s normalization is highly prescriptive in that it sets up a rationale for preserving a life only if the life has a certain degree of both bodily and intellectual control.

Ironically, all the characters who "befriend" and "love" Ken are those who eventually support his wish to die: the young, attractive female Dr. Scott; a petite white female student nurse named Joey; his white male lawyer; and a black Caribbean hospital porter called John. John emphasizes the film's agenda when, while trying to get Joey to go out with him, he asks her, "How much does it cost to keep [Ken] alive; thousands of dollars a week?"

JOEY: That's not the point.
JOHN: Well the point is that in Africa people die of the measles, ya know,
    little babies even. Only cost a few pennies to keep 'em alive. No,
    there's got to be something crazy somewhere, man!
JOEY: Well that's wrong too.

Here, then, John aligns the cost of medical treatment with the ethics of whether they should keep Ken alive: in other words, financial cost equals ethics. The choice of low camera angle and John and Joey's extreme friendliness to Ken reinforce the power of John's and Joey's viewpoints. Consequently, as Ken's friends advocate his death on purely economic grounds, their argument gains validity as a central theme of the film's criticisms against medicalization and, by implication, marks impairment as expensive and unproductive. Equally, Joey's support for Ken soon becomes positive support for his wishes to die. By characterizing Ken as physically dependent, the film reveals how modern medicine incurs financial problems in its shift from curing infectious diseases to containing and curing chronic degenerative illness. Significantly, Joey wishes Ken "good luck" when he goes to court (a makeshift court in the hospital library) to plead for the right to die.

Whose Life consists predominantly of long takes, some lasting up to nearly two minutes and emphasizing that Ken's needs are time-consuming. One such scene starts with a fairly static long take of Joey giving Ken his coffee, which Ken spills. Ken then falls out of bed while Joey cleans him. The simple visualization that Ken needs special canned (sterile) coffee makes specific the high cost of keeping him alive; he requires not just technology but special people and special nourishment. When Ken starts to fall out of bed, the pace of the music increases, the positions and angles of the camera shift sharply, and the cuts become increasingly rapid. Between Ken's starting to fall, and his falling and being put back in bed into his former position, there are twenty-seven shots that together last under seventy seconds. They consist of straight-on medium shots of Joey, who is panicking; long shots of male and female nurses coming to rescue Joey/Ken; and shots of Ken's body slipping down to the floor, from the bed, from under the bed, and from the opposite side of the bed. Most important, though, are the point-of-view shots from where Ken is, shots that involve the camera panning left, tilting ninety degrees, rapidly, and shots canted from the floor as Ken's head rests upon it. The disorientation suggested by the movement of the camera, and the pace and rapidity of the shots, combine to emphasize the helplessness and terror that a lack of body control—in Ken and the disabled—entails in circumstances where control would be advantageous. Rather than offering the rare point-of-view shot from the perspective of a person with an impairment, this sequence depicts Ken as simply helpless; he becomes a spectacle for the camera, initially, and then for the medical gaze: Emmerson, his students, and Dr. Scott walk in upon Ken hanging from his bed.

Upon falling out of bed, Ken first seems to feel embarrassed, but his emotion turns to outrage when Emmerson walks in with the student doctors. Ken orders them all out. Christopher Ricks's assessment of Keats's art and its use of embarrassment is applicable here to how Ken feels, and what the art of the film achieves, when he states that embarrassment is connected with feelings of "defenselessness" and that art "uses embarrassment to help [the spectator] deal with it, not by abolishing or ignoring it, but by recognizing, refining and putting it to good human use" (1). Ken's embarrassment is rooted in his defenselessness. The art of the film assumes and takes advantage of the audience's defenselessness against developing quadriplegia (an impairment) to make the audience feel as uncomfortable in observing Ken's defenselessness as Ken is in experiencing it. A socially constructed reaction such as embarrassment, in this case, is the embarrassment of witnessing the deformed or non-controllable body, as individualized in Ken. When Ken decides that it is "right" for his embarrassment to be removed (by his committing suicide), the film imposes closure. This resolution relieves an audience's embarrassment and discomfort and restores the ideal world (of entertainment and normality). The embarrassment in the scene is not only what the audience witnesses but also what the audience's required emotional response is, because embarrassment is both personal *and* social in all contexts. No other single scene in the film more explicitly combines its philosophy and imagery to greater effect.

Mary Douglas claims that the human body is a symbol of society and that "we cannot possibly interpret rituals concerning excreta, breast milk, saliva and the rest unless we are prepared to see in the body a symbol of society, and to see powers and dangers credited to social structures reproduced in small on the human body" (115). Although Douglas talks of the typical—normal—body, the anxiety about the impaired body can be understood only as part of a range of available bodies that act as potential cultural symbols. Ken's body has been normal and now is not; its value as a symbol is both as a metaphor and as a potentially lived reality.

In keeping with Douglas's argument, it is impossible now to enjoy death or dignity as a "natural" part of living. After all, it is death that has become Ken's root desire. In contrast, Emmerson, in an earlier scene with his student doctors, cites death as "the enemy," whereas death is, more radically for Foucault (*Power and Knowledge*), the last resistance to power. This gives rise to a crux in interpretation: as seen through a social model of disability analysis. The film posits death as the release from abnormality and not as Foucault meant it: as a last stand against the tyranny of normality. Ken's body symbolizes failure because his body projects anxiety about the social state in order to criticize medicalization.

Ken's dependence and inability to protect himself from potential danger relate to his lack of freedom of choice (the "right to die") in that Ken is also a metaphor for a society "paralyzed" by its construction of people so dependent (while nevertheless keeping them alive) that they become "useless eaters."

Returning to the earlier scene, once Ken is back in bed, Dr. Emmerson tells him that he will be a quadriplegic for life and that it is hoped he will be transferred in the near future to another ward or hospital for continuing rehabilitation. Ken retorts, "[Y]ou mean you just grow the vegetables here, the vegetable store is somewhere else." Here, Ken's humanity contrasts the content of his own words, but, more importantly, while this conversation continues, a new "vegetable" is brought in to an ICU cubicle alongside Ken's (in view through the panopticon-like glass construction that ICU is). The film shows the medical production line of "vegetables" being created and damned in the same process of medicalization Ken has undergone. Emmerson—in a medium shot from the side—is again lit in a cinematically sinister manner with the left side of his face in near darkness which, when combined with his ethnic (Italian-American) features, gives him an appearance of being obsessed—achieved by the formulaic mise-en-scène taken from horror films. This is in sharp contrast to Ken, who is well lit in close-up (for extra intensity and feeling, the shot is straight on), with no shadow on his face. Thus the lighting lends purity to Ken's words, rendering him vulnerable, whereas Emmerson appears corrupt. Later in the film, during the court hearing, Ken classifies Emmerson's wishes as committing him to "a life sentence."

In another scene when nurses change his bed, then wash and dress him, the film infantilizes Ken. It is important to note that bodies are mediated by social relationships and that Ken's is constructed in the film as the root of his social exclusion. Only when what Goffman calls "body idioms"—movement, gestures—and "body gloss"—the desire to enact those "idioms"—are perceived as natural, rather than constructed, does the loss of one's own standard "idiom" or "gloss" become problematic (qtd. in Burns 38–85). A physical change can be interpreted as a loss; however, it becomes the reason for living—or dying in Ken's case—only if the physical change is metonymic of the loss of one's natural state. *Whose Life* inadvertently demonstrates the acceptance of such norms as natural through the film's portrayal of Ken rationally deciding to commit suicide because of his inability to maintain the "idioms" and "glosses" that were part of his existence before the accident. If one constructs the body as the "showcase of the self"—which is in turn a "showcase of a successful life"

(Seymour 13)—then one perpetuates an essentialist reading of the dependent body as inherently negative.

Additionally, clothes increasingly signify the worth of the individuals within them, the degree of success and worth manifest in their apparent cost or individuality. Ken's apparel singles him out as both a social and a physical failure. All the characters in the film wear clothes that vary and signify the social multiplicity of individuals, compared to Ken in his hospital uniform. Before Dr. Scott has an evening out with Ken's lawyer, she first visits Ken in her elegant evening dress: this scene only shows that the doctor has an external (private) life as well as a professional (public) life. Sander Gilman argues that human identity lies in the individuality of the body and that the outer man is a graphic reproduction of the inner man, allowing an interpretation of Ken's body as symptomatic of his limited character and performance capabilities. Ken's body has become his sole characteristic while all the other characters signify that to be a social being requires a multiplicity of social performances. Here and in most other impairment-oriented films (Barnes 36–38)—for example, *My Left Foot* (1989)—the individual with an impairment becomes circumscribed by his or her body, and, as Gilman argues, the danger is that the cultural image can become the self-definition—self-hatred. *Whose Life* does not question how the image becomes the self-definition through social discourse and its processes; it merely reinforces the circumscription as the logical, natural, essentialist definition that is generic to impairment.

Robert Murphy states:

> [T]he quadriplegic body can no longer speak a "silent language" in the expression of emotions or concepts too elusive for ordinary speech—for delicate feedback loops between thought and movement have been broken. Proximity, gesture and body set have been muted, the body's ability to articulate thought has been stilted. (101)

Thus the body, if muted, can place an obstacle on social relationships, but the muted version should not become the full expression of the individual. If muted bodies are mutations comprehensible only as outsiders to interactive social relations, then an acceptance of bodily difference becomes increasingly difficult. The film advocates the muted body as the equivalent of the dead body. For example, several characters "speak" Ken's body language for him: Nurse Joey feeds Ken a chicken leg and she then licks her fingers; John wipes away Ken's tears for him; and Ken has to ask a nurse to get his lawyer's card out of his bedside cabinet and telephone him. The repetition of others carrying out bodily reactions and simple tasks either for, or in contrast to, Ken places him further into the realms of "the dependent useless eater": the "useless eater" is visually equated with the dead body. In addition, any understanding of dialysis—depicted in the film—would lead the spectator to realize that even Ken's bodily functions occur on his behalf. In this case a machine is the surrogate.

Ken's physical poise prior to his accident is energetic and strong, showing assurance in its movements and posture. He holds his head high and he has a darkish beard covering a strong chin. Once the accident occurs, his posture reflects the change in the nature of his personality: Ken's constant supine position emanates hopelessness, and he is often portrayed in a manner that is not, medically speaking, related to his quadriplegia. After the accident Ken's chin always rests on his chest and his beard has paled—apparently in order to signify the waning of his masculine health. Yet Ken can hold his chin up (he is shown having physiotherapy to strengthen his chin/neck) in a way that would drastically change the way the spectator perceives his posture and, by extension, his character. His given (changed) character is inextricably linked with his posture to reinforce the ideology of the film that his condition is hopeless and abject.

Most other disability films (Barnes 36–38) use the same techniques and constructions to make their disabled characters abject. The impaired are easily fatigued, totally dependent, socially isolated, asexual, and infantilized, and have an impaired posture (see *The Raging Moon* [1970] and *The Elephant Man* [1980]). Consumer culture needs a plastic body that will buy decay-delaying products: consumer culture needs the consumer to be productive as well as merely a consumer (unlike Ken in *Whose Life*). Ken cannot consume freely and repeatedly. Ken does consume but does so by using a high-cost, low-demand technology (i.e., dialysis). Thus Ken consumes in a way that drains capital from a more rapid product consumerism. Even so, Ken still has a function in consumerism, as does the film itself, to take the point of Mike Featherstone et al. (eds.) that consumer culture "needs to stimulate the fear of decay and incapacity which accompanies old age and death by jolting individuals out of complacency and persuading them to consume body maintenance strategies" (186). Ken, and the film, facilitate this process by signifying all that is horrific about not controlling one's own body functions and not having specific control over one's own body idioms. This perspective extends to fashion and body garments within *Whose Life*, where, for example, Ken is almost always in his hospital gown—in his wheelchair he has a particularly tasteless dressing gown over it—which ensures that he is never represented as anything other than a sick person. Equally, the "sick person" implies loss of bodily control, dignity, privacy, and freedom, but also implies decay and mess due to its chaos of fecal and urinary excreta (bodily decay). The failure of the impaired body to play the "sick role" (cited in Murphy 19)—where the individual promises to make the effort to recover in return for the temporary abdication of responsibility to work—clearly participates in the overall negation of impairment as a validated state. And within *Whose Life* this notion (and process) of the "sick role" becomes the crux of Ken's argument to die, as he will never "recover" from his present bodily reality.

The film disables and objectifies Ken as a body and as an individual through movement, and primarily through the visualization of the movement of others. The mise-en-scène of movement, to degrade Ken, lies both in the characters' direction and in the movement of the camera, in the lighting and in the editing. Only when Ken gets closer to winning his battle to die (the ultimate in non-movement) do the camera angles and lighting and sound slow down. The mise-en-scène is striking in that a large number of scenes together create a style of camera movements that, in itself, validates movement over stillness (right up until stillness—death—is seen as the perfect denouement).

The immobile body is expertly negated in *Whose Life*—among a myriad of other scenes that include ballet and Ken's prior ability to sculpt, draw, and be sexually "alive": in one very short scene in which Ken's lawyer, Carter Hill, tries to talk to an uncooperative Dr. Emmerson, Emmerson, trying to dissuade Hill from continuing to represent Ken's case, walks very rapidly along a hospital corridor. The two then turn a corner. The scene is shot from behind the two professionals as they quite literally hop-skip-and-jump up five steps and immediately turn another corner. Next to the five steps, to the left of them and the screen, is a hospital porter slowly pushing another patient in a wheelchair up a ramp. The design and existence, socially and filmically, of the juxtaposition of steps/ramp project obvious parallels. The virtual non-movement of the wheelchair-user up the ramp juxtaposes the short period that Emmerson and Hill take to climb (jump) the stairs. And this clarifies the difference in ability and efficiency between the two types of mobility: the "normal" and the "abnormal." In this sequence the camera moves as rapidly as the non-disabled characters, with the whole Emmerson and Hill conversation filmed on the move, *cinéma vérité* style. Significantly, as if to reinforce the idea of the burden of impairment, one non-disabled character "forfeits" his mobility to cater to the needs of the wheelchair user.

Although Ken fleetingly mentions that all he wants is choice, his liberal demands are lost in the plethora of "normal body" images that the film puts forward for him to have the right to terminate any choice at all in the future: the "right to die." Ken's body, at the same time as being represented as a reality, is also a symbolic representation of the danger to society of medical technology. From a social model of disability viewpoint, the film negatively and one-sidedly fails to consider independent—or any—living as an option.

Georges Canguilhem's claims that "strictly speaking a norm does not exist, it plays its role [, a role . . .] which is to devalue existence by allowing its correction" (77). Ken's body is devalued by not embodying the adult human "norm" of the ordinary male/masculinity. Although Canguilhem's point is that all existence is devalued—even those who can closely fit the norm—I argue that the norm is specifically used on film to devalue the disabled body. Canguilhem's suggestion that the norm devalues the norm is important in that the norm devalues itself by making an individual's body an object rather than a subjective, lived experience. The devaluation of the normal body by the normal body occurs through its generalization, as in this film when the impaired and the nonimpaired characters are offered up to the viewer in order to be compared and contrasted. I argue that the liberation of the disabled body from a negative generalization (medicalization and normalization) would, above all else, free the body of normality from the tyranny of itself. If Ken were allowed/ encouraged to live, without stigma, then the film would suggest that all impaired (and disabled) people could live free of the dread of embarrassment of either others or themselves.

In conclusion, I argue that the "good cripple" for culture comes across on film as the cripple who does his/her utmost to overcome his/ her abnormality of body, in contrast to the "bad cripple" who is happy to be a cripple. Ken Harrison overcomes his abnormality by preferring death to impairment in *Whose Life*. The film represents the impaired and abnormal body as the paradigm through which normality is created, validated, defined, and reinforced as superior by having the impaired body disqualified and invalidated by its inability to be, as a consequence, normal. A list of films that follow this logic would be so extensive and diverse in so many ways—including impairment subject, country, era, genre, and form—that its length alone would reveal that the nature of disability representation is astoundingly static.

Works Cited

Armstrong, David. *Political Anatomy of the Body.* Cambridge, UK: Cambridge University Press, 1983.

Barnes, Colin. *Disabling Imagery and the Media.* Halifax, UK: BCODP & Ryburn Publishing, 1992.

Burns, Tom. *Erving Goffman.* London: Routledge, 1992.

Canguilhem, Georges, with an Introduction by Michel Foucault. *The Normal and the Pathological.* New York: Zone Books, 1989.

Douglas, Mary. *Purity and Danger.* London: Routledge, 1966.

Featherstone, Mike et al., eds. *The Body: Social Process and Cultural Theory.* London: Sage, 1991.

Foucault, Michel. *The Birth of the Clinic: An Archaeology of Medical Perception.* Translated by A. M. Sheridan Smith. New York: Vintage Books, 1994.

———. *Discipline and Punish: The Birth of Prison.* London: Penguin, 1977.

———. *Madness and Civilization.* New York: Pantheon, 1965.

———. *Power and Knowledge: Selective Interviews and Other Writings 1972–1977.* New York: Pantheon Books, 1980.

Gilman, Sander L. *Disease and Representation.* Ithaca: Cornell University Press, 1988.

Murphy, Robert F. *The Body Silent.* New York: Norton, 1991.

Norden, Martin. *The Cinema of Isolation: A History of Physical Disability in the Movies.* New Brunswick, NJ: Rutgers, 1994.

Ricks, Christopher. *Keats and Embarrassment.* Oxford: Clarendon Press, 1974.

Seymour, Wendy. *Bodily Alterations.* London: Allen and Unwin, 1989.

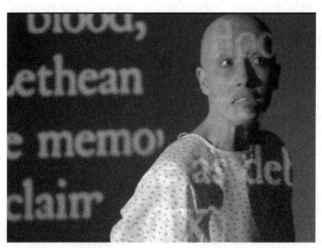

Text eclipses the ill body of Vivian Bearing (Emma Thompson). *Wit*. By Margaret Edson. Adapted for film by Emma Thompson and Mike Nichols. Directed by Mike Nichols. Home Box Office Network, 2001.

"And Death —capital D—shall be no more—semicolon!"

Explicating the Terminally Ill Body in Margaret Edson's W;t

VIVIAN: I want to tell you how it feels. I want to explain it, to use *my* words. It's as if . . . I can't . . . There aren't . . . I'm like a student and this is the final exam and I don't know what to put down because I don't understand the question and I'm *running out of time.*

—Margaret Edson, *W;t*, 1999

Introduction

Physical pain, as cultural critic Elaine Scarry writes, "has no voice" because it constitutes a sentient experience that "comes unsharably into our midst as at once that which cannot be denied and that which cannot be confirmed" (3, 4). Representation, on the other hand, seeks to give voice to lived experiences, to translate those experiences into action that circulates among authors, actors/characters, and spectators/readers who are themselves engaged in the process of making meaning. The antithetical relationship between physical pain and its representation, says feminist theorist Elisabeth Bronfen, ensures that "the violence of the real is translated only precariously into representation" (53). As Bronfen explains, "representation attempts to attach the dying, decomposing body, destabilizing in its mobility, to a fixed semantic position" (53). Bronfen suggests that attempts to fix the body-in-pain to a "semantic position" necessarily are doomed to fail because "signifying nothing, [pain and death] point to the indetermination of meaning so that one can speak of death only by speaking other. At the point where all language fails [pain and death are] also the source of all allegorical speaking" (54).[1]

For both Scarry and Bronfen, physical pain initiates a representational vanishing point, a site within representation at which sentient experiences (seem to) cease to exist. As a felt-experience rooted within the body, physical pain destabilizes any representational apparatus that seeks to codify and contain its meaning. As an empirically verifiable experience, death too enters "precariously into representation" (Bronfen 53), its visibility rendered unstable by the "indetermination of meaning" that constitutes the very nature of the experience. Unrepresentable because they signify no tangible referent in the physical world, then, physical pain and death enter into representation through extended allegories, whereby sentience takes the form of a concrete image, its abstract qualities personified by characters who signify "meanings independent of the action in the surface of the story" (Holman and Harmon 11).[2]

---

1. While I would not want unconditionally to conflate physical pain and death, given that there are many sentient experiences (e.g., torture) that do not necessarily posit an equivalency between the two, terminal illness (the focus of this essay) constitutes a sentient experience that links pain and death. As Scarry has written, "pain is the equivalent in felt-experience of what is unfeelable in death" (31). Therefore, the apparent collusion between theories of bodily pain (Scarry) and death (Bronfen) here is an intentional means of framing the larger argument I assert in the body of the essay.

2. Terminal illness constitutes perhaps the most frequently allegorized sentient experience in film. Although the medium of film is, as Mary Ann Doane writes, "characterized by an illusory sensory plentitude (there is 'so much to see')" (231), cinema has historically relied on a limited range of allegorical narratives to "translate" the lived experiences of terminal illness. Some films intimate that terminal illness grants wisdom and serenity to an individual whose life prior to diagnosis was chaotic, due to misplaced priorities (e.g., and *Terms of Endearment*). Other films posit terminal illness (and the concomitant death of the terminally ill individual) as the means through which conventional social structures (especially heteronormativity and the "nuclear family") are recuperated (e.g., *Stepmom*, *An Early Frost*, and *In the Gloaming*). And still other films identify terminal illness and death as retribution for transgressions of firmly entrenched social norms (e.g., the Camille narrative, as in *Beaches* and *As Is*). While each of these examples spins a slightly different "existential" narrative about the personal/collective meanings of terminal illness and death, all have one telling common denominator: they elide any consideration of how terminal illness impacts the fleshy, material body. In each of these examples, the material body and the lived experiences of illness become vehicles through which to convey a philosophical/spiritual message about the "meaning of life," rather than a means to analyze the body's journey through sickness and death. Stated differently, in each of these films a character personifies illness, rendering the real (but abstract) experience of pain concrete through an allegorical narrative that references experiences outside the body (of the text).

Not surprisingly, critics of Margaret Edson's W;t[3] read the play/film[4] as an allegory of death.[5] The play and film follow Dr. Vivian Bearing—a professor of seventeenth-century literature and a specialist on the poetry of John Donne—through her diagnosis of, treatment for, and eventual death from fourth-stage ovarian cancer. In a discussion of the play, high school teacher Carol Jago suggests that "[a]nyone who has seen or read W;t has no doubt that playwright Margaret Edson knows quite a lot about literature, but also about life" (21). Similarly, in *The North American Review*, critic Robert L. King suggests, "If W;t's premise seems contrived and Bearing's interests arcane, the play in performance is a deeply felt, human and humane experience" (49). For *American Theatre* critic James S. Torrens, the "humanity" of the play rests on a thematic link between Donne's poetry and Bearing's medical condition. As Torrens explains, "At the conclusion [of W;t Edson] ties up a thematic thread of the story, John Donne's habit of hiding from God behind his wit, with a children's tale that E. M. Ashford [Bearing's graduate school mentor] reads to the barely conscious Vivian Bearing. It is a fable of young animals trying to run away from their parents and always being found—an allegory, says Ashford" (28).

Such readings of W;t are, I argue, deceptively (and erroneously) simple precisely because they ignore the more complex representational strategy undergirding the film's narrative. I contend that W;t constitutes a rare addition to the corpus of films about terminal illness, an example of what Scarry says is "an isolated play, an exceptional film . . . that is not

---

3. Readers might note that the titles of the stage play and the teleplay differed in one important respect: the teleplay substituted an "i" where in the original stage play title a semicolon appeared (i.e., W;t). Throughout this essay I employ throughout the title of the original stage play, semicolon included, not in order to render hazy the important and noteworthy differences between W;t-as-stage-play and Wit-as-teleplay (a topic that I take up and explore in the section titled "Textual Differences" below); rather, I retain the original spelling in recognition of the central role that close textual reading and, in particular, punctuation plays in Vivian Bearing's interpretation of Donne's Holy Sonnets (and in my own reading of W;t that follows).

4. Of course, it is important to acknowledge that while Emma Thompson and Mike Nichols are the credited adapters for the teleplay version of W;t, this teleplay is almost identical in both structure and content to the original stage play (with only one major exception, which I discuss below in the section titled "Textual Differences"). For that reason (as well as for the sake of clarity and simplicity), I refer to Edson as the "author" of both the teleplay and the stage play throughout.

5. Interestingly, Edson has herself encouraged such readings. In an interview with *American Theatre* writer Adrienne Martini, for example, Edson has commented, "The play is about redemption, and I'm surprised that no one mentions it. . . . Grace is the opportunity to experience God in spite of yourself, which is what Dr. Bearing ultimately achieves" (24, 25). Given that Edson is the author of the play, some credence must be attributed to her comments here. However, the play encourages a New Critical reading (one akin to Bearing's reading of Donne's poetry), and critics must resist the urge to equate the meaning of the play/film with the author's feelings, intentions, or worldviews (what New Critics disdainfully regarded as the "Intentional Fallacy"). Instead, the play must be regarded as "a public text that can be understood by applying the standards of public discourse" (Bressler 41) (here, specifically, the public discourse of literary explication).

just incidentally but centrally and uninterruptedly about the nature of bodily pain" (10). What makes *W;t* so rare is the author's insistence on the analogical, rather than the allegorical, properties of sentience. The film attempts to render felt-experience meaningful by comparing a wholly unfamiliar and strange experience (i.e., sentience, pain, death) with something more familiar, at least for the I-narrator of *W;t*, Bearing: literary explication. By juxtaposing personal diary and literary explication in the direct-address asides (the film's central dramatic conceit), Edson suggests that poetics offers an analogical means through which to read the terminally ill body/text.[6]

In the film, Bearing's New Critical approach to literature is central to the plot, as it informs her understanding of Donne's Holy Sonnets and her experiences with terminal cancer. By alternating between scenes in which Bearing's oncologists diagnose and treat her body and scenes in which Bearing herself explicates Donne's poetry, *W;t* foregrounds the parallels between the sentient experiences of terminal cancer and the analytical process of literary explication. But like allegory, analogy ultimately proves insufficient for explaining the felt-experiences of terminal cancer as each of Bearing's attempts to draw parallels between textuality and ontology fail. While analogy proves as insufficient as allegory at explaining the felt-experiences of terminal cancer, *W;t* does recognize (through Bearing's direct-address asides) that "the only external sign of the felt-experience of pain . . . is the patient's verbal report" (Scarry 6). Through these direct-address asides, *W;t* charts the struggles that derive from any attempt to document the ravages that terminal illness exacts upon the material body. I argue that *W;t* does not provide a "documentary" through which the experience of living with cancer is translated onto celluloid; rather, the film voices a metafilmic commentary on how instances of pain and suffering complicate the process of cinematic creation.

---

6. The distinction that I seek to draw between analogy and allegory is slight but significant. Analogy, as Holman and Harmon illustrate, constitutes a literary device "by which something unfamiliar is explained or described by comparing it to something more familiar" (20). On the other hand, allegory is a "form of extended metaphor in which objects, persons, and actions in a narrative are equated with meanings that lie outside the narrative itself. Thus, it represents one thing in the guise of another—an abstraction in that of a concrete image" (11). Both analogy and allegory rely on comparison as the means through which to convey meaning. Both point to the similarities between two objects/things that are alike in certain respects. But whereas analogy foregrounds the comparison as a means through which to generate meaning about and facilitate understanding of an experience/object that is unfamiliar, allegory "attempts to evoke a dual interest, one in the events, characters, and setting presented, and the other in the ideas they are intended to convey or the significance that they bear" (11).

Bodily Poesis

Bearing is a New Critic—a point that is made clear early in the play during a flashback scene depicting Bearing's first encounter with her graduate school mentor, the esteemed E. M. Ashford. In the scene, Ashford criticizes Bearing's essay on Donne's Holy Sonnet Six, claiming, "You have entirely missed the point of the poem, because, I must tell you, you have used an edition of the text that is inauthentically punctuated" (13). Ashford reveals her own training as a New Critic:

> You take this too lightly, Miss Bearing. This is Metaphysical Poetry, not The Modern Novel. The standards of scholarship and critical reading which one would apply to any other text are simply insufficient. The effort must be total for the results to be meaningful. Do you think the punctuation of the last line of this sonnet is merely an insignificant detail?
>
> The sonnet begins with a valiant struggle with death, calling on all the forces of intellect and drama to vanquish the enemy. But it is ultimately about overcoming the seemingly inseparable barriers separating life, death, and eternal life. In the edition you chose, this profoundly simple meaning is sacrificed to hysterical punctuation.
>
> And death—*capital D*—shall be no more—*semicolon!*
>
> Death—*capital D*—*comma*—thou shalt die—*exclamation point!*
>
> If you go in for this sort of thing, I suggest you take up Shakespeare. (13–14)

In this passage Ashford abides by a strict and rigorous attention to detail in her systematic dissection of texts. Dripping with disdain, her comments about both The Modern Novel and Shakespeare also convey the gate-keeping mentality with which she approaches the study of literature. In Ashford's mind, "good" and "bad" literature are as clearly demarcated as "authentic" and "inauthentic" punctuation.

Through discussions about her research and teaching, Bearing reveals how thoroughly she has internalized the close textual reading strategies professed by her esteemed mentor. Toward the beginning of *W;t*, Bearing describes her "immeasurable contribution to the discipline of English literature" (17): "a volume on the twelve Holy Sonnets in the 1633 edition, which I produced in the remarkably short span of three years" (19). With great pride Bearing reveals to the audience that in the volume, titled *Made Cunningly*, she "devote[s] one chapter to a thorough examination of each sonnet, discussing every word in extensive detail. . . . It is exhaustive" (19). That each chapter of Bearing's book centers on one sonnet—as opposed to a theoretical concept, a thematic concern, generic conventions, or a cultural phenomenon—echoes not only Ashford's earlier edict ["You must begin with a text" (13)] but also the New Critic's guiding premise ["The natural and sensible starting point for work in literary scholarship is the interpretation and analysis of the works of literature themselves" (Wellek and Warren 139)]. That Bearing dissects each sonnet word by word (and punctuation mark by punctuation mark) in "extensive detail" demonstrates the *"uncompromising* way" (Edson 15) that New Critics (such as Ashford) seek "truth" in intricate phraseology, punctuation, scansion, rhyme, and/or meter. In other words, Bearing's close attention to (textual) detail demonstrates, as Cleanth Brooks once wrote, that for a New Critic, "The meaning must issue from the particulars" ("Irony" 75).

In her teaching Bearing demonstrates the same rigorous attention to textual detail. Toward the middle of *W;t,* Bearing "stands still, as if conjuring a scene" (48), in this case a scene from one of her undergraduate seminars on metaphysical poetry in which Bearing lectures her uninterested students on the minutiae of Donne's Holy Sonnet Five:

> The speaker of the sonnet has a brilliant mind, and he plays the part convincingly, but in the end he finds God's *forgiveness* hard to believe, so he crawls under a rock to *hide.*
>
> If arsenic and serpents are not damned, then why is he? In asking the question, the speaker turns eternal damnation into an intellectual game. Why would God choose to do what is *hard,* to condemn, rather than what is *easy,* and also *glorious*—to show mercy?
>
> (Several scholars have disputed Ashford's third comma in line six, but none convincingly.)
>
> But. Exception. Limitation. Contrast. The argument shifts from cleverness to melodrama, an unconvincing eruption of piety: "O" "God" "Oh!"
>
> A typical prayer would plead "Remember me, O Lord." (49–50)

Throughout this lecture Bearing remains an earnest New Critic, holding steady to the belief that "the goal of formal analysis is to show how the various elements in the poem fit together, how the parts cohere to produce the whole" (Keesey 67). Word by word, Bearing winds her way through the sonnet, searching for the answer to the speaker's question ("If arsenic and serpents are not damned, then why is he?") in the formal features of the poem. For Bearing, the denotations and connotations of specific words (e.g., "But. Exception. Limitation. Contrast.") provide insight into the speaker's attitude/tone (e.g., "The argument shifts from cleverness to melodrama.").

Interestingly, during the lecture scene Edson makes explicit the analogy between the analytical process of literary explication and the sentient experience of terminal cancer. Bearing begins the lecture with a brief introduction to the metaphysical school, its central conceit ("wit"), and its "greatest wit" (John Donne) (48). Afterwards, "The lights dim. A screen lowers, and the sonnet 'If poisonous minerals,' from the Gardner edition, appears on it" (49). As Bearing nears the climax of her lecture where she will reveal the "truth" expressed by the poem ("how the parts cohere to produce the whole"), she "moves in front of the screen, and the projection of the poem is cast directly upon her" (50). At this moment in the film, textuality and ontology collude through the visual projection of Donne's sonnet onto Bearing's terminally ill body. The distinguishing features of metaphysical poetry transfer from Donne's sonnet to Bearing's body, indicating that the lecture—itself an attempt to "embody" the poem—is, for Bearing, analogous to her attempts to understand the lived, bodily experiences of terminal cancer. The analogy, then, reveals Bearing's desperate attempts to use her training as a literary critic to render her sentient experiences tangible.[7]

Textual Embodiment

In addition to developing a somewhat interesting thematic parallel, the collusion of textuality with ontology, and of formal analysis with medical practice, serves as a potential means through which Bearing can gain access to the sentient experiences of terminal cancer. Late in the film

---

7. One scene later Bearing reiterates the interrelationship between textuality and ontology when she remarks on "the journal article [Kelekian and Jason] will no doubt write about me": "But I flatter myself. The article will not be about *me*, it will be about my ovaries. It will be about my peritoneal cavity, which, despite their best intentions, is now crawling with cancer. What we have come to think of as *me* is, in fact, just the specimen jar, just the dust jacket, just the white piece of paper that bears the little black marks" (53). Bearing compares her material body to "the white piece of paper that bears the little black marks" and renders her body a poem/text whose meaning derives from the interrelation between its component parts. Like Bearing, Kelekian and Jason believe that if they dissect Bearing's body into its component parts (tumors, symptoms, organs, etc.), then that body can be reassembled into a coherent (if not ultimately healthy) whole. The medical data implicitly compare to literary interpretation—a similar type of truth statement expressed through the constituent parts ("the little black marks") that constitute the body/text ("the white piece of paper").

Bearing reveals in direct-address asides, "I want to tell you how it feels. I want to explain it, to use *my* words" (70). Although the specific referent for the repeated pronoun "it" is unclear within the context of this aside, several options present themselves. "It" could refer to the physical pains associated with her illness since, several lines later, Bearing explains, "I am in terrible pain. . . . Say it, Vivian. *It hurts like hell. It really does*" (70). "It" could also refer to the more general experiences of living with terminal cancer. In that same direct-address aside, for instance, Bearing explains, "Susie says that I need to begin aggressive pain management if I am going to stand it. 'It': such a little word. In this case, I think 'it' signifies 'being alive'" (70). Or "it" could refer to the process of death. All these possible referents have one telling common denominator: sentience. Through the film, then, Bearing seeks "to use [her] words" to express the experiences of terminal cancer, bodily pain, and death.

Ironically, although close attention to textual detail once allowed Bearing to "draw so much from the poems" (48), that same attention to detail now works to complicate her understanding of the body-as-text.[8] From the opening scenes of the film, Edson emphasizes the inapplicability of formalist reading strategies to sentience by highlighting how terminal illness strips language of its traditional meanings and methods of signification. In one scene, for example, Dr. Harvey Kelekian, "chief of medical oncology, University Hospital" (3), explains Bearing's diagnosis while she, only half-attentive, dissects the diagnosis word by word:

> KELEKIAN: Now then. You present with a growth that, unfortunately,
> went undetected in stages one, two, and three. Now it is an insidious
> adenocarcinoma, which has spread from the primary adnexal mass—
> VIVIAN: "Insidious"?

---

8. In his review of *W;t*, Dr. Abraham Philip offers an alternative reading of how irony functions in the play:

> The most awesome irony is that while Vivian Bearing is sterile (emotionally, physiologically, and symbolically)—she never had a love affair, has not given birth or accepted anyone into the essence of her body—she ultimately succumbs to ovarian cancer, a malignancy of a life-giving or renewing organ. (3261)

On the most superficial level this reading does characterize the action of the film—that is, Philip has his facts straight, so to speak. But what disturbs me about this reading is how it so blatantly and unapologetically recapitulates harmful cultural narratives about femininity, the body, and illness (specifically the Camille narrative). Implied in Philip's reading is the suggestion that Bearing's cancer is metaphorically the result of her inability to conform to the "natural" roles prescribed by her sex—that is, an emotional, passive (note Philip's use of a certain passivity of action in the following: "she has never accepted anyone into the essence of her body") mother figure. Although the play does not, this reading that has found its way into the *Journal of the American Medical Association* speaks to the stronghold the Camille narrative continues to have over representations of unruly (here, specifically, intellectual) women and terminal illness.

KELEKIAN: "Insidious" means undetectable at an—
VIVIAN: "Insidious" *means* treacherous . . . Insidious. Hmm. Curious word
   choice. Cancer. Cancel. (7–8)

Several lines later, as Kelekian describes the effects of the proposed treatment cycle, Bearing muses: "Antineoplastic. Anti: Against. Neo: new. Plastic. To mold. Shaping. Antineoplastic. Against new shaping" (9). As she did with Donne's poetry, Bearing assumes she can render her terminally ill body intelligible and meaningful through the precise explication of its particulars. She adopts a questioning, analytical stance in relation to her object of scrutiny (i.e., her material body and its health), interrogating Kelekian's word choice and dissecting the complicated medical jargon he employs. Ever the devout New Critic, Bearing in both instances plays with Kelekian's language, mulling over the denotative meanings and etymological origins of specific terms in order to arrive at the "truth" of her condition (namely, the extent of tumor growth and her prognosis).

This detailed explication proves insufficient for explaining the sentient experience of terminal cancer when, in the scene following Kelekian's diagnosis, Bearing "hesitantly" explains to the audience, "I should have asked more questions, because I know there's going to be a test. I have cancer, insidious cancer, with pernicious side effects—no, the *treatment* has pernicious side effects" (12). Interestingly, Bearing here echoes Kelekian's explanation of her diagnosis and treatment almost verbatim, conceding to the very language that she interrogated and contested in the previous scene. When she strays from Kelekian's "script," she quickly corrects herself ("no, the *treatment* has pernicious side effects"), indicating the degree to which the embodied experiences of terminal illness resist (if not annihilate) the expressive language of literary criticism and necessitate the construction of a "less evocative" but "more potent arsenal of terminology" (43–44). Stated differently, Bearing appropriates the language of her oncologist, much as she does in the lecture scene where she explains the words of Donne.

Bearing frequently draws lines connecting literary devices to her medical condition in an effort to discover the "truth" of her sentient experiences, but these parallels too prove insufficient. After the "Grand Rounds" scene, for example, Bearing explains the role that she plays in the medical drama: "I receive chemotherapy, throw up, am subjected to countless indignities, feel better, go home. Eight cycles. Eight neat little strophes. Oh, there have been the usual variations, subplots, red herrings: hepatoxicity (liver poison), neuropathy (nerve death). (*Righteously*) They are medical terms. I look them up" (41). In this passage Bearing tellingly likens her "treatment modality" (Kelekian's words, 8) to a "strophe," or "stanza," and compares the side effects of the "chemotherapeutic agent" (again, Kelekian's words, 8) to "subplots." By offering these analogies to literary devices, Bearing emphasizes again her desire "to explain it, to use my words."

However, these analogies to literary devices only illustrate how completely alien Bearing's sentient experiences of terminal cancer are. Like the strophe/stanza, Bearing's "treatment modality" consists of a series, or "recurrent grouping" (Holman and Harmon 454), of individual units (in poetry, verse lines; in oncology, chemotherapy cycles). But whereas in poetry the interaction among various strophes produces unity, coherence, and "truth," in oncology the treatment modalities often lead to a disintegration of unity, coherence, and truth (i.e., health). Herein lies another irony in the film: as Bearing remarks, "My treatment imperils my health" (47). As a side effect of the chemotherapy, Bearing suffers from "[f]ever and neutropenia" (44); in fact, Bearing ultimately succumbs not to the cancer—at least, not directly—but to the liver failure and subsequent cardiac arrest induced by chemotherapy (81). She also endures fierce vomiting spells during which she can only "[moan] and [retch] in agony": "Oh, God— . . . Oh, God. Oh. Oh . . . Oh, God. It can't be . . . Oh, God. Please. Steady. Steady" (32).[9] For Bearing, the "treatment modality" proves to be anything but "neat little strophes," as they subvert their own purpose (making the body healthy) and force the body to overflow its boundaries (through vomiting). Unlike strophes, which provide order and coherence to a poetic text, the chemotherapy cycles render the body-as-text less manageable and understandable, and the analogy ultimately proves ineffectual for explaining to the audience "how it feels."

Edson highlights Bearing's increasing inability to express in her words how cancer "feels" by reducing the intellectual acumen of the direct-address asides, as well as by gradually de-emphasizing the role of those asides as the plot unfolds. As Bearing's pain increases, her attention to semantic detail becomes increasingly less pronounced: "Oh, God, it is so painful. So painful. So much pain. So much pain . . . Am I in pain? I don't believe this. Yes, I'm in goddamn pain. (*Furious*) I have a fever of 101 spiking to 104. And I have bone metastases in my pelvis and both

---

9. Here, Bearing reverts to the same kind of eruptive emotion evidenced in the "inaccurately punctuated" edition of Donne's poetry mentioned above (in which the translator was prone to "hysterical punctuation"). The implicit parallel that Edson draws between bodily pain and textual inaccuracies signals what Scarry has termed "the unmaking of the world"—that is, how physical pain initiates "an immediate reversion to a state anterior to language, to the sounds and cries a human being makes before language is learned" (4). In other words, the dissolution of Bearing's literary acumen (i.e., her rigorous standards for objective, non-emotive criticism) mirrors the disintegration of her material body.

femurs. (*Screaming*) There is cancer eating away at my goddamn bones, and I didn't know there could be such pain on this earth" (71). Unlike earlier asides, this outburst does not consist of clever turns of phrase or semantic squabbles; instead, Bearing equivocally repeats the same declaration over and again, "So painful," without specifying the location, extent, or nature of the pain. The comparison between these two very different direct-address asides clearly demonstrates how Bearing's vocabulary over the course of the film "[takes] a turn for the Anglo-Saxon" (32), how words and language once considered her "only defense" (44) lose meaning.

Near the end of the film Edson breaks completely with the asides when Bearing, overwhelmed by pain, relinquishes her role as the I-narrator. In her final spoken lines Bearing "weakly" addresses the audience: "These are my last coherent lines. I'll have to leave the action to the professionals. It came so quickly, after taking so long. Not even time for a proper conclusion" (72). Her lines signal a radical shift in the nature of *W;t*'s narrative—from a story *by* Bearing to a story *about* her. Herein lies a third irony of the film: that a woman who has built her entire professional reputation on the precise usage of language is, in the end, rendered silent. Without words to express the sentient experiences of terminal cancer, and without the physical capacity to endure the tremendous pain, Bearing consents to a large dose of morphine for pain management and eventually slips into a coma from which she will never awaken (72). This shift in narrative strategy startles spectators partly because Bearing "guides" them from the opening lines of the film, and partly because she loses coherence and voice before she can offer a "proper conclusion" (i.e., some "truth" statement about the meaning of life, death, or both).

Textual Differences

To this point, I have focused on how *W;t* thematically presents the body-in-pain through an analogous relationship between ontology and New Criticism.[10] In the final section of this essay, I want to turn my attention

---

10. Edson has commented that at first she was a bit leery of the adaptation, noting, "I thought they would have to jazz it up, add different themes and different places and a car crash" (qtd. in Peyser). Sharing Edson's skepticism was actress Emma Thompson, who was approached by director Mike Nichols to star in and co-author a screenplay version of *W;t*. As Thompson revealed to *Newsweek* reporter Marc Peyser, "It's quite rare that plays work when filmed. They're designed for a different kind of experience." Despite Edson's and Thompson's misgivings, the HBO adaptation of *W;t* has been labeled a "faithful adaptation" of the stage play and has received near-unanimous praise from reviewers. *People Weekly* critic Terry Kelleher dubbed *W;t* "one of the finest

to one noteworthy difference between the stage and screen versions of
W;t—the final sequence of events that depicts Bearing's death—in order
to speak specifically to the cinematic mode.

At the close of the play Edson abandons analogy, opting instead to
posit an allegorical narrative by which Bearing's death personifies the
Judeo-Christian belief in eternal life and salvation. After Bearing has
coded and been pronounced dead,

> SUSIE lifts the blanket. VIVIAN steps out of the bed. She walks away from
> the scene, toward a little light. She is now attentive and eager, moving
> slowly toward the light. She takes off the cap and lets it drop. She slips off
> the bracelet. She loosens the ties and the top gown slides to the floor. She
> lets the second gown fall. The instant she is naked, and beautiful, reaching
> for the light—Lights out. (85)

What is perhaps most striking about this final sequence of events is
Bearing's concession of the narrative-I position, indicated by her silence.
The lack of voice accentuates her passive narrative position and indicates
how death renders her an object made meaningful. The shedding of her
hospital gown visually marks the shedding of illness and bodily pain
as well as identifies death as a release from worldly/material suffering
(during the disrobing process, Edson describes Bearing as "attentive,"
"eager," "beautiful"). Death, though, does not simply signify an end to
worldly suffering; it also gestures toward the beginning of eternal life and
redemption, a point made manifest in Bearing's move toward a white
light which symbolizes a spiritual realm, a realm beyond the material
one, that gives purpose and meaning to life.

The final sequence of filmic events differs markedly from that of the
play. In the film, once Bearing has coded and been pronounced dead, the
camera records a long shot of Bearing's hospital room. In the immediate
foreground Bearing's lifeless, seminude body is sprawled out across a
gurney; in the background Susie stands motionless over Bearing's body,
looking down upon her. After lingering over this tableau for a few beats,
the camera abruptly shifts perspective, cutting to a bird's-eye view of the
gurney. Once again, the camera maintains this shot for a brief moment
before cutting to a wide exterior shot of the hospital room, filmed from

---

films I've seen in recent years—on big screen or small," citing Thompson's "consummate skill
and unshakable commitment" to the role of Bearing as one of the highlights of the film. Similarly, *Variety* reviewer Eddie Cockrell described HBO's adaptation as "[a] shrewd and triumphant
retooling of Margaret Edson's 1997 Pulitzer Prize–winning play" and noted that while "[t]he risks
in filming such a theatrical experience are enormous," "the original material has been carefully
and smartly reworked by Thompson and Nichols."

Heath Diehl | 121

the adjoining corridor. From this angle spectators see Susie through the closed glass doors leading into Bearing's room; silently but with purpose she closes the drapes. The next cut returns spectators to the interior of the hospital room. This time, however, the camera captures a tight close-up of Bearing's face in death. Her eyes are closed, her head turned slightly to the right, as if in death Bearing avoids the persistent gaze of the camera. Her head is bald, her skin pallid, and her lips parted slightly. Slowly the view cross-fades to a black-and-white, bust-shot photograph of Bearing in life. In the photograph her gaze is firmly directed into the lens of the camera, her expression held between a smirk and a grimace. The only soundtrack that runs beneath this series of cuts and cross-fades is Bearing's voice-over recitation of Donne's Holy Sonnet Six, "Death, be not proud." Immediately following the final lines of the sonnet the screen fades to black and the credits begin to flash.

The final sequence of filmic events clearly suggests that analogy remains the chief tool of *W;t*'s narrative method;[11] indeed, aside from the lecture scene during which Donne's sonnet is visually projected onto

---

11. Despite the noteworthy differences between film and play that I outline here, some critics insist on attributing an allegorical narrative to the conclusion of the film. In one particularly scathing, and I would argue ill-informed, review, *Entertainment Weekly* columnist Ken Tucker writes:

> I saw the original Off-Broadway production of *Wit* [sic], which starred Kathleen Chalfant in a heroically unsympathetic performance that Thompson has softened. Don't get me wrong—Thompson is excellent—but in reshaping Edson's play, she and Nichols emphasize the element that bothers me about *Wit* [sic]. It's the play's central deviousness: While filled with admiration for Donne's poetry, *Wit* [sic] ultimately says that well-reasoned, ferociously disciplined scholarship is inferior to what one character calls "the meaning-of-life garbage"—that is to say, that Professor Bearing's life would have been less lonely, more full, if she had loved her students as much as her subject. To which I say: Oh, phooey.

Here, Tucker suggests that in reworking the play for the small screen, Thompson and Nichols foregrounded the allegorical narrative deviously undergirding Edson's stage play. As I note above, this reading has been fostered by Edson, who claims that the play is principally about grace and redemption, though few (if any) critics have commented on that fact.

For me, Tucker's statement speaks more to the persistence of allegory as a means to understand texts about terminal illness than it does to the "truth statement" advocated by the film. Indeed, the few moments in the drama when Thompson and Nichols might appear to advocate what Tucker terms "the meaning-of-life garbage" (e.g., when Bearing and Susie share a Popsicle or when Ashford reads *The Runaway Bunny* to Bearing) are undercut by Bearing's simple but telling aside, "That certainly was a *maudlin* display. Popsicles? 'Sweetheart?' I can't believe my life has become so . . . *corny*" (69). A few lines later Bearing admits that such overwrought dramatics "can't be helped" since "[w]e are discussing life and death, and not in the abstract either; we are discussing *my* life and *my* death, and my brain is dulling, and poor Susie's was never very sharp to begin with, and I can't conceive of any other . . . tone" (69). My point here is that, for Bearing, the effusive, existential statement that Tucker attributes to the play is never an option (her "I can't conceive of any other . . . tone" implies a tone other than that engendered by her overweening intellect). Other characters (Susie when she rubs the lotion on the hands of a comatose Bearing) may succumb to the "meaning-of-life garbage," but for Bearing these moments are perhaps unavoidable, but nonetheless "corny."

Bearing's ill body, this scene offers the most explicit comparison of material body/ontology and sonnet/New Criticism. The film's juxtaposition of Bearing's lifeless body with Donne's "Death, be not proud" reinforces the analogy. However, death and the concomitant disappearance of the material body (one variable in the initial analogical equation) necessitate a shift in analogy. In the absence of the material body—an absence visually recorded in the cross-fade from motion picture to still photograph—the conditions of analogy shift from expressed (simile) to implied (metaphor), so that the body is not *like* the sonnet but instead the body *is* the sonnet.

Because the film not only foregrounds literary explication as its central thematic and narrative concern but also advocates that methodology for its readers, to explicate the body-in-pain spectators must employ the same reading practices Bearing uses when she interprets Donne's Holy Sonnets. The central presupposition of New Critics is that every "good" poem must achieve "organic unity," defined as "the concept that all parts of a poem are interrelated and interconnected, with each part reflecting and helping to support the poem's central idea" (Bressler 43). In "The Formalist Critics," for example, Cleanth Brooks articulates some "articles of faith" that guide and direct the work of formalist critics, chief among them being "the problem of unity—the kind of whole which the literary work forms or fails to form, and the relation of the various parts to each other in building up this whole" (52). To achieve organic unity, the critic must identify the central tension in a poem and then, by exploring particular devices of irony, paradox, and wit through which that tension is conveyed, the critic must resolve the tension and arrive at a statement of the poem's chief effect.

I contend that the central tension in *W;t* is expressed through the antithetical relationship between physical pain and its representations. On one hand, pain (to paraphrase Scarry) has no voice because it is located within the invisible (and unknowable) terrain of the material body; on the other hand, representation foregrounds the voice as one central device through which meaning is produced. This struggle between voice and silence perhaps is most succinctly articulated in the epigraph that opens this essay. For Bearing, who has built her professional career on a precise and judicious application of language, the experience of terminal cancer and its radical medical treatment is devastating because those experiences are, as Scarry claims, "world-destroying" (29). Bearing's unbearable pain compromises her ability to translate experience into language, a point underscored by the repetition of ellipses in the epigraph. Like her students who struggle with close textual analysis, Bearing "flounders" (48) in her attempt to express what pain feels like.

The film sustains this narrative tension in the final scene through the persistence of asides. As a narrative convention, the aside presupposes a certain degree of agency. As Kaja Silverman explains in *The Acoustic Mirror*, "Western metaphysics has fostered the illusion that speech is able to express the speaker's inner essence, that it is 'part' of him or her. It locates the subject of speech in the same ontological space as the speaking subject, so that the former seems a natural outgrowth of the latter" (43). Typically, the act of speaking (i.e., the narrative-I) confers upon an individual the status of "subject." The voice is, in this way, identified as the central locus for the production of both identity and subjectivity, and the realization/execution of that voice is assumed (by the individual and those with whom that individual engages) to be evidence of the individual's subject status. Thus the I-subject of the speech and the I-as-point-of-view speaking subject are conflated, or, in Silverman's parlance, are located in "the same ontological space." Direct-address asides emphasize this process of conflation so that Bearing's recitation of "Death, be not proud" projects the body-in-pain/-death as a speaking subject.

At the same time, several additional aspects of the mode of address undercut the sense of agency implied by Bearing's direct-address asides. This final aside is spoken posthumously, and death, as Bronfen persuasively argues, typically effaces "the subjectivity of the dying woman, her position within the death process, her body, and her pain" (49–50). In addition, the recitation is framed by the objective rather than the subjective/nominative case. By speaking Donne's words, Bearing marks her body as an object to which something is don(n)e, as a text to be read. Through careful instruction and rigorous example, Bearing aids and abets spectators in reading the body, but she herself retains little power over the outcome of the interpretive process or her medical treatment. Note, for instance, her dismay at "leav[ing] the action to the professionals" without "even time for a proper conclusion" (72).

The use of portrait photography in the final moments of the film visually underscores the oscillation between subject and object. On one hand, the photograph produces a fixed visual record of the material body, one framed in space by the ocular perspective of the photographer and one framed in time by the present progressive tense of the shutter's click. The spatial and temporal fixity of the photograph places in relief the literal death and disappearance of Bearing's material body; in other words, the permanence of the former sharply contrasts with the provisionality of the latter. On the other hand, photography manufactures presence as an endlessly reproducible visual image of the material body. Through the process of cropping, photographic negatives can be framed and reframed to accentuate a particular bodily feature or to emphasize a unique camera angle. By manipulating light and shadow during the developing process, the photographer can (sometimes radically) alter the visual composition of a negative, and digital enhancement can modify the photographic image. Thus the "reproductive possibilities of photography" (Phelan 38) suggest that the process of signification, of meaning making, does not presuppose a one-to-one correlation between signifier and signified. Even in the absence of the material body (signified), the photograph (signifier) continues to re-produce Bearing's body as a meaningful text-to-be-read.

Formalist approaches to literature insist that narrative tensions must be both explicated *and* resolved (several times throughout the film Bearing and Ashford claim that their methodology produces meaning as Truth); however, I argue that W;t presents an unresolvable tension. To suggest that the narrative tension in W;t is left unresolved, though, is neither an uncritical reiteration of Scarry's and Bronfen's theses nor a nihilistic proposition of my own (i.e., pain can never be translated into representation). Rather, I suggest that the film constitutes an exercise in wit, one in which representational (rather than metaphysical) quandaries are posed but never resolved. In this respect the film calls attention to itself as a form of representation that is doomed to fail in its address (given its subject matter: pain and the treatment of terminal cancer), but one that can nonetheless chart the struggles within its mode of address that derive from any attempt to document the ravages that terminal illness exacts upon the material body.

From the initial scenes of the film, Edson calls attention to the cinematic apparatus not simply as a vehicle through which to convey the story, but rather as a force that shapes the action. In her first aside Bearing apologetically notes, "It's not my intention to give away the plot; but I think I die at the end" (6). Later in this same aside Bearing reveals, "I've got less than two hours. Then: curtain" (7). Similarly self-reflexive comments recur throughout the film, such as when Bearing refers to her hospital gown as a "costume" (6), designates flashback sequences as "scenes" (63), and challenges the absent author (Edson) by noting, "If I were writing this scene, it would last a full fifteen minutes. I would lie here, and you would sit there" (35). By foregrounding the operations of the dramatic and then the cinematic apparatus, Edson effectively disallows an empathetic bond between spectators and character. In effect, spectators' attention is divided between the unfolding narrative and its self-reflexive construction. If spectators are made aware of the operations of the cinematic apparatus, then they also are made aware of their own situatedness as onlookers of the drama. But, given the nature of Bearing's profession (teaching) and given the shape of *W;t*'s plot (much of it reads like a lecture in seventeenth-century poetry and New Critical explication),[12] spectators are not simply voyeurs but rather students, and *W;t* constitutes the final exam.

Conclusion

W;t challenges traditional theories of the body-in-pain which suggest that the two primary means of representing the felt-experiences of pain are the weapon (or causal agent— cancer) and the damage (or effects/wounds—vomiting, nerve death, liver damage). Indeed, the final scene of the film invokes neither the weapon (since cancer is an internal medical condition that happens at the microscopic level of cellular activity) nor its damage (since the camera refuses to linger over Bearing's corpse). Rather, it proposes a third means of representation, one that locates itself precisely within the moment that pain is inflicted and death is experienced. In the film the cinematic apparatus provides a multitude of possibilities for how to represent the body-in-pain, just as New Criticism provides a multitude of tools for rendering the poetic text meaningful. The text provides a cautionary note: when the focus of the representation is misdirected (on either the weapon or the damage), the body-in-pain remains untranslated and sentience remains unsharable. And while analogy ultimately fails to convey to spectators what it "feels like" to be terminally ill and to receive radical and invasive medical treatment, the self-reflexive analogy in *W;t* more directly acknowledges the failure to produce meaning, knowledge, and Truth than does allegory.

The film also challenges the traditional ways in which the patient (especially the female patient) is codified and contained within medical discourse (itself a specific mode of representation) and rendered an object of the (usually male) physician's gaze.[13] Bearing's lifeless body, then, sig-

12. Edson herself describes *W;t* as "90 minutes of suffering and death, mitigated by a pelvic exam and a lecture on 17th-century poetry" (Zinman 25).

13. Outside theatre circles, *W;t* has captured the attention of medical practitioners for its relentless and "deft satire of doctors, who are depicted as concerned but detached, viewing their patient more as a scientific case study than as a person" (Hornby 297). In fact, it is precisely Edson's cogent critique of palliative care that has prompted a number of this country's top medical schools to use *W;t* as a teaching tool for residents and interns. As Marianne Szegedy-Maszak explains in her article "A Lesson Before Dying": "At 30 of the top U.S. medical schools, the play is performed as part of a broader national effort to teach medical students—and their professors—that the heroic saving of life is only half their job. The other half is dealing with the dying when a cure proves impossible" (48).

For more responses to the play from the medical community, see: M. J. Friedrich, "Wit: A Play That Raises Issues," 1611–12; Suzanne Gordon, "Viewpoint," 9; Dr. Abraham Philip, "Cancer

nals the ways in which illness and the representational forms of illness render the patient an "unwitting accomplice" in her treatment and return to health.[14]

Edson suggests that one need not hide from the inherent failures of representation, but rather should acknowledge them. *W;t*'s chief effect is simple. Suspiciously simple. At the close of the film, spectators perhaps want (or need) further clarification. But it is too late. Like Bearing, the audience has run out of time and the cinematic encounter is over. The final image of the still photograph of Bearing, whose insistent gaze bears down at viewers, questions what audience members have "learned." The final exam is over; to wit: time's up.

Patient," 3261.

14. Through the explicit display of the female body, the final image of the film also gestures toward the ways in which gender socialization renders the female body a shameful terrain that must be hidden behind both clothing and euphemism—that is, the way in which biological processes that are unique to women (e.g., ovulation, menstruation, conception, menopause) are consistently and unwaveringly linked to the "failure and dissolution" of the material body (Martin 32). It is precisely this history of shame that often compromises women's health care, leaving many maladies (especially those centered on "taboo" areas such as the breasts and vagina) undetected until they are too advanced to treat.

Works Cited

Bressler, Charles E. *Literary Criticism: An Introduction to Theory and Practice.* 2nd edition. Upper Saddle River, NJ: Prentice Hall, 1999.

Bronfen, Elisabeth. *Over Her Dead Body: Death, Femininity, and the Aesthetic.* New York: Routledge, 1992.

Brooks, Cleanth. "The Formalist Critics." In *Literary Theory: An Introduction.* Edited by Julie Rivkin and Michael Ryan. Malden, MA: Blackwell, 2000. 52–57.

———. "Irony as a Principle of Structure." In *Contexts for Criticism.* 2nd edition. Edited by Donald Keesey. Mountain View, CA: Mayfield Publishing Co., 1994. 74–81.

Cockrell, Eddie. "Wit." Rev. of *W;t,* by Margaret Edson, adapted for film by Emma Thompson and Mike Nichols. *Variety* (19–25 Feb. 2001): 39. *Proquest General Periodicals.* CD-ROM. UMI-Proquest. February 2001.

Doane, Mary Ann. "Film and the Masquerade: Theorizing the Female Spectator." In *The Sexual Subject: A Screen Reader in Sexuality.* London: Routledge, 1992. 227–43.

Edson, Margaret. *W;t.* New York: Faber and Faber, 1999.

Friedrich, M. J. "*Wit:* A Play That Raises Issues of Emotional Needs of Patients." *JAMA: The Journal of the American Medical Association* 282.17 (3 Nov. 1999): 1611–12.

Gordon, Suzanne. "Viewpoint: Nursing and *Wit.*" *American Journal of Nursing* 99.5 (May 1999): 9.

Holman, C. Hugh and William Harmon. *A Handbook to Literature.* 6th edition. New York: Macmillan, 1992.

Hornby, Richard. "The Two August Wilsons." Rev. of *W;t,* by Margaret Edson. *The Hudson Review* (Summer 2000): 291–98.

Jago, Carol. "Death, Be Not Proud." *English Journal* (Sept. 2000): 21–22.

Keesey, Donald. "Formal Criticism: Poem as Context." In *Contexts for Criticism.* 2nd edition. Edited by Donald Keesey. Mountain View, CA: Mayfield Publishing Co., 1994. 65–73.

Kelleher, Terry. "Wit." Rev. of *W;t,* by Margaret Edson, adapted for film by Emma Thompson and Mike Nichols. *People Weekly* (26 Mar. 2001): 30. *Proquest General Periodicals.* CD-ROM. UMI-Proquest. March 2001.

King, Robert L. "*W;t* and Others." Rev. of *W;t,* by Margaret Edson. *The North American Review* (Sept./Oct. 1999): 49–52.

Martin, Emily. "Body Narratives, Body Boundaries." In *Reading Women's Lives.* 3rd edition. Edited by Mary Margaret Fonow. Boston: Pearson Custom Publishing, 2001. 31–38.

Martini, Adrienne. "The Playwright in Spite of Herself." *American Theatre* (Oct. 1999): 22–25.

Peyser, Marc. "From Broadway to Boob Tube." Rev. of *W;t,* by Margaret Edson, adapted for film by Emma Thompson and Mike Nichols. *Newsweek* (19 Mar. 2001): 56–59. *Proquest General Periodicals.* CD-ROM. UMI-Proquest. March 2001.

Phelan, Peggy. *Unmarked: The Politics of Performance.* London: Routledge, 1993.

Philip, Abraham. "Cancer Patient." Rev. of *W;t*, by Margaret Edson. *JAMA: Journal of the American Medical Association*. 283.24 (28 June 2000): 3261.

Scarry, Elaine. *The Body in Pain: The Making and Unmaking of the World*. New York: Oxford University Press, 1985.

Silverman, Kaja. *The Acoustic Mirror: The Female Voice in Psychoanalysis and Cinema*. Bloomington: Indiana University Press, 1988.

Szegedy-Maszak, Marianne. "A Lesson Before Dying." *U.S. News and World Report* (25 June 2001): 48–49.

Torrens, James S. "Triple Play." Rev. of *W;t*, by Margaret Edson. *America* (22 May 1999): 27–28.

Tucker, Ken. "Poetic Justice." Rev. of *W;t*, by Maragret Edson, adapted for film by Emma Thompson and Mike Nichols. *Entertainment Weekly* (23 Mar. 2001): 91–92. *Proquest General Periodicals*. CD-ROM. UMI-Proquest. March 2001.

Wellek, René and Austin Warren. *Theory of Literature*. New York: Harcourt, Brace, 1949.

Zinman, Toby. "Illness as Metaphor." *American Theatre* (Oct. 1999): 25.

Bess (Emily Watson) flees torment from local children. *Breaking the Waves.* Directed by Lars von Trier. Zentropa Film Entertainment, 1996.

EUNJUNG KIM

"A Man, with the Same Feelings"

Disability, Humanity, and Heterosexual Apparatus
in Breaking the Waves, Born on the Fourth of July,
Breathing Lessons, *and* Oasis

> For the love of beauty is a deep-seated urge which dates back to the beginning
> of civilization. The revulsion with which we view the abnormal, the malformed
> and the mutilated is the result of long conditioning by our forefathers. The
> majority of freaks themselves are endowed with normal thoughts and emotions.
> —Dwain Esper, *Freaks* Prologue

In the well-known American classic film *Freaks* (1932), characters with disabilities working in a circus claim revenge on "the normals" because of the way the normals swindle and attempt to kill Hans, "the midget" (Harry Earles). He has an "innocent" desire for a "beautiful" and "big" non-disabled female aerialist, Cleo (Olga Baclanova). The opening prologue of the film, excerpted in the epigraph above, cautions viewers that their revulsion toward the film will no doubt invoke a mere historical construct. The prologue was not a statement made by the director Tod Browning himself, but instead was added by distributor Dwain Esper later in the 1940s for the exploitation circuit[1] to "pacify the audience" (after MGM gave him a twenty-five-year license on the film). Although David Skal and Elias Savada desribe it as a "cynical attempt to position the picture

---

I thank Sally Chivers and Nicole Markotić, Michael Gill, David Mitchell, Tobin Siebers, Mark Sherry, Sharon Snyder, the fellows of the Global Ethnic Literature Seminar at the University of Michigan at Ann Arbor, and the anonymous reviewers for their thoughtful suggestions and discussions.
    1. Eric Schaefer describes the exploitation films as having a "forbidden" topic, as the subject matter includes "sex, sex hygiene, prostitution and vice, drug use, nudity, and any other subject considered at the time to be in bad taste" (5). The classical exploitation films were also made cheaply and distributed independently. After Dwain Esper, an exploitation film director, acquired *Freaks*, he gave the film new titles, including *Forbidden Love*, *The Monster Show*, and *Nature's Mistakes*, in the 1940s to appeal to the exploitation film viewers (387).

with a moralistic, 'educational' defense" (223), Esper's textual scroll captures how the historical construction of "the love of beauty" as a cause of revulsion toward the "abnormal" evokes the audience's empathy with the "freaks" who have "normal thoughts and emotions." This comment aligns the able-bodied audience with the disabled man (Hans) who experiences "normal" (able-bodied and heterosexual) desire. Ironically, while attempting to challenge the love of beauty, the film's narrative depends upon a "normal" sexual desire for the non-disabled feminine beauty of Cleo in order to humanize Hans. As the opening scroll ends, disability and undesirability converge: "We present the most startling horror story of THE ABNORMAL and THE UNWANTED" (Esper, Prologue).

After the appended prologue, the external frame story of the film starts with a carnival barker gesturing toward a box to which guests respond in horror. The scene implies the tragic destiny of a "once-beautiful woman" turned into a "monstrosity." Later the audience learns that the monstrosity on display is the woman Cleo, mutilated because she has mistreated one of the "freaks," Hans. The fact that this able-bodied woman was turned into a "monster" as a moral punishment implies a reversal of revulsion that capitalizes on a misogynistic tone in the main story that follows. The film shapes Hans's manhood (as gendered humanity) through his aspiration to love Cleo while he is engaged to Frieda (Daisy Earles), also a "midget." In a crucial scene where Hans is first linked sexually to Cleo, he is attracted to her body, and his fiancée Frieda is jealous. Hans gazes at Cleo when she intentionally drops her cape in front of him in order to seduce him to gain access to his inherited fortunes. When he lifts the cape for her, Cleo turns her back to him, smiles, kneels down, and allows him to drape it on her shoulder. Hans nervously asks, "Are you laughing at me?" When Cleo asks why she would laugh at him, Hans replies, "Most big people do. They don't realize I'm a man, with the same feelings they have." The scene's depiction of Frieda is ambiguous. Frieda is a "good woman," presented as a counter-image to Cleo whose "inner" badness is made conspicuous and combined with her future embodiment of monstrosity. The film does not necessarily depict Frieda as asexual; however, she is not "woman enough" to establish Hans's normative heterosexuality because she does not appear to be an "object" of his sexual desire.

By taking for granted men's desire for women of a certain size and shape, the film attempts to overcome disability, and through this effort it lends to Hans' status as a "real" man. More importantly, it visualizes the assumption that, because of their presumed undesirability, disabled people are doomed to be insufficiently or inadequately gendered unless they receive sexual enabling. Problematically, the setup of this gender entitlement through momentary yet necessary sexual transgression contradicts the opening statement about the film's intention to enlighten the audience with the idea that revulsion toward "the abnormal" and "the love of beauty" is a historical product rather than human nature.[2] In *Freaks*, Hans is made vulnerable to Cleo's exploitation because his sexual desire transgresses the boundary of his community of disabled people. At the end of the film, having failed to be sexually incorporated into the normate world but also having paid the price for his attempt to seek out love with an able-bodied woman, Hans successfully and safely returns to Frieda to form the ultimate heterosexual bond. This move secures the sexual boundary of disabled people and the binary between disabled and non-disabled femininity that both enables and threatens disabled manhood.

Cinematic representation of disabled men's sexuality often aims to externalize their humanity by presuming that heterosexual male desire is universal. The dichotomy between a sexually promiscuous, non-disabled woman and a chaste, disabled woman plays a pivotal role in establishing this desire. As briefly illustrated in the example of *Freaks*, this essay closely interrogates the connections between heterosexualizing apparatuses and disabled manhood and womanhood in four films: *Breaking the Waves* (1996), *Born on the Fourth of July* (1989), *Breathing Lessons: The Life and Work of Mark O'Brien* (1996), and *Oasis* (2002). By "heterosexualizing apparatuses," I refer to filmic story telling and visualizing methods including the employment of certain characters, plot development and cinematography that inscribe heterosexual desire, thus setting up the prior trouble with (or absence of) heterosexuality in association with disability. In the first three films commercially and medically available forms of sexual services provide heteronormative means to integrate disabled men who are otherwise positioned outside the realm of sexuality. These films display this logic in different ways and, at the same time, provide critical reflections on the supposed necessity of such integrating intervention, according to a view that physical disability naturally desexualizes. I argue that in two of these films, one featuring a disabled man in religious Scotland

---

2. Sharon L. Snyder and David T. Mitchell see this contradiction as an unchallenged myth of the oversexed nature of dwarfs, saying, "[W]hile *Freaks* depicts the social rejection of people with disabilities as inhumane, it leaves more established myths—such as the oversexed nature of dwarfs and the desire of disabled people for revenge against the able-bodied—unchallenged" (380). Snyder and Mitchell argue that the film displays two impulses to normalize and to exoticize its disabled acting ensemble. I add an important point here: the female characters with and without disabilities play an important role in Hans's momentary but necessary enabling in a way that fortifies the separated worlds between the "freaks" and the "normals." Hans needs both women, as his reunion with Frieda is presented as a true form of resolution.

(*Breaking the Waves*) and the other featuring an American disabled male veteran after the Vietnam War (*Born on the Fourth of July*), newly disabled men are positioned in a desexualized terrain from which they must be rescued and then escorted into the heterosexual world through different forms of prostitution. Next I examine a documentary film about the life of an American disabled man (*Breathing Lessons*). This film explicitly discusses sexual exploration using sex surrogacy services. By connecting discourses of sexual liberalism within and outside the film, I examine how disabled manhood and desire are reconfigured within sexual-access rhetoric. I question the way in which disabled men's sexuality is assisted and imagined through the terms of heterosexual normativity in cultural representations. Finally, turning to the South Korean film *Oasis*, I examine the representation of a socially outcast male character's violation of a disabled woman and his love and care for her following the violation. I demonstrate how his actions humanize him and in turn enable the disabled woman's humanity visualized through her able-bodied fantasies.

Lovemaking and Curing Disability Through Surrogate Prostitution

While *Freaks* relies on the binary of a desirable, promiscuous, deceitful, able-bodied woman and an undesirable, innocent, disabled woman propping up a disabled male character's humanity, *Breaking the Waves* (1996) deftly fuses good womanhood into a disabled woman's body that has been prostituted in order to intervene in a man's physical and sexual disablement. The first film produced as part of his "Good Woman trilogy" or "Golden Heart trilogy"[3] (with *The Idiots* [1998] and *Dancer in the Dark* [2000] following), Lars von Trier's Dogme 95 film depicts disability in relation to religion, love, salvation, and gender politics, all of which create a separate sexual realm for a disabled man. Within ambiguous power dynamics between a "feeble"[4] woman and a physically disabled man,

---

3. "Golden Heart" is a Danish children's story about "the role of a martyr in its most extreme form" (von Trier). A little girl goes into the woods with a few things, including pieces of bread, in her pockets. On her travels she gives away all she has to people in need. Naked and bereft, Golden Heart says to herself "I'll be fine anyway" (Faber 59–60). Alyda Faber compares this children's story with Shel Silverstein's *The Giving Tree*, the story of "goodness as female self-sacrifice" (60).

4. Bess's mother calls her "feeble girl" when she discovers her promiscuous behaviors. Bess is also described as "psychotic" in the film. The juxtaposition of the emotionally vulnerable individual attached to the physically disabled person is employed as the representational strategy to highlight the "sublime innocence" of the relationship which also appears in reversal in *Oasis*. One can identify Bess as a disabled character because the narrative refers to her becoming "mentally ill" after her

the film initially juxtaposes sexuality and disability as conflicting forces. Scholarship on *Breaking the Waves* focuses on divinity, female characterization and religious suppression of sexuality, and *eros* as sacrifice (Keefer and Linafelt 1999); sexual transgression (Heath 1998); and valorized male domination and sexual violence with redemptive meaning (Faber 2003). To elaborate the last example, Alyda Faber argues that in the film, "Bess's goodness [is represented] as masochistic debility, a dubious construction" that is "a persistent male creation of women's social reality" (59, 74). However, not much attention is paid to the disabilities of either male or female characters in the film. The way the film represents disability, I argue, is a crucial setup in order to reconfigure the values of sexuality, spiritual cures, gender norms, and desire.

Set during the 1970s in Scotland, the film interweaves "the cure of disability" with the concept of the sexual surrogate body of a prostitute. In a closed village populated by characters with fundamental Christian beliefs, Bess McNiell (Emily Watson) marries an unwelcome outsider and oilrig worker Jan Nyman (Stellan Skarsgård). When Jan returns to his work at the oilrig, he is paralyzed from the neck down in a work accident; Bess believes that the accident is her fault because she had asked God to bring him home. While Jan is frustrated with his new body, Bess does not seem to be upset by the fact that her husband is disabled. Telling her the news of his paralysis, the doctor gives her the legitimacy to grieve by stating that it would have been better if he had died. But what matters to Bess is the fact that he is alive and will live. Here Bess celebrates Jan's survival and transgresses the commonly imagined "misery" of disablement, which the doctor labels as a "life not worth living."

The most overpowering and devastating consequence of disablement for Jan is the fact that he is, presumably, deprived of having sex. Sexuality in the film is made incompatible with his disability, thus creating a condition that requires mediation. Suffering over the fact that Bess will also be deprived of sexual acts, he laments to her: "I'm finished Bess. You could take a lover without anybody noticing. But you can't divorce me. They'd never let you." After resisting this idea of finding a lover as an alternative to religiously prohibited divorce, she leaves him alone in the room. Jan attempts to commit suicide in order to free Bess, thinking that it is the only way to liberate her from a matrimonial bond. Jan's nurse,

---

brother dies and her husband becomes physically disabled. She often becomes "delusional" when she impersonates God's voice. The film critic Bryant Frazer suggests that to the villagers, Bess is a suitable case for treatment because she fails to follow the rule that women must be silent in church. That Bess seeks to hear from God through her own self-voicing is perhaps not considered deviant but rather religious in that local context. However, later on, her sexual acts lead her to become an outcast.

Bess's loving sister-in-law Dodo McNiell (Katrin Cartlidge), intervenes and prevents Jan's suicide and then persuades him to live by telling him that Bess would do anything for him. Dodo unknowingly facilitates Jan's suggestion that Bess have sex with a stranger when she also tells Bess, "You could give him the will to live. That's more than any doctor could do." Then Jan again attempts to persuade Bess to go out and find a man to have sex with:

> Love is a mighty power, isn't it? If I die, it will be because love cannot keep me alive. But I can hardly remember what it's like to make love, and if I forget that then I'll die. . . . Bess, I want you to find a man to make love to and then come back here and tell me about it. It will feel like you and me being together again. Now, that . . . that will keep me alive. . . . It will be you and me Bess. Do it for me.

Bess now believes that she is put to the test by God of proving her love for Jan. The voice of God (spoken aloud by her), shown as a sign of her delusion, is the only command she obeys, while she defies the church and medical authority. First, she attempts to carry on her mission by having sex with her physician, Dr. Richardson (Adrian Rawlins), as demanded by God to prove that she loves Jan. Her attempt fails because the doctor does not cooperate, so she fabricates an implausible coital story for Jan, to his disappointment. Desperately believing that an actual sexual foray may improve Jan's deteriorating health, Bess gives a male fellow bus traveler a "hand-job." This scene initially solidifies Bess as Jan's surrogate body, sent into the world outside the hospital in order to explore the sexual pleasures that, in his mind, his disability has made impossible.

Seeing him improve after he hears the bus story, Bess now believes that she can save Jan. She transforms her attire and makeup to look like—to become—a prostitute. When her physician confronts her about her prostitution, Bess adamantly but softly tells him, "I don't make love with them. I make love with Jan and I save him from dying." The project of saving Jan through her sexual acts and her narrations to him of what the sex is like renders all possible johns as Jan's surrogates. While most of the characters around Bess, including her mother and Dodo, disapprove of Jan's "sick fantasy" and condemn her "stupidity," Bess continues to seek sexual activities as Jan's condition worsens. Her behavior alone, not that of the many anonymous customers who indulge in "sinful" activities, creates a scandal in the religious community, to the extent that she is forbidden to enter the church.

When Dodo tells her that Jan, now in critical condition, is dying, Bess hurries to a ship, where she was previously assaulted and barely escaped, to engage in another sexual exchange, thinking this will save Jan's life. Bess no longer believes that she needs to even tell Jan stories of her exploits. In her mind the act itself transforms Jan's health. In this climactic moment of crisis Bess is dreadfully and violently assaulted by a group of sailors. Barely surviving the attacks, she returns to Jan's hospital, where she dies of her injuries. Bess paradoxically achieves the status of "good" woman by prostituting herself because she believes herself to be under the power of divine command. As expected, the film depicts Jan recovered from his critical condition, sitting in a wheelchair and later walking with crutches, assuring the audience that her sacrifice indeed saved him and he is on the way to being entirely cured of his disability.

The film speaks within the tradition of prostitution as spiritually and psychologically therapeutic to men, not only by restoring Jan's masculinity but also by maximizing the degree to which Bess's prostitution cures his paralysis. At her burial site church elders declare Bess a sinner and consign her to hell. Wishing to free Bess from religious dogma once again, Jan steals her corpse and holds a funeral for her on a ship so that he can then release her body into the sea. The next morning Jan and everyone else on the ship hear a heavenly bell ringing in the middle of the sea. The film ends with the miracles of Jan's recovery (if one had believed the physician's prognosis of him as terminally quadriplegic) and Bess's salvation, celebrating the fact that her love is ultimately rewarded by a higher power.

"The film creates an image of Bess as the template of bittersweet sexuality," Faber argues, "that heals and wounds deeply—from her childlike 'sexless' sweetness in the opening scenes to her disillusioned suffering in the hospital after she has been tortured and raped" (67). Faber further argues, "von Trier creates the image of Bess as sexual martyr through a peculiar valorization of feminine abjection as madness, formlessness, malleability, hysteria" (69). Disturbed by a sadistic God as crafted by von Trier, Faber invokes Kristeva to criticize the film by stating, "The spectacle of feminine masochism becomes irresistible in sensations of horror and suffering in the spectator, hence the irresistible 'truth' of feminine abjection within the male rational order" (73). However, the associations among Bess's disability, prostitution, and abjection are not free from the longstanding yet unfounded psychoanalytical condemnations of disability as a fragile, hypersexual condition. Faber describes Bess's anguish when Jan leaves town to return to his oilrig work as an "animal intensity of emotions" and her prostitution as a symbol of a self-destructive psyche (69). Faber's argument about gendered sexual violence and male domination is accurate; however, her argument is deeply influenced by the conventional understanding of disability as necessarily damaged and abject. The violence Bess undergoes in her search for sexual "pleasure" is neither necessitated by her project of salvation nor leads directly to masochism. Rather, the violence of the sailors and the community's stigmatization of her and other prostitutes in the name of religion exist beyond Jan's and Bess's psychological characterizations in the film.

The medical and religious communities' perception of disablement as desexualization creates anxiety toward Bess's sensual pursuit of sexual pleasure. Within that closed fissure, prostitution yields the only pseudo-solution for both a sexual woman and a man with disabilities. Other changes that follow Jan's disablement enter the narrative only when he is frustrated in front of his friends by not being able to lift a beer can. While both the marriage and Jan's non-disabled body are privileged by the community as the only sanctioned places for sexual pleasure, Jan is seemingly left without a choice for Bess's continued sexual pleasure since, constrained by rigid religious tenets, they cannot divorce. His masculinity is diminished in front of a group of male friends; he is compelled to be a man who can satisfy his wife only by relying on other, non-disabled male bodies. How, then, is Bess convinced that her sexual experiences with strangers can provide Jan a cure with—or even without—delivering these narratives of sexuality to Jan? Rather, how does the director present the film as "a simple love story" and say, "I prefer to work with unassailable ideas. And I wanted to do a film about goodness" (von Trier 12)? Faber argues that von Trier's characterization of Bess reiterates a common image of the female martyr, constructing her power as debilitating masochism (59). In contrast, however, the film relies on the common and persistent belief that impairment damages the personhood of disabled men in its incompatibility with sexuality, creating a necessity for cure.

Prostitutes as Rehabilitators

Unlike *Breaking the Waves*, which centrally engages the question of salvation and sexuality when a disabled woman engages in prostitution to cure her disabled husband, Hollywood cinema has symbolically capitalized on disabled men purchasing sex as part of the process of physical and psychological rehabilitation after disablement. *Coming Home* (1978), *Born on the Fourth of July* (1989), *The Waterdance* (1992), and *One Flew over the Cuckoo's Nest* (1974) have an inconspicuous commonality beyond simply portraying disabled male characters. The films all posit prostitution/ stripping and a non-disabled female sex worker as a fleeting and necessary rite of passage in the physical and psychological rehabilitation of disabled men. In *Coming Home*, for example, before showing Luke Martin (Jon Voight) engaged in passionate and fulfilling sexual activities with Sally Hyde (Jane Fonda), the film depicts him casually greeting a white prostitute in his apartment.[5] He awaits his regular prostitute, but when a new woman comes instead, he does not reject her after learning that she is experienced in having sex with disabled customers. This very brief exchange indicates that purchasing sexual service has become an ordinary aspect of his life of rehabilitation outside the hospital; it is also a sign of his active sexual life after disablement. Unlike many films depicting non-disabled men who hire prostitutes for pleasure, thus imperiling their morals and their reputations, Luke's role—seemingly as a regular john— does not diminish his morality or personable characteristics. Rather, presented as a positive sign of his rehabilitation, the scene crucially challenges common assumptions that disabled people are uncomfortable with their sexuality because of their disability. Thus the scene prepares the audience to encounter his full ability to make love to the woman he actually loves. His ability to satisfy Sally is contrasted with her psychologically traumatized yet physically able-bodied husband's inability to do so. Luke is presented as confident and skilled in enticing Sally into his first sexual affair immediately after his brave, solo antiwar protest, prompted by the suicide of one of his friends, also a Vietnam veteran.

Although the connection between male disabled characters and female able-bodied prostitutes is pervasive in film, the relationship between disabled masculinity and prostitution is not monolithic. For example, *Scent of a Woman* (1992) depicts the engagement of a blind man, Lieutenant Colonel Slade (Al Pacino), with a high-class prostitute—who does not appear in the film—as a last wish to experience sexual satisfaction before he attempts suicide. However, he had frequently hired prostitutes' services before his disablement, and his descriptions of the experience to a young, inexperienced Charlie (Chris O'Donnell), whom Slade hires as a personal guide, build him up as a passionate and virile character rather than merely rehabilitating him. Slade is rehabilitated through playing the

---

5. This film's depiction of Sally and Luke's sexual fulfillment has been celebrated as the tradition of "alternative phallic heterosexual narrative." Subsequently, *Murderball*'s (2005) sexual story of disabled men was presented as life-affirming as opposed to "dogmatic asexuality" (Garland-Thomson 122). I question the alternative nature of such heterosexuality and the problematization of asexuality; however, my emphasis on the role of a prostitute does not negate the representational importance of the sexual relationship between Sally and Luke. My analytic focus concerns the presence of prostitution as a precursor to idealized heterosexuality through which Luke's sexual ability is confirmed.

role of father to Charlie, who is in trouble at his prep school for failing to reveal the names of fellow students whom he saw committing acts of vandalism. After Slade's heroic defense of Charlie and his integrity at his disciplinary hearing, the previously suicidal Slade meets a female love interest and becomes lively and flirtatious.

The prostitute-as-rehabilitator logic plays out more simply and melodramatically in *Born on the Fourth of July* than in *Coming Home* or *Breaking the Waves*. Ron Kovic (Tom Cruise) returns paralyzed from his tour of duty in the Vietnam War. While trying to adjust to civilian life with his new body, he is initially disturbed by the U.S. antiwar atmosphere. However, fraught with guilt about killing villagers and a fellow soldier, he slowly realizes the problem of warfare and grows cynical about his past role as a soldier and his country's current participation in global conflict. One night, after fighting with another marine in a bar and falling from his wheelchair in the middle of a dancing crowd that literally looks down upon him, Ron returns home intoxicated and angry. He holds his religious mother's cross in his hand, ranting to her about the war and the government's deception, writing off his past religion and patriotism altogether. He then holds his catheter in one hand and the cross in the other and shouts, "It's a lie. . . . There is no God, no country . . . just me and this dead penis." While effectively establishing able-bodiedness and the phallus as hidden pillars of the nation-under-God, the scene shows that Ron has lost all his normative foundational identities but has not yet found ways to understand his new body or to gain a new perspective, a critical reimagining, of American society. When a calmer Ron says to his father, "I wanna be a man again," Ron's struggle with his disability is summarized as his sexual frustration. The meaning of disability is translated as the loss of his phallus, and the translation presents a potential solution as Ron's father prescribes him a visit to Mexico for a "rest."

In the scenes that follow, the film depicts a Mexican town as "paradise" for American disabled veterans, mostly represented as white, surrounded by prostitutes of color who appear to restore the veterans' manhood. Ron's journey to become "a man again" takes him to a brothel. While Ron is lying in bed with a naked prostitute, Maria Elena (Cordeliá Gonzáles), he stops her from unbuttoning his pants, saying that "there is nothing down here at all, nothing happens." Maria assures him, "We are gonna have a good time." While Maria continues to make a moaning sound sitting on top of him, the camera focuses on his face covered with tears. It appears that Ron has successful penetrative sex with Maria, fulfilling her promise of "a good time." While it does not make clear how the audience should interpret his tears, the film portrays the experience of purchased sexual service as a complicated event (Ron loses his virginity, and he later futilely seeks out a romantic relationship with Maria). Paired with a fight in the desert with another veteran, which makes Ron face his own sinister past of the time he spent in combat, this ambivalent sexual experience serves as a gateway through which Ron can be reintegrated into civil life as a prominent antiwar activist upon his return.[6] After this Mexican double-rendezvous, Ron is fully rehabilitated into manhood and transformed politically; he visits and apologizes to the family of the fellow soldier whom he killed.

Peter Lehman provides a relevant explanation of the film's symbolization of Ron's phallic rehabilitation: the "melodramatic penis on the one hand challenges conventional representations, and on the other hand constitutes a troubled site of representation that contains disturbing contradictions" (26). In *Born on the Fourth of July*, the penis becomes a metaphor for damaged masculinity as visualized through the catheter swinging in Ron's hand. Maria's orgasmic performance and upright posture on top of Ron during intercourse represent Ron's erect penis to the viewers, thus visualizing Ron's return to self-assurance in his masculinity through sexual performance.

Ron's experience with Maria can be seen as transformative—as much as it is vain and temporary—with a full range of race, national space, and class significance embedded within that transaction. Ron's American whiteness serves as an asset that compensates for his disability in the sexually saturated exotic space of a brothel and on the streets where women of color are passively portrayed as lined up and waiting to be chosen. The gender and the whiteness of disabled men are consolidated and reasserted when desexualized disabled bodies need to be rehabilitated through prescriptive heterosexualization. In this process certain

---

6. Nick Allen's film review describes this scene as exactly such a rehabilitating pathway. He writes: "Cruise reaches dark recesses as the tears flow for real during his liaison with a Mexican whore[;] it is here in a[n] oasis of hope in the desert that the character finally decides to face his predicament." In the autobiography by Ron Kovic with the same title, Kovic describes the experience in Mexico and the "whorehouse" in the Village of the Sun. When he first had an encounter with a sex worker, it was she who cried at the sight of his disability and left him. He proceeded to find another sex worker, Maria, who asked him to come back the next day and live with her. In the autobiography Kovic narrates his time with Maria in the third-person voice. In contrast to the portrayal of the penetrative sex in the film, he notes that he did not take off his pants but shared intimate time touching upper bodies, rolling, and talking. However, unlike his naïve courting gesture in the film, Kovic never returned to Maria, knowing that she did not really mean her invitation. Rather, he sought out a new woman every night until he found himself thrown out of a bar with another disabled veteran who had a violent fight with "one of the whores" by punching her. Kovic and the disabled veteran became lost in the desert after they left the bar together (Kovic 126–28), and they found their way back to the Village of the Sun. The autobiographical depiction of the encounters with sex workers maintains an unflappable tone about the disposable nature of relationships and the violence prevalent in the sex industry.

cultural depictions enforce the sexuality of disability as a unique aspect that differs from non-disabled existence, like many other benign factors of life experience of disabled people. This is not to suggest that all filmic depictions of disabled people's sexuality unfold in the same way. And certainly many films challenge the heteronormative framework of disabled people's sexuality, such as the affirming portrayal of the asexuality of a woman with autism in *Snow Cake* (2006) and the portrayal of a sexually inactive, short-statured man in *The Station Agent* (2003) which has an ending that implies a potential sexual relationship. Queer intimacy and disability are portrayed in several films, such as *Gaby, A True Story* (1987); *Philadelphia* (1993); *Girl, Interrupted* (1999); and *F**k the Disabled* (2002). What is at the center of my inquiry is the logic behind the relationships among disabled masculinity, heterosexuality, and the normalization of humanity displayed in certain films. Prostituted women who participate in this process are marginalized as instruments of such humanizing projects without being fully characterized.

Sexual Surrogacy

*Simulating Sexual Relationships and the Limits
of Sexual Liberalism*

Jessica Yu's documentary film *Breathing Lessons: The Life and Work of Mark O'Brien* (1996) addresses the unlikelihood of heterosexual bonding of a disabled man through a technique of verisimilitude. *Breathing Lessons* provides an opportunity to give one account of the emergence of sex surrogacy to "specially" manage disabled men's sexuality. Here, the well-known American disabled poet, journalist, and activist Mark O'Brien[7] depicts sex surrogacy as one liberating aspect of his life in Berkeley.[8] In describing his experience of hiring a sex surrogate, Mark explains his interest in hiring her again:

> Cheryl was very kind to me. She kissed me on the chest after we had intercourse. I felt my chest was very unattractive. But she kissed me right there. The intercourse was so quick. It wasn't as great as I thought it would be. But being naked in bed with a woman who was being extremely friendly

---

7. In order to differentiate between the documentary character and the writer, I use "Mark" to refer to the character in the film and "O'Brien" to refer to the author of the essay.

8. For a more complete discussion of O'Brien, including his sexuality, gender identity, and literary works, see Tobin Siebers, "Sex, Shame, and Disability Identity."

was the most fun I've ever had. I think I'd like to do it again.

However, as Mark continues his narration, he demonstrates less enthusiasm for the encounter because of the temporary nature of the pleasures he experienced:

About a year after I saw her I just felt terribly depressed. I had expected somehow that seeing the surrogate would change my life. I had started wearing cologne, and I thought everyone would be able to tell I was sexy and handsome, but nothing happened.

With this narration a series of point-of-view shots feature, in slow motion, a pair of female legs walking in a short skirt. This image shows the audience what Mark longs for, and it invites the audience to empathize with him when he tells the story of one woman whom he loved. Although Mark expected that sex with a surrogate would transform his life, he observes that no overall change has actually occurred, and he still experiences isolation due to a lack of social infrastructure because he spends most of his life apart from people his own age. Unlike Ron in *Born on the Fourth of July*, who shows anger toward his emasculated body, Mark explains his anger as directed toward society, and toward women: "I just felt very crazy. I was angry at all women 'cause I'd fall in love with several attendants and they all said it was a business relationship."

In this way the film problematizes the limited access of disabled men to sexual experiences. This sexual oppression is also investigated in the scholarship on disability and sexual access. While Western disability activism has focused on access to public space, utility, resources, and societal power, it has also considered sexuality as a site requiring access for disabled people. The notion of sexual access is theorized as equal access to sexual relationships and sexual activities (Shuttleworth and Mona). In any sexual experiences and relationships, general access to all activities that include transportation, education, employment, virtual and physical access to socializing spaces, diverse modes of communications, availability of accommodations, subcultural spaces of diverse sexual orientations, and the right to domestic and community living must be brought into and considered as part of the picture. However, the consideration of gendered sexual politics has been ambiguous, since many options to enable sexual experiences through services depend on the image of the biologically different needs and risks of disabled men and women.

Sexually liberal discourses for disabled people's sexual access have also engaged with various options, especially for people "who may not have access to sexual partners and who are seeking greater personal fulfillment" (Shapiro 78). Suggested options include government-sponsored personalized funding for hiring sex therapists or sex surrogates (Shapiro); displaying pornographic magazines and adding "adult viewing channels" in nursing homes (Edwards 18); free escort services, creating private spaces in institutions for sexual intercourse, and equal access to sex workers (Hamilton); a specialized "Touchers Project";[9] legalizing prostitution for disabled people;[10] behavior management and support group therapy (Shaw); and match-making services such as DateAble, "a dating service with heart." Some disability organizations such as Accsex Network, headquartered in Australia, argue for accessible brothels and for funding so that disabled people have the means to consume pornographic materials.[11]

All these practices are interrelated with the gendered cultural representations of disability and the imagined need to be sexualized in order to be fully rehabilitated. If the focus on sexual access is limited to the disabled male's access to commercially and medically available sex services, the importance of current diverse forms of the sexual/asexual lives of disabled people is inevitably underestimated. In addition to the commercially available options, the social construction of disabled sexuality as a separate entity seems to call for specialized medical or commercial intervention.

Although many disabled veterans have received sexual rehabilitation education in medical settings, the employment of sex therapy to allow disabled people sexual experience or "fulfillment" along with rehabilitation is a relatively recent idea. Sexology experts have rarely invested in a major way in sex therapy for disabled people, except when it involved cataloguing so-called "deviant" sexual beings. Early sex therapy, in the days as far back as Victorian times, focused on reducing sexual desire because

9. In June 2003, a Swiss organization in Zurich called Pro Infirmis launched the "Touchers Project." Pro Infirmis's Zurich branch announced the pilot scheme, which involved training twelve professional "Touchers." The Touchers were then expected to offer sexual and emotional relief to the Zurich disabled community. Services included massage and erotic games but not "sexual relations." However, financial donations dropped significantly after the project was publicized. The project and the organization were swamped with an uproar of criticism. Pro Infirmis said that it will continue to try to address the issue and that it intends to find legally recognized and independent financial support for the project (Swissinfo, "Zurich Disabled").

10. I observe that there is a stronger connection and easier acceptance of this connection between disabled men's "consumption" of prostitution than non-disabled men's. See Kim and Sherry (2006).

11. BBC News Asia-Pacific reported on an Australian brothel (2003): "The Pink Palace in Melbourne is thought to be the first in the country to carry out such modifications and campaigners for the disabled in the hope that others will follow suit. The new features also include enlarged doors to accommodate wheelchairs and installed a sit-down shower. George Taleporos, a researcher into sexuality and disability, said many disabled people used prostitutes and brothels because it is difficult to date in the usual way."

women's sex drives were considered dangerous (Kilmann and Mills 16). In contrast, sex therapy in contemporary history is dedicated mostly to the problems of able-bodied males and their general anxiety about fulfilling cultural standards of masculine sexuality. In *Human Sexual Inadequacy* (1970), Masters and Johnson introduce the concept of surrogacy as a therapeutic method. Their term "partner surrogate"[12] indicates a partner—usually female—provided for an unmarried man in treatment who has no one to provide the psychological and physiological support deemed necessary during the acute phase of his therapy (135). The term "surrogate" can also apply to instances when a woman plays a sexual role in the place of an "authentic" partner. The surrogate's function is "to approximate insofar as possible the role of a supportive, interested, cooperative wife" as a means of psychological support, without judging the physiological function of the man (150). In the rationale of sex therapy, emphasizing the therapeutic effect and the enhancement of self-esteem shifts the focus away from a desexualizing social context and instead individualizes the problem. The rhetoric of sex therapy often assumes that disabled people experience discomfort with their own bodies and suggests that this discomfort is the cause of an unsatisfactory sexual life.

Several years before the documentary was released, O'Brien wrote about his experience of hiring Cheryl in his essay "On Seeing a Surrogate," and he is more reflexive in his writing than he seems to be in the film. After his first session with Cheryl he writes, "For the first time, I felt glad to be a man," implying the connection of sexual experience to his manhood. Later he reflects, "but my life hasn't changed." Then he further poses a question along the lines of a continuum of sex surrogacy and prostitution:

> Where do I go from here? People have suggested several steps I could take. I could hire prostitutes, advertise in the personals, or sign up for a dating service. None of these appeal to me. Hiring a prostitute implies that I cannot be loved, body and soul, just body or soul. I would be treated as a body in need of some impersonal, professional service—which is what I've always gotten, though in a different form, from nurses and attendants.

Here O'Brien presents the critical insight that the therapeutic idea of sex service is related to other forms of professional medical services.

---

12. "Sex therapist" can occasionally refer to the person who engages with the client in a form of body labor, but it more likely refers to a person in a medical setting who works with patients and prescribes a range of therapy to a surrogate partner.

Although the concept of sex surrogacy arose from medical discourses put forth by a team therapist and a licensed and/or certified professional with an advanced degree, sex surrogacy is now more likely to be part of the continuum of the sex-service industry than it is to be found in clinical discourse in North America and Western Europe. Disability communities' employment of sex surrogacy as a method for enhancing disabled people's sexual access is situated within the massive, worldwide effort to profit financially from sex and the specialized branding based on customer groups. At the same time, pro-prostitution discourses use the disabled population to justify the necessity of sex labor. Even though medical rhetoric removes some forms of stigma and moral judgment associated with the sex trade, it is important to note that sex surrogacy, when positioned alongside medicalized professional services, further contributes to the medical model of disability as suggested by O'Brien.

After winning an Oscar for *Breathing Lessons*, director Jessica Yu offered her "deepest thanks to Mark O'Brien, 41 years paralyzed in an iron lung." She continues, "Mark, it was not your bravery but your humanity that earned this award." The film introduces sexual surrogacy as a way of depicting his humanity, sexual desire, and sadness without investigating their complicated social contexts (*Breathing Lessons*, "Introduction"). Furthermore, the documentary—aiming to emphasize Mark's humanity through his heterosexual desire toward an able-bodied woman—nonetheless does not include his critical viewpoint about sex surrogacy as just another form of professional service. The film ends the sequence with his passive remarks that hand over the authority to recognize disabled people as sexual beings to a ubiquitous, able-bodied "they" who determine desirability:

> They tell us to think of ourselves as sexual and beautiful but it doesn't do any good. Unless someone else sees us as sexual and beautiful. You just can't demand love. You have to be lovable. I'm still trying to figure out how to do that.

The documentary's simplified version of O'Brien's narrative repeats a pattern that appeared in *Freaks'* highlighting of desire as a tool for humanizing men with disabilities and constructing disability as causing sexual frustration.

The film narrative ignores O'Brien's reflexive thoughts about sexual desire and broader social contexts expressed throughout his essay and poetry. He poses a question that potentially challenges the logic of heterosexual rehabilitation in his essay:

What do I seek? I don't know. Someone who likes me and loves me and who will promise to protect me from all the self-hating parts of myself? An all-purpose lover-mommy-attendant to care for all my physical and emotional needs? What one friend calls a "shapely savior"—a being so perfect that she can rescue me from the horror that has been imposed upon me and the horror I've imposed upon myself? Why bother? I ask myself. I don't. Not anymore.

His ceasing to desire sexual experiences is a complicated decision shaped within the social oppression of disabled people, isolation, his own complicity, and heteronormative sexuality as able-bodied sexuality. The rescue rhetoric that he problematizes also alludes to an image of a sexual, able-bodied woman since he states that he does not feel attracted to disabled women (although he later admits that he is attracted to one of his female therapists who has a disability).

The management of sexuality through "scientific knowledge and the complexity of normative systems" strongly determines what constitutes the experience of "an ordinary sexual life" (Hamilton 44). When one recognizes that the history of disability oppression includes gender, race, sexuality, and class, then contemporary sexual experience becomes more than just another site of exclusion. Acts of sexual exchange produce or are based upon power differences that subsequently create needs and desires. In addition, a hierarchical set of bodies and norms at the core of disability oppression maintain these power differences. In "Sex and the Emergence of Sexuality," Arnold Davidson explains how, in the last half of the nineteenth century, a set of psychiatric concepts emerged that made sexual identities a matter of impulses, tastes, aptitudes, satisfactions, and psychic traits (96). Subsequently, sexuality became an object of clinical knowledge. As a result of this emergence, an entirely new grouping of sexual diseases and disorders came into existence that intersects with disability categories (96). For example, it was not uncommon for medical diagnoses up through the nineteenth century to include drawings depicting hermaphrodites and deaf-mute persons as sexual perversions, directly translating bodily differences into abnormal sexuality (118). In a similar way, scientific inquiries committed themselves to proving gender difference in order to produce the knowledge required for a fully operational binary system of masculinity and femininity—both terms interrelated with heterosexuality (Butler, *Gender Trouble* 22). The category of disability functioned as a dumping ground for people who did not fit into the normative sex/gender/heterosexuality system. Simply put, without the classification of the abnormal, there was no way to classify "normal" sexuality. In other words, medical knowledge created the category of normative sexuality by creating the category of deviant sexuality.

This construction then allowed for the suppression of disabled sexuality in the eugenic sense through the medical control of disabled populations via marriage restrictions, segregation, and sterilization methods. A combination of active suppression and political fear shaped disabled sexuality as a menace. In this regard the formation of disability is strongly related to the scientific development of sexology as well as to the emergence of the "normative body" as defined by its functions, reproductive privileges, and heteronormative desires and behaviors. O'Brien's experiences with a sex surrogate and the filmic representation of the experiences are located within this intersection of the simultaneous and mutual construction of disability and sexuality. This intersection presents the desexualization and hypersexualization of disabled people and their disqualification from mating with non-disabled, heterosexual counterparts not as coincidental but as necessary in maintaining the mutuality of able-bodiedness and heterosexuality.

An Oasis Needs a Desert

Because disabled female sexuality is socially invisible, filmic narrative requires excessive effort to demonstrate its existence and significance. The internationally screened South Korean film *Oasis*, produced in 2002, depends on the absence of disabled women's voices in public about their desires, diverse sexual experiences, and frequent violence. The film closely depicts a disabled woman's life and its common experiences of family rejection and exploitation, inaccessible environments, and the stigmatizing gaze of and hatred from the public.

In the beginning of the film Hong Jongdu (Sol Kyung-gu) is released from prison after serving time for manslaughter in a hit-and-run accident; he learns that his family moved during his incarceration without leaving any forwarding address. When he locates them, he is greeted with hostility and disgust. Jongdu is a societal misfit because his behavior and mannerisms do not follow social decorum. Jongdu visits the family of the deceased from the accident and finds the daughter, Han Gongju (Moon So-ri), a woman with cerebral palsy, living alone. As part of a courting ritual, Jongdu brings her flowers, which her neighbor takes to her. After the neighbor is gone from her house, he breaks into her house, tells her that he is interested in her, and posts his phone number on her mirror. He then goes on to sexually assault her. Frightened, Gongju resists the attack and loses consciousness in her terror. Jongdu regrets his behavior immediately, slaps his own face, and tries to wake her up by spraying water on her face. Jongdu runs away, leaving her on the bathroom floor. The audience members later see her phoning him. When he visits her again, she asks, "Why did you bring me flowers?" The scene suggests that her unfamiliar experience of receiving sexual attention from a man blurs the boundaries between violence and affection, because the image of the flowers gains importance through the trope of courting. While the film disallows communication between the audience and the central disabled character with a speech difference, viewers depend on Jongdu to intrinsically understand her and to reiterate what she says.

It is important to take a look at several dehumanizing events antecedent to Gongju's phone call to Jongdu: Her neighbors use her small apartment to have sexual intercourse away from their children while ignoring her presence in her room. She is forced to pretend that she lives in her brother's house (a better house which her brother's family took away from her when she received it as a disability welfare benefit); she must pretend that she lives there so that when the social worker comes to inspect her house, the worker can confirm that Gongju, the beneficiary, lives there. These scenes portray her social barrenness and exploitation, the movie positing the encounter with the unlikely Jongdu as her oasis. Similarly, Jongdu suffers ostracism from his family, who has taken advantage of him in the interest of the family and its survival. When his older brother, the breadwinner of the family, kills Gongju's father in a traffic accident, the family conspires to lie to the police that Jongdu was the driver. Then audience members find out that unproductive Jongdu already has a prior conviction of rape, and the family believes that sending him, instead of the family breadwinner, to prison is the best choice for the sustenance of the family.

The combination of Jongdu's and Gongju's vulnerability and exploited status allows the film to highlight their relationship as innocent when viewed in the midst of their families' and neighbors' rejection and dehumanization. Nevertheless, the director relies on gendered violence occurring between the two outcasts to challenge contemporary Korea's indifferent, exploitative, and hypocritical workings of family. The film draws on Gongju's disability in order to complicate Jongdu's character and to avoid an overly simplified identification of good or evil. The film portrays Gongju vividly only during her intermittent fantasies of having a nondisabled body and dancing and playing with Jongdu. He is vulnerable and exploited, and he earns the audience's sympathy through his passionate attention to Gongju. After the initial assault he is no longer violent and transforms into a caring person.

The popular media perceived *Oasis* as explicitly about disability, and the film does provide a unique representation of disability in relation to the "reality" of disabled lives. Being far from melodramatic in portraying a disabled woman's life in contemporary Korea, *Oasis* pretends to be closer to reality by using documentary-style filming. The use of a handheld camera, realistic diegetic sounds such as TV and radio rather than music, the predominance of dark scenes through low-key lighting, the choice of a less stylistic mise-en-scène, and the casting of unfamiliar actresses and actors—with the exception of the two protagonists—all mimic reality or at least create a sense of verisimilitude. The film's unprecedented choice of a woman with spastic cerebral palsy as the main female character gives *Oasis* its distinctive flair that differentiates it from other trends in the visual portrayal of disability. Disabled women in the Korean film tradition have been dominantly portrayed with muteness, deafness, and blindness. Nevertheless, because few other images and narratives about disabled people's lives are available, the fiction film is understood as providing an informative, factual depiction of the sexuality of disabled women. Critics read this film in relation to the real lives of disabled women with regard to their isolation and alienation. However, in the midst of scarce cultural representations of disabled women, the director, Lee Chang-dong, faced fierce criticism from a group of disabled women. Activist Pak Chuhui writes that she was appalled by the film's blatant misrepresentation of disabled women's sexuality—particularly since the sexual violation leads to a positive relationship. Although what constitutes misrepresentation or correct representation is fraught with the impossible determination of reality, and although women do quite frequently form relationships with their violators, Pak's claim challenges the validity of the film's representation of disabled women's lives. In a theatre in Seoul a group of disabled women went to watch the film, and they felt threatened by the audience's laughter at Gongju's spastic facial movements and at the attack scene that depicts Jongdu as comical.[13] Because of Jongdu's embarrassment the non-disabled audience is supposed to see the attack as one of the benign mistakes of a fool that makes his antisocial characteristics more humane. The lack of his awareness of the seriousness of the situation makes him a cognitively or at least socially disabled character, later fully humanized through the representation of his care for Gongju. Further, the film presents the sexual attack as an ambivalent interaction and as an innocent

---

13. Personal communication with disabled women's rights activist Jung Youngran.

act that uniquely acknowledges Gongju's personhood and femininity while also signifying Jongdu's naïveté. In one poster advertising the film, Jongdu is lifting Gongju. Viewers see the expression of joy in his face but are not able to see Gongju and her expression. She is held and elevated by him as a way of being fully embraced, illustrating that the focus of the film is not Gongju and her disability but Jondu's transformation. In contrast, in the promotion picture two characters are sitting on a bench, posing with their hands together on their thighs. Gongju's disability is no longer present, and Jongdu seems to be compliant. This picture visualizes the rehabilitated humanity of both characters through their intimate bond and caring, manifested when the bodily characteristics of disability and social deviancy are removed.

Later in the film, as they continue to grow closer, Gongju engages in consensual sexual intercourse with Jongdu at her apartment. Her brother and his wife come in unannounced, interrupt the act, and accuse Jongdu of rape. They do not think of Gongju as a consenting adult in a sexual relationship. The representation of her consensual sexual intercourse with him being misunderstood as rape ironically parodies the earlier attack scene that frames sexual assault as an expression of compassionate interest. During the police investigation, the interrogating detective reproaches Jongdu in front of Gongju: "Are you a pervert? How do you even get aroused seeing that kind of a woman?" His statement captures the social configuration that denigrates disabled women as "unqualified" for sexual assault. Gongju's struggle to voice that what happened was not rape is too easily dismissed by her family and police.

The film ends with Gongju cleaning her bright room, waiting for Jongdu to return from prison where he has been sent for a rape conviction as a result of the above-described scene. Gongju's brother and his wife are antagonists, obstructing the supposedly unselfish relationship between Gongju and Jongdu. What may appear to be sexual assault is portrayed in the movie as being at worst "innocent curiosity" instead of intentional violation toward a lonely and sexually ignored female character. The film tries to challenge public assumptions that disabled people are asexual or victimized. Instead, by portraying the two "deviant" characters having a "normal" desire for love, the film affirms the prevalent denial of the sexuality of disabled women. The film substantiates the idea that sexual violence helps disabled women "escape" from undesirability and become "true women." The film plays on the belief that disabled women are not recognized as sexual; therefore sexual abuse of disabled women is utilized as a way of recognizing their heterosexuality, because sexual objectification is considered a part of heterosexual experience. By reifying the relationship between two "abject" characters, the film reinforces the invisibility of sexual violence against disabled women and the unlikelihood that they will have intimacy in their lives.[14]

Despite the prevalent understanding of disabled people as asexual, the asexuality of disabled people is a relatively new concept in South Korea as explored by disabled women's activism. Moreover, until recently, asexuality itself has not emerged as a problem of disabled people that must be fixed in social discourse. Interestingly, efforts toward heterosexualization in Korean cultural representations simulate that disabled women lie outside the gender matrix. Normative sexuality, already gendered, is repeated within the cultural representation of the sexual practices of gendered and disabled individuals. Because the sexualization of individuals with disabilities occurs on the basis of a presumed asexuality, almost every sexual exchange with the opposite sex is perceived as exerting a positive influence on disabled people. Because the recognition of woman as sexual object is seen as delivering the social approval of femininity and adulthood, the arena of women's sexual objectification emerges as an important and violent place for the integration of disabled women in Korea.

Conclusion

While prostitution and sex surrogacy offer fleeting but strong connections to manhood for disabled men in cultural representations, they enable disabled manhood at significant political cost by ignoring gender and race in heterosexual politics, such as those illustrated in *Born on the Fourth of July*. Overwhelmed by the presence of disability, forwarding the value of heterosexuality is reconfigured as a curing intervention to the "damaged," "emasculated" other. Simultaneously, the imagined need for the heterosexualization of disabled men reinforces the belief that disability naturally desexualizes the body. *Breaking the Waves* presents an unconventional relationship between prostitution and a disabled man by making the disabled wife a sexual mediator. It embraces the concept of the sur-

---

14. Gender theory points out that a "sphere of legitimate intimate alliance is established through the producing and intensifying regions of illegitimacy" (Butler, *Undoing Gender* 105). And this is why inclusion of illegitimate alliance in legitimate areas cannot eliminate illegitimacy of certain alliances. The intimacy and normalcy of undesired and sexually disenfranchised outcasts do not bring about a change in sexual hierarchy, a hierarchy which is enabled through the creation of sexual disenfranchisement in the first place.

rogate body employed for sexual experience and also demonstrates how interchangeable a wife and a prostitute can be. In this film the belief in the curative powers of sexuality makes it possible for Bess's narration of sexual conduct to "cure" Jan's paralysis. Indeed, by the end of the film Bess has accomplished the ultimate sacrifice when her death enables Jan to walk. The film offers a complicated incompatibility between disability and sexuality, highlighting the mediating role of prostitution while leaving unchallenged the "authentic" sexual pleasure that "surrogate" sexual experience summons.

The heterosexualization of desire requires and institutes the production of a binary gender system, where masculine and feminine are understood as expressive attributes of male and female (Butler, *Gender Trouble* 17). Likewise, gender differentiation "is accomplished through the practices of heterosexual desire" (22–23). Robert McRuer argues, however, that compulsory heterosexuality also depends on able-bodied norms (2). In providing the groundwork for understanding how able-bodiedness and heterosexuality are intertwined, he argues that both systems work to (re) produce the able body and heterosexuality (31). The cultural location of gender and heterosexuality in able-bodied norms creates a gap between individuals with disabilities and their cultural mapping to become fully gendered according to this binary logic. Film representation of disability seizes the imagined desire to fill this gap with characters' pursuits of iconic gender qualifications, as if the narrative can rehabilitate its characters. Thus able-bodied heterosexuality is further strengthened to the degree that heterosexualization completes the making of the rehabilitated self with disability. Sexualization through prostitution succeeds to some degree in transforming the disabled person into a fully heterosexual disabled man, thereby reflecting the tendency to think of gender as it is expressed in sexual practices. Inevitably, the traces of purchasing sex and the prostitute disappear rather quickly in the film after they have been utilized and exhausted.

While the Western disability sexual rights movement tends to challenge the norm of able-bodiedness, it does not as often seek to challenge the power relations inherent in "normative sexuality," because this norm is configured as the position many disabled people wish to access. To view disabled people as a group of people sharing the same sexual oppression (i.e., exclusion from heterosexuality) is misleading and ignores tremendously diverse positions of disabled people in relation to heteronormative society. O'Brien's complex desire to be wanted and to feel like a man, as well as his coming to terms with an "asexual"[15] life, captures the failure of the heterosexualizing project. Similarly, in the South Korean context, Gongju's relationship with Jongdu in *Oasis* illustrates the complexity of her sexual social relations. When heterosexual apparatuses can remedy disabled manhood and womanhood, sexuality is narrowly considered to be a psychologically and physically necessary aspect. This logic does not valorize the diverse sexual lives of disabled people—heterosexual, homosexual, bisexual, asexual, celibate, or otherwise. Rather, such circumscription begins with the contradictory assumptions that disabled people are undesirable, and thus ordered to be asexual, and that asexuality is a deprived way of life. Moreover, gendered, racialized, and medicalized forms of sexual intervention in cultural representations construct disabled sexuality itself.

As films represent disabled people exploring sexuality, who should own the subjectivity to find erotic energy and pleasure while deciding how to identify self-image and locate the body within and outside the realms of sexuality? Hypervisible, simplistic, and heteronormative sexualizing apparatuses in films emphasize the desexualized status of disabled people, forging the imperative to bring disabled people into the normalized sexual realms in order for them to be humanized and recognized.

---

15. O'Brien alludes to his asexuality when he declares that he no longer waits for his desire to be fulfilled. In this case his celibate life does not come from the absence of sexual desire; rather, it is a result of social desexualization. However, I argue not that asexuality is inherently negative or even indicative of the absence of desire itself, but that it must be respected as one form of identification and embodiment.

Works Cited

Allen, Nick. Rev. of *Born on the Fourth of July.* http://www.fast-rewind.com. Accessed November 21, 2003.

BBC News Asia-Pacific. "Brothel Offers Easy Access for Disabled." http://news. bbc.co.uk/1/hi/world/asia-pacific/1219878.htm. Accessed October 23, 2003.

Breathing Lessons: The Life and the Work of Mark O'Brien. "Introduction." Fanlight Production. http://www.fanlight.com/catalog/films/180_bl.shtml. Accessed December 5, 2003.

Butler, Judith. *Gender Trouble: Feminism and the Subversion of Identity.* New York: Routledge, 1990.

———. *Undoing Gender.* New York: Routledge, 2004.

DateAble. "Welcome to DateAble, Inc.: A Dating Service with Heart." http://www. dateable.org. Accessed October 15, 2003.

Davidson, Arnold. "Sex and the Emergence of Sexuality." (1987). In *Forms of Desire: Sexual Orientation and the Social Constructionist Controversy.* Edited by E. Stein. New York: Routledge, 1992.

Edwards, Douglas J. "Sex and Intimacy in the Nursing Home." *Nursing Homes: Long Term Care Management* 2 (Feb. 2003): 18–21.

Faber, Alyda. "Redeeming Sexual Violence? A Feminist Reading of *Breaking the Waves.*" *Literature and Theology* 17.1 (2003): 59–75.

Frazer, Bryant. Rev. of *Breaking the Waves. Deep Focus.* http://www.deep-focus. com/flicker/breaking.html. Accessed December 5, 2003.

Garland-Thomson, Rosemarie. "Shape Structures Story: Fresh and Feisty Stories of Disability." *Narrative* 15.1 (2007): 113–23.

Hamilton, Carol. "Doing the Wild Thing: Supporting an Ordinary Sexual Life for People with Intellectual Disabilities." *Disability Studies Quarterly* 22.4 (2002): 40–59.

Hawkins, Joan. *Cutting Edge: Art-Horror and the Horrific Avant-Garde.* Minneapolis: University of Minnesota Press, 2000.

Heath, Stephen. "God, Faith, and Film: *Breaking the Waves.*" *Literature and Theology* 12 (March 1998): 99.

Keefer, Kyle and Tod Linafelt. "The End of Desire: Theologies of Eros in *The Song of Songs* and *Breaking the Waves.*" In *Imag(in)ing Otherness: Filmic Visions of Living Together.* Edited by S. Brent Plate and D. Jasper. Atlanta: Scholars Press, 1999.

Kilmann, Peter. R. and Katherine H. Mills. *All about Sex Therapy.* New York: Plenum Press, 1983.

Kim, Eunjung and Mark Sherry. "International Sex Industry." *Encyclopedia of Disability,* Vol. IV. Edited by Gary Albrecht, Jerome Bickenbach, David T. Mitchell, Walter O. Schalick III, and Sharon Snyder. Thousand Oaks: Sage Publications, 2006. 1436–42.

Kovic, Ron. *Born on the Fourth of July.* New York: Akashic Books, 2005.

Lehman, Peter. "Crying over the Melodramatic Penis: Melodrama and Male Nudity in Films of the 90s." In *Masculinity: Bodies, Movies, Culture.* Edited by Peter

Lehman. New York: Routledge: 2001. 25–42.

Masters, William H. and Virginia E. Johnson. *Human Sexual Inadequacy.* Boston: Little, Brown, 1970.

McRuer, Robert. *Crip Theory: Cultural Signs of Queerness and Disability.* New York: New York University Press, 2006.

O'Brien, Mark. "On Seeing a Surrogate." *The Sun* 174 (May 1990). http://www.pacificnews.org/marko/sex-surrogate.html. Accessed April 10, 2009.

Pak, Chuhui. "There Is No Oasis." Rev. of *Oasis. Konggam* 6 (2003): 10–14.

Schaefer, Eric. *"Bold! Daring! Shocking! True!: A History of Exploitation Films, 1919–1959.* Durham: Duke University Press, 1999.

Shapiro, Lawrence. "Incorporating Sexual Surrogacy into the Ontario Direct Funding Program." *Disability Studies Quarterly* 22.4 (2002): 72–81.

Shaw, Jeanne. "When You're Asked to Speak about Sex, Intimacy, and Alzheimer's." *Journal of Sex Education and Therapy* 26.2 (2001): 140–45.

Shuttleworth, Russell P. and Linda Mona. "Disability and Sexuality: Toward a Focus on Sexual Access." *Disability Studies Quarterly* 22.4 (2002): 2–9.

Siebers, Tobin. "Sex, Shame, and Disability Identity: With Reference to Mark O'Brien." In *Disability Theory,* by Tobin Siebers. Ann Arbor: University of Michigan Press, 2008. 157–75.

Silverstein, Shel. *The Giving Tree.* New York: HarperCollins, 1964.

Skal, David J. and Elias Savada. *Dark Carnival: The Secret World of Tod Browning.* New York: Anchor Books, 1995.

Snyder, Sharon L. and David T. Mitchell. "Re-Engaging the Body: Disability Studies and the Resistance to Embodiment." *Public Culture* 13.3 (2002): 367–89.

Swissinfo. "Disabled Organization Withdraws Sex Project." *Swissinfo* (September 11, 2003). http://www.swissinfo.org/sen/swissinfo.html?siteSect=105&sid=4222207. Accessed September 12, 2003.

———. "Zurich Disabled Get Sexual Relief." *Swissinfo* (April 8, 2003). http://www.swissinfo.org/sen/swissinfo.html?siteSect=105&sid=1715377. Accessed November 21, 2003.

von Trier, Lars. "Naked Miracles." Interview by Stig Björkman. *Sight and Sound* 6 (1996): 12.

The filmmakers procure authenticity for Maggie (Hilary Swank) by having her purchase her training bag with rolled coins. *Million Dollar Baby*. Directed by Clint Eastwood. Warner Bros., 2004.

ROBERT McRUER

Neoliberal Risks

Million Dollar Baby, Murderball, and
Anti-National Sexual Positions

Million Dollar Baby, a Warner Bros. production released in December 2004, could be said to sell itself short, as far as its title is concerned. The production budget alone exceeded the titular $1 million thirty times over. Undoubtedly far more important to Warner Bros. and to director Clint Eastwood, however, was the film's domestic and foreign gross: exceeding $200 million U.S. dollars. This baby—to invoke an ableist metaphor appropriate to the film's anti-disabled ethos—had legs.

Of course, "million dollar baby" itself, as a metaphor, is intended to mark something so unique as to be well-nigh priceless; the million dollar figure, in other words, is paradoxically here a measure used to call up for audiences a value seemingly beyond measure. Despite this apparent desire for the immeasurable, however, the film is ultimately (and unsurprisingly) fairly recognizable as a banal Hollywood blockbuster. Maggie Fitzgerald (Hilary Swank) is a poor boxer who beats the odds against her to achieve international success; her success is largely propelled by the fact that she has convinced trainer Frankie Dunn (Eastwood) to work with her, even though he initially claims he will not "train girls." In the final third of the film, after a spinal-cord injury resulting from an accident in the ring, Maggie—unable to move her arms and legs without assistance—asks Frankie to help her end her life. Frankie struggles briefly with his decision and then complies.

A rags-to-riches story, a story of pluck and perseverance, and ultimately a story of triumph and bittersweet loss—there was very little about *Million Dollar Baby* that contemporary moviegoers had not seen dozens if not hundreds of times before. Even the disability protests of the film that

159

emerged soon after its release, in fact, could be positioned in relation to both the film's measurability and its accolades: yet another film adored by the majority and opposed by only a supposedly small minority, *Million Dollar Baby* overcame opposition to be showered with Oscars at the 2005 Academy Awards—Best Supporting Actor (Morgan Freeman), Best Actress, Best Director, and of course Best Picture.

My apparent cynicism, or pessimism of the intellect, in temporarily positioning even the vibrant disability protests of *Million Dollar Baby* in relation to the film's recognizability should not belie one of this essay's goals, which is precisely to account for the gap between the almost-universal adoration of the film, emanating from the moviegoing public at large, and the almost-universal condemnation of it, emanating from disability activist communities. The disability critiques of *Million Dollar Baby* (some of which I will work through in this analysis) are not difficult to understand; indeed, although my own experience is by no means representative, I generally found even in casual conversation that fans of the film quickly understood why disabled people were critical of it: Maggie's death by lethal injection following her spinal-cord injury is both unnecessary and completely dependent on the cultural assumption that disabled lives are not worth living. Disability activists had nothing like the media control of Warner Bros. or Eastwood, certainly, but fans who nonetheless came in contact with disability critiques (a relatively small number compared to the film's viewership as a whole) were not incapable of comprehending them. Instead, fans were for some reason simply resistant to having their pleasure in *Million Dollar Baby*, their recollection of what they experienced watching it, interrupted. This article, positioning *Million Dollar Baby* within the cultural logic of neoliberalism, attempts to understand why. In the process my goal is ultimately to counter cynicism, affirming and extending the immeasurable value of an increasingly global—and at times, as I imagine briefly in conclusion, daringly antinational—disability movement.

That *Million Dollar Baby* could generate comforting recollections difficult to relinquish after a pleasurable first viewing suggests that, on some level, the film succeeds by mobilizing nostalgia. *Million Dollar Baby* is, however, as Fredric Jameson might say, "technically not a nostalgia film," ("Postmodernism and Consumer Society" 117) since it takes place in contemporary settings—largely contemporary Los Angeles, but also London and Las Vegas. The skyscrapers of contemporary downtown L.A. are visible in at least one key scene, as Frankie wanders back to the Hit Pit Gym after Maggie attempts suicide (biting through her tongue to induce lethal bleeding). But in general, *Million Dollar Baby* is a textbook example of the films Jameson famously describes as nostalgic regardless of their contemporary setting: "the very style of nostalgia films invad[es] and coloniz[es] even those movies today which have contemporary settings: as though, for some reason, we were unable to focus our own present, as though we have become incapable of achieving aesthetic representations of our own current experience" (117). Jameson uses Lawrence Kasdan's 1981 film *Body Heat* to exemplify the phenomenon he theorizes, but it's almost uncanny how much his description applies to *Million Dollar Baby:*

> [The film does] without most of the signals and references which we might associate with the contemporary world, with consumer society—the appliances and artifacts, the high rises, the object world of late capitalism. Technically, then, its objects [are contemporary] products, but everything in the film conspires to blur that immediate contemporary reference and to make it possible to receive this too as a nostalgia work—as a narrative set in some indefinable nostalgic past, an eternal 1930s, say, beyond history. (117)

Tellingly, given Jameson's invocation of an eternal 1930s, one reviewer noted that *Million Dollar Baby*'s Hit Pit Gym, in particular, seemed purposefully designed to represent "any decade from the 1930s to the present": "The only direct time-period reference is to prominent real-life 1980s fighter Tommy 'Hitman' Hearns, who the film's characters state has been retired for many years" (Johnson). Of course, women's boxing in a professional boxing association is ostensibly a contemporary topic, and the world represented—inside and outside the boxing ring, in the hospital, and in the rehabilitation center—is apparently a post-civil-rights-era world of multiracial harmony. Gender and race are actually factors, however, that contribute to *Million Dollar Baby*'s status as a nostalgia film: both certainly have incredibly cacophonous, complicated, and ongoing histories in Los Angeles, Las Vegas, and London, but in the world beyond history that the film conjures up, that complexity must be disavowed. In other words, we may know, as Mike Davis and numerous other commentators have demonstrated, that a masculinist and structural racism undergirds downtown and other spaces in "Fortress L.A." (Davis 221), but in this nostalgic story it does not.[1]

---

1. Mike Davis's *City of Quartz* remains the foundational study of the relations between spatiality, political economy, and culture in Los Angeles; see also Edward W. Soja, *Postmodern Geographies;* Allen J. Scott and Edward W. Soja (eds.), *The City;* and Raúl Homero Villa and George J. Sánchez (eds.), *Los Angeles and the Future of Urban Cultures.* Fredric Jameson's own work on Los Angeles also emphasizes the fortress-like qualities of downtown spaces such as the Bonaventure Hotel, which "repels the city outside" and constitutes an enclosed and disorienting space of spectacle within, a space that is

The film is most obviously and directly nostalgic when the setting moves away from Los Angeles, however, in the two scenes where Frankie (once with Maggie, once—following her death—poignantly without) enjoys homemade lemon meringue pie ("none of that canned stuff," Maggie had insisted) in a diner not far from the small town in Missouri where Maggie grew up. Or, I might say, given how absolutely earnest *Million Dollar Baby* is about its fabricated authenticity, not far from the small town in "Missour-ah" where Maggie grew up (Swank's accent may be inconsistent in the film, but this particular home-grown pronunciation, direct from the backwoods and hills of the Show-Me State, comes through every time). I return to that imagined community later, but consider first a minor moment of rupture in *Million Dollar Baby's* fabricated authenticity. With that moment of rupture or interrupted nostalgia as a starting point for my analysis, I relocate *Million Dollar Baby*, and what David T. Mitchell and Sharon L. Snyder might call the "narrative prosthesis" that drives it (*Narrative Prosthesis* 6–10), within our contemporary moment, paying particular attention to how this is a neoliberal text representing a docile and quite disciplined national identity and, indeed, national sexuality.

After a nod to the remote possibility that there is actually some crip humor in *Million Dollar Baby*, I conclude by briefly considering some of the ways *Murderball*—an independent documentary focused on the aggressive contact sport known as "quad rugby"—functions as the antithesis of *Million Dollar Baby*. *Murderball* was released in the summer of 2005, directly after *Million Dollar Baby's* triumphs at that year's Academy Awards; the documentary was received, on the whole, much more positively in disability communities (there were certainly no protests by disability activists outside theatres, and intracommunity reviews like Ed Hooper's in the *Ragged Edge*, declaring *Murderball* "quite simply the best film ever made on disability," were not uncommon). Keeping an eye on just how flexible the cultural manifestations of neoliberalism can be, however, I am interested in considering in conclusion both how *Murderball* might function

---

temporally dislocated and even nostalgic in ways similar to the films he discusses (*Postmodernism* 42). Although I am drawing on Jameson's insights for this essay, I want to register at least some caution in regard to his recruitment of "schizophrenia" as a metaphor for postmodern subjectivity (he is extending and commenting on the work of Jacques Lacan, Gilles Deleuze, and Félix Guattari) ("Postmodernism and Consumer Society" 118–23; *Postmodernism* 26–34). The historical emergence of able-bodiedness has been disappeared, and able-bodied identity, like heterosexuality, tends, now, to be conceptualized as universal or simply "natural." (I discuss this more thoroughly in *Crip Theory*, 1–19.) Given that the naturalization of able-bodiedness allows capitalism to function more efficiently, it seems possible to examine the temporalities of late capitalism critically while simultaneously connecting those temporalities to able-bodied hegemony, rather than simply metaphorizing the postmodern condition in toto as somehow "disabled."

as the antithesis of *Million Dollar Baby* and, more controversially perhaps, how it might not.

Neoliberal Currency

The rupture I highlight comes in a scene where Maggie buys her very own training bag for boxing. She has saved the pennies and dimes she has made working as a waitress, and deposits them in a pile, loose and in rolls, on the counter when she pays for the training bag. "It is a strange thing to do," a writer at Movie Mistakes tells us, but "Maggie bought the coin rolls from a 'bank or other vendor.'" Moviemistakes.com is a popular website (with about 30,000 hits daily) owned and operated by an individual movie buff whose intent is not simply to trash films, but—in a way—to generate alternative pleasures; "open your eyes," the site uses as its motto, suggesting in decidedly antinostalgic fashion that seamless representations do not exist. The webmaster for Movie Mistakes is no Bertolt Brecht; he identifies himself, indeed, simply as a "film lover" who tends to like most films that he sees, and he minimizes his critique of the industry. The site itself, nonetheless, does invite a kind of Brechtian reflection on the mechanisms that should, for the ideal viewer of most of the films catalogued, remain obscured by pleasurable content.[2]

Initially, the writer at Movie Mistakes insisted that the coins in *Million Dollar Baby* were clearly "props": "The coin rolls [Maggie] has are the sealed type that can only be produced by a machine and not those that are produced when you roll coins from a coin jar. She would have had to purchase the rolls directly from a bank or other vendor to achieve this and she clearly did not roll them herself." Realizing that this is precisely what Maggie has done, the writer concludes that this is exceedingly "strange." Indeed, to dwell on this strangeness, from the filmmakers' perspective, there's not really a convincing scenario—or rather, there is no scenario convincing from within the realist aesthetic upon which the film depends—where Maggie would have gotten these coins from a vendor. Maggie apparently exchanged paper currency for coins despite the fact

---

2. That the site invites Brechtian reflection does not of course guarantee that those considering the "errors" identified at moviemistakes.com, including the designers and writers, respond to that implicit invitation. There is, in fact, nothing essentially subversive about moviemistakes.com, and the errors catalogued there can easily be used to market a film, or a subsequent DVD release, without disruption of its larger ideological project. Nonetheless, even if I am writing at the limit of the critical reflections the site could be said to authorize, its motto undeniably encourages alternative, and even disloyal, ways of apprehending texts, which would of necessity include the reading I offer here.

that there could not conceivably be a training bag vendor, in Los Angeles or elsewhere, who would appreciate having the transaction conducted in pennies. The only conceivable scenario for this exchange would shatter the illusion of realism and require Swank playing alongside her character: "Listen, I need to buy some rolled coins so that on-screen, when I get my training bag, I look like an authentic, hard-working, salt-of-the-earth, small-town girl with a dream. Can you help me out?" This exchange, then, is in a sense located solely (and necessarily) outside the text of the film: the filmmakers procure authenticity for Swank's character by having her use coins to purchase her training bag.

This particular scene is so precious, in my mind, given how completely it works as a metaphor for the whole film: the maudlin disability story that concludes the film should be just as recognizable as a movie mistake—that is to say, *Million Dollar Baby* gives us the same old mass-produced disability story that you can get prepackaged, ready-made at the Hollywood bank (in exchange, this time for 30 million U.S. dollars). And as currency of a sort, this disability story circulates, but—like anything that comes in contact with actual currency—with its value homogenized.

The irony that I am excavating here is indebted to Karl Marx's understanding of money and value. According to Marx, "Money degrades all the gods of mankind and turns them into commodities. Money is the universal and self-constituted value set upon all things. It has therefore robbed the whole world of both nature and man, of its original value" (41). As I have already suggested, the filmmakers for *Million Dollar Baby* desire, on a narrative level, to conjure up an experience or life (Maggie's) and paradoxically value that experience as beyond all measure and certainly outside of relations of exchange—Maggie's story should not be legible within the degraded processes Marx traces. The coin blooper, however, can be deployed to make comically visible the ways in which disability representation—especially corporate Hollywood representation—is inescapably caught up in the homogenization of value Marx describes. It would take some pretty serious reading against the grain to find alternative economies of disability—the heterogeneous, excessive values that disabled people and movements have generated—in this film (outside, in the streets, protesting it, yes; but in it, no).[3]

---

3. For a consideration of homogenized value and of the ways in which individuals or groups shape alternative, excessive values, see Matthew Tinkcomm's *Working like a Homosexual*, especially the Introduction (1–34). Tinkcomm analyzes the ways in which capital requires workers to shape themselves into blank commodities and to produce objects that erase the history of their production; he considers as well the ways in which camp productions exceed those demands and generate alternative, queer values. For a more general or global consideration of the generation of excessive

In a more complex sense, though, the coin scene is precious for making temporarily visible the confluence of market and state that *Million Dollar Baby* and most Hollywood films—whether they are about disability or not—would mask. The Dream Factory purports to churn out stories about, well, dreams, not theses about the ideologies founding contemporary political economy or exposés about how Hollywood capitalizes on the cultural politics of disability. Minted or authorized by the state for circulation in the market, these coins are not supposed to distract our attention from the sweet pleasures of lemon meringue pie, authentic Irish flute music, and excited crowds cheering our Maggie on, or from the bittersweet pleasure, in the end, of Frankie setting a disabled Maggie free as he delivers a lethal dose of adrenalin (disability activists, of course, called this "murder," but the ideal or preferred viewer, fighting back the tears, is supposed to see the death as a kind of freedom).

Hiding in plain sight as a prepackaged blooper, however, the coin props beg the question of the interest that state and market might have in a text such as this. It's worth pointing out that most scholars in disability studies really do not need me, in this article, to excavate the disability movie mistake that is *Million Dollar Baby*; give any disability studies scholar a computer, a microphone, or a spotlight, and I'm confident she'll convincingly critique the film in a few minutes or so.[4] Considering, however, the ways that *Million Dollar Baby* functions as neoliberal currency, as a prime example of what Amitava Kumar calls "the literature of the New Economic Policy" (xxi)—or more provocatively, "World Bank Literature" (xvii)—is, perhaps, work that remains for us to do.[5]

I contend that disability is located at the absolute center of the emergent "literature" Kumar names. *Million Dollar Baby* and the disability story it tells in fact school us, all of us (regardless of where in the world we view the film), in what it meant to be American at the particular moment *Million Dollar Baby* was made, when neoliberalism had achieved hegemony and the state (particularly the dominant U.S.

---

values, see Michael Hardt and Antonio Negri's *Multitude*.

4. This point is borne out by the cluster of essays critiquing *Million Dollar Baby* in the summer 2006 issue of *Disability Studies Quarterly* (Dolmage and DeGenaro). Of course, what is true of disability studies scholars (that they do not need me to rehearse disability critiques of the film) is not necessarily true of film studies scholars or cultural studies scholars more generally; this essay presumes, however, that even scholars positioned mainly outside disability studies have begun to recognize its main tenets and ways of reading.

5. Reading *Million Dollar Baby* as literature of the New Economic Policy entails taking seriously Rosemary Hennessy's response to Amitava Kumar's question "where is the literature of the World Bank?" Hennessy writes that "the literature of the World Bank can be found in the World Bank [that is, in documents generated by the World Bank]"; however, "the World Bank's literature may be lodged insidiously in places where we had not thought to look" (40–41).

state) was no longer working to sustain any sort of check on corporate capital but was instead allied with capital in an ongoing, and geographically uneven, reconsolidation of class power. Neoliberal theory,
propagated by the state and other contemporary institutions (such as
the World Bank), promised for almost three decades that its implemen-
tation would cause wealth to trickle down to all of us, but don't get
your coin rolls out too soon: in practice, neoliberalism generated the
largest redistribution of wealth upward that the world has ever known.
Kumar and many others, asking about the representation of such promises (asking—essentially—how World Bank literature functions), have
attempted to theorize the ways in which consent was secured culturally
to these processes. I confess that I dislike *Million Dollar Baby* enough to
wish I could blame it all on this one film, which disability activist John
Kelly hilariously described to me as a sad excuse for an after-school special, but of course my larger point invoking World Bank literature is that
neoliberal lessons were perpetuated by an array of texts like this film
(including, I would say, almost all the other disability films showered
with, or considered for, awards in 2005: *The Sea Inside, Ray, The Aviator*).[6]
Million Dollar Baby, in other words, strikes me as in no way unique but
rather as representative (as other texts are representative) of the cultural
logic of neoliberalism.[7]

---

6. These award-winning 2004 films were all disability biopics: *Ray* focused on the life of blind
musician Ray Charles; *The Aviator* depicted the life of entrepreneur and millionaire Howard Hughes
(particularly presenting Hughes's life with obsessive-compulsive disorder); *The Sea Inside*, as I discuss briefly below, put forward the story of a Spanish quadriplegic, Ramón Sampedro, petitioning
Spanish courts for the right to end his life.

7. Neoliberal capitalism, like all the forms of capitalism that have preceded it, is constantly in
crisis; indeed, the "cultural logic of neoliberalism" emerges to manage (always partially and always
incompletely) the crises generated by a fundamentally unjust, inequitable system. I have used the
past tense in the preceding paragraph to highlight that *Million Dollar Baby* speaks to the neoliberal
crisis at the moment of its release. Less than four years later, of course, a global financial crisis began
to reveal even more explicitly the fissures in neoliberal logic; this crisis was partly characterized by
a refreshing and new (or reinvigorated) skepticism regarding many of the main tenets of neoliberalism (tenets that I discuss more directly in the next section). The skepticism or fear emerging from
the global crisis contributed to Barack Obama's victory in the 2008 U.S. presidential election. In the
wake of all these events, some have even declared the death of neoliberalism (despite the fact that
Obama, upon taking office, surrounded himself with some of the major figures working to consolidate neoliberalism over the past few decades). At the time of this writing, the global financial crisis is
ongoing and there is a great deal of uncertainty as to what will happen next. I currently align myself
with those arguing that announcements of the end of neoliberalism are very premature. Although
I am hopeful about the possibilities opened up by the current crisis, it still seems to me that the
reconsolidation of class power that neoliberalism marked continues (indeed, that seems to me an
understatement), even if it is currently taking new forms with the Obama administration.

Hit Me with Your Best Shot

Deregulation, Privatization, and Their Discontents

Taking five of the key principles of turn-of-the-century neoliberalism, I sketch out in this section some of the ways in which they are operative in *Million Dollar Baby*, with my contention that the film teaches us what it means to be participants in this system, or—more directly and insidiously—what it means to be an American, remaining in the background throughout. By invoking "what it means to be an American," of course, I put forward the conflation of the United States with "America" that is part of the political unconscious of any film like *Million Dollar Baby*, a point to which I will return. For now, however, I stress what it means to be an American simply because neoliberalism functions differently in different national locations. Jump cut, for instance, to the Spanish courtroom scene in *The Sea Inside*, where lawyers for Ramón Sampedro (Javier Bardem) are arguing—before literal representatives of the state's juridical power—for his right to end his life. "We are a civilized nation," the lawyers insist—words that mark a key moment of consolidation for Spanish neoliberalism, but that would be completely beside the point in *Million Dollar Baby*.[8] *Million Dollar Baby*'s lesson plan, on the other side of the Atlantic, is somewhat different, and it is a lesson plan that has no interest (in all senses of the term) in proving the impossible thesis that "America" is "a civilized nation."

The five principles of neoliberalism I draw on for this section were drafted and disseminated by Elizabeth Martinez and Arnoldo García, in a brief written specifically for activists countering neoliberalism. It is a brief intended, as the Zapatistas of Chiapas would have it, "for humanity"; indeed, Martinez and García attended the Intercontinental Encounter for Humanity and Against Neoliberalism in July 1996, hosted by the Zapatistas in La Realidad, Chiapas (since that *encuentro*, the Zapatistas' Subcomandante Marcos has dispatched numerous communiqués from Chiapas addressed "to the people of México," or even "to the people of the world").[9] There is a vast and indispensable scholarly literature on neoliberalism at this point—a literature that is one of the conditions of possibility for my own scholarship.[10] I draw on Martinez and García in this

---

8. For an indispensable discussion of neoliberalism in Spain, see Gabriel Giorgi's article "Madrid en Tránsito." Giorgio's analysis has strongly influenced my thinking on the uneven global geographical development of neoliberalism and the ways in which postmodern identities are incorporated into geographically located manifestations of neoliberalism.

9. On the Zapatistas, Subcomandante Marcos, and disability, see my "Wish You Were Here."

10. See, for instance, Lisa Duggan, *The Twilight of Equality*; David Harvey, *A Brief History of Neoliberalism* and *Spaces of Global Capitalism*; Amitava Kumar, *World Bank Literature*; and Neil Smith, *The*

section, however, to conjure up the productive labor of activists and to highlight the alternative forms of circulation and value imagined and put in motion by the Intercontinental Encounter for Humanity and similar events (circulation alternative, in particular, to the homogenizing circulation of capital).

You can't stop people from sharing, Naomi Klein and numerous others imagining alternative globalizations might say, and sharing Martinez and García's talking points against neoliberalism is precisely what happened not long after the Chiapas gathering: the five points I draw on here circulated values irreducible to a cash nexus to and through innumerable progressive locations. The sites where the piece is now available, for instance, include "CorpWatch: Holding Corporations Accountable," "Global Exchange: Building People-to-People Ties," "Global Issues That Affect Everyone," "AIDC: Alternative Information and Development Centre," "illegalvoices.org: Anarchist People of Color," and "Double Standards." These locations are all Internet-based, but it is of course impossible to measure fully just how far these resistant ideas have traveled.[11] Martinez and García, finally, are part of the National Network for Immigrant and Refugee Rights, and I also draw on their talking points because, as I move in the conclusion toward "anti-national" sexual positions (Puar 27), it is important to think about how and why the nation might be undone by bodies moving otherwise, bodies moving beyond the borders of the contemporary nation-state.

The first neoliberal lesson of *Million Dollar Baby*, as Martinez and García's talking points would have it, is that the market is everything. If there is a simple or single ideological message in *Million Dollar Baby*, it's that in America you get your shot: you take a risk, you put yourself out there, and if it pays off, it pays off, but regardless, you get your shot. The second lesson is that you best get that shot in a deregulated environment. Even if there are rules (and certainly there are referees everywhere in the film), it's clear that the rules are there to be broken, and nobody *really* abides by them, least of all those who would take risks and get ahead. Maggie's spinal-cord injury itself comes as the result of a broken rule (an illegal and decisive blow), and her opponent Billie the Blue Bear (played by real-life boxer Lucia Rijker) has secured her reputation and gotten to the top by flouting regulation. Maggie too doesn't play by the book (or, we might

---

Endgame of Globalization.

11. Hardt and Negri's work on the productive power of multitude is animating my formulations in this paragraph; see also Naomi Klein, *Fences and Windows*. While I am drawing on Martinez and García's talking points, I have reordered them for the purposes of my own argument about *Million Dollar Baby*'s neoliberal lessons.

say, she thinks outside the box), from her relentless insistence that Frankie train her (despite his policy against training women) to her tendency to take opponents down in the first round.

The first two points—the market is everything and deregulation is best—are the most esoteric of *Million Dollar Baby*'s neoliberal lessons; the other three points are both more direct and clearer as to the role that disability has in these processes. If neoliberalism, like sadism, demands a story, then it's a story that functions on a familiar narrative level, at least as far as disability is concerned. Mitchell and Snyder's theory of "narrative prosthesis" suggests that disability functions "as a crutch upon which literary narratives lean for their representational power, disruptive potentiality, and analytical insight" (49). Extending their theory we might recognize that the story or narrative of American neoliberalism absolutely depends upon disability. I list Martinez and García's final three lessons here and then explain this thesis more carefully. Third, privatization is an unequivocal good; it is functioning, unquestionable common sense. Fourth, social services are inefficient, corrupt, and unnecessary, sapping not just the coffers but also the vitality of a given culture. And fifth, personal "responsibility" should be valued far above any more expansive notion of the common or public good. Or rather, the common good is best realized by individuals acting "responsibly."

The third and fourth points—that privatization is an unequivocal good and that social services should be slashed—are interrelated, and each point, as far as *Million Dollar Baby* is concerned, comes with a representative disabled figure. Maggie's mother, Earline Fitzgerald (Margo Martindale), is represented as fat; her fatness is relentlessly discussed, exaggerated, and positioned as disability; and she is on both welfare and Medicaid (locating Earline here is one of the primary ways the film positions her fatness as disability). Earline represents the other side of that small Missour-ah town, the part of town the nostalgic mist can't reach. Audiences don't know what she needs medicine for; we simply know that she needs medicine and that she's very concerned, if she's perceived as making too much money (after Maggie buys her a house), that the medical and pharmaceutical services she accesses will be terminated. Despite how comically she's portrayed (it's not funny in the slightest, but she's intended to be read as a comic character), Earline's worries are legitimate. They are worries for innumerable disabled people trying to access what Lisa Duggan has called the incredible shrinking public sphere (22).

According to Jay Dolmage and William DeGenaro, in an analysis of how class and disability intersect in *Million Dollar Baby*, Earline represents for audiences a working-class body paradoxically "incapable of labor," suggesting that "people with disabilities cheat the system for money because they won't work, while at the same time people with disabilities could never be capable of working." I am calling this a neoliberal lesson because it is a stereotype located in an era when social services were being slashed and when consensus around those cuts was being secured culturally by positioning figures such as Earline not as members of the public themselves, but as always and everywhere threatening to the general public's well-being. Maggie's disability, in contrast to Earline's, has no connection to the public, or rather no connection to the public as comprehended by state and market: when Earline expresses a concern that the hospital and rehabilitation center will use up all of Maggie's financial resources, Maggie—in her most docile moment—informs Earline that the Women's Boxing Association (WBA) is paying for everything (it's Maggie's most docile moment, even though, or precisely because, it appears to be her most confrontational). The good disabled subject, with her entirely privatized care, confronts the bad disabled subject, who not only drains American resources, but might be merely faking it. The confrontation between the two representatives of contemporary disability comes to a head with Maggie's angry final lines to her mother: "Momma, you take Mardell and JD and get home 'fore I tell that lawyer there that you were so worried about your welfare you never signed those house papers like you were supposed to. So anytime I feel like it I can sell that house from under your fat, lazy, hillbilly ass. And if you ever come back, that's exactly what I'll do."

As innumerable disability critics have pointed out, of course, Maggie's top-notch private care, actually, sucks. To list just a few of the disability critiques that have circulated quite freely: the doctors and nurses seem not to know how to prevent or to treat bedsores, except by letting gangrene set in so that they can amputate Maggie's leg; the wards Maggie inhabits are dark and isolated; at times it seems that the workers' responsibility, in relation to Maggie, can be summed up with the two words "suicide watch" (and even with that limited job description, no one is in the running for Employee-of-the-Month). No disability activist I talked to could think of a single rehabilitation memoir that had the newly disabled figure going it solo, yet Frankie, in his brief suggestion that Maggie might go to school, is actually the only one moving through this facility who ever talks to Maggie about imagining and managing life after rehab.[12] No counselors, no disabled community or professionals, nothing. The

---

12. Prominent counter-examples of the ways in which disability solidarity, as well as—often—direct critiques of the rehabilitation center itself, include John Hockenberry's discussion of rehab in *Moving Violations* (28–41) and Simi Linton's in *My Body Politic* (4–17).

soundtrack for the film—composed by Eastwood himself and orchestrated by Lennie Niehaus—is, predictably, at this point, almost entirely slow violins (the music is described by the closed captions on DVD, again predictably, as "meditative and melancholy"). Another soundtrack is possible, however, and it's not *unthinkable*, if we approach the film from the perspective of alternative, disabled values, to come away from *Million Dollar Baby* singing an adaptation of Bruce Springsteen's classic "War (What Is It Good For?)" (even though it is admittedly the opposite of the message you're supposed to read into the rehab sequences): "Privatization? Huh. Yeah, what is it good for? Absolutely nothin!" Maggie's mother, however, keeps you from going there: clearly, for the intended viewer, it's *social spending* that is out of control if U.S. taxpayers' dollars are paying for the prescription drugs of people like Earline. Millions and millions of dollars, actually, if in fact Earline stands in for innumerable other poor women or men on Medicaid and welfare.[13]

Fifth and finally, and related to the above example, personal "responsibility" is valued above any notion of the common or public good, which is essentially how both Maggie's and Frankie's stories play out—Maggie recognizes that she has had her shot and "responsibly" (according to the logic of the film) works to ends her life; Frankie recognizes that, despite the sovereign regulations imposed by the Catholic Church (he attends regularly despite being represented from the beginning as a skeptic), the responsible thing for him is to help her achieve that end.[14] The hegemony of personal responsibility means that neoliberalism's good disabled subject would appear to have three chapters in her narrative: onset of disability, brief privatized care, elimination. But hey, in America, she got her shot.

No Sex Please, We're Disabled

Million Dollar Baby's status as American literature of the New Economic Policy helps to provide some evidence as to why there is such a proscription on sexuality in this text. Anne Heche and Harrison Ford, Helen Hunt and Jack Nicholson—May/December heterosexual couplings in Hollywood are just about a prepackaged dime a dozen.[15] But for some reason,

---

13. For a good analysis of the role that the "welfare queen" has played in public discourse in the past few decades, see Ange-Marie Hancock's *The Politics of Disgust*.

14. Duggan discusses the role "personal responsibility," coupled with privatization, plays in the consolidation of neoliberalism in *The Twilight of Equality* (12–15).

15. The list of Hollywood films with couples made up of an older man and younger woman is potentially endless; the two I nod toward here are *Six Days Seven Nights* (1998) and *As Good As It Gets*

the erotics of Frankie's repeated phrase "my darling, my blood" notwithstanding, Eastwood and Swank must not have sex. "You're everything I got, boss," Maggie says at one point, but if she's making a pass, Frankie fails to take the hint. The film nonetheless (again, as a contemporary nostalgia film) is haunted by how relationships are supposed to be, normatively, even though there is not a single successful heteronormative coupling in *Million Dollar Baby*. The closest we come to a successful performance of heterosexuality is Maggie's sister Mardell (Riki Linhomme), who—when she is introduced in the first of the Missouri sequences—is waiting for JD (Marcus Chait), the father of her baby, to get out of prison. Mardell and JD are later present for the exorcism of the bad disabled subject and are clearly not held up as models to be emulated; they exit the rehab center—and the film—with Earline after Maggie's outburst. The closest we come to a successful performance of heterosexuality as far as Frankie and Maggie are concerned is the one moment of potential crip humor that I mentioned. When Maggie wakes up in rehab, she starts the banter between the two:

> "Growin' a beard, boss?"
> "I thought it might help me with the ladies."
> "Can't say it does."

But, of course, given the prosthetic role a disabled Maggie needs to play in this narrative, again the flirtation must go nowhere.

I contend that disability as prosthesis in the narrative of American neoliberalism disallows Maggie and Frankie's romantic or sexual connection. There may be no couple, in *Million Dollar Baby*, that comes remotely close to getting the repetition of compulsory heterosexuality exactly right, but the film is haunted nonetheless by a proper sexuality that would provide stability in a world made unstable by the cultural, political, and economic dislocations of the last three decades. In this sense *Million Dollar Baby* is like the 2004 U.S. election year it immediately followed, since the year had thousands of frightened voters heading to the polls to restore the sanctity of the supposed traditional family through ballot initiatives that would prohibit same-sex marriage or codify statewide definitions of marriage as "the union of one man and one woman."

The primary subplot of *Million Dollar Baby* arguably attests well to its thematizing of sexual and gender propriety. Audiences have learned over

---

(1997). In *Crip Theory*, I discuss the ways in which *As Good As It Gets* serves as a particularly good representation of how compulsory heterosexuality and compulsory able-bodiedness are currently intertwined (1–32).

the course of the film that Frankie is alienated from his wife and daughter (the letters that he writes to his daughter, in particular, are returned unopened). This subplot is resolved (only partially, and of course inadequately) by the final scene that nostalgically locates Frankie back in the Missouri diner, eating lemon meringue pie served up by a nameless figure who nonetheless, in her amorphousness, becomes contemporary patriarchy's desired Everywoman: mother/daughter/lover/waitress, phantasmatically protecting neoliberal masculinity and familial relations from the dissolution that perpetually threatens them.

Frankie's assistant, Eddie "Scrap-Iron" Dupris (Freeman), provides the voice-over narration for *Million Dollar Baby*. In this concluding scene, as Scrap imagines Frankie somewhere far away, "in a place set in the cedars and oak trees," it's made clear that the narration has "really" been a letter to Frankie's daughter, to let her know, as the final words of the film would have it, "what kind of man your father really was." The nameless figure serving Frankie pie in the diner may never be definitively identified as Frankie's daughter, but she doesn't have to be. Scrap's letter, regardless of the difference Frankie's wife and daughter have marked throughout the film, reaches its target: an American audience invoked as understanding proper sexual and gendered positions, the properties we should associate with the American heartland (i.e., the stability of American values and the reliability of home cooking, not rural poverty or impairment), and the difference between good and bad (disabled) subjects.

This is where *Murderball* is in some ways (and again only partially) the antithesis of *Million Dollar Baby*, despite *Murderball*'s extreme (and indeed much more explicit) nationalism. *Murderball*'s nationalism is represented most obviously by the ongoing battle over whether the United States, Canada, or some other nations's quadriplegic rugby team will emerge victorious (despite staging a classic U.S. sports film rivalry between "America" and another country, it is ultimately New Zealand that wins at the 2004 Athens Paralympic Games). If there's a pleasurable moment of rupture in *Murderball*'s nationalist narrative, however, a moment when the state is not directly figuring the positions these men will occupy, it's the now-famous and graphic discussion of sex in the center of the film: "so does the girl always have to be on top?" one of the women chatting with a quad rugby team player asks at that point in the film. "A lot of girls like to be on top," is his provocative and—in the wake of *Million Dollar Baby* and other contemporary texts suggesting implicitly or explicitly that "America" cannot sanction non-normative sexual positions—seductively anti-national response.

Neoliberalism is nothing if not flexible, however, and that moment of rupture in the construction of national identity and sexuality is in tension with (and contained by) the absolutely integrationist final scene at the White House, with the team receiving accolades directly from George W. Bush. It's a scene that has not received much attention in the largely celebratory disability response to *Murderball*, although—at least in the urban locations where I initially viewed the film and in university classrooms (and disability studies classes) where I later discussed it with students—it is not uncommon for the scene to elicit jeers or hissing from viewers. The insidious conflation of "America" with the United States in a film like *Million Dollar Baby* is interrupted for many viewers of *Murderball* by the Bush scene. The jeers and hissing mark a moment of disidentification with the "America" imperialistically imposed upon the world during the Bush II administration and a moment of potential identification with the many non-U.S. critics of his policies. More importantly, the visceral reactions to the Bush scene are in stark contrast to the laughter and other sounds of pleasure that generally accompany the discussion of sexual possibilities. Affectively, for many viewers, the moment of national and "American" consolidation figured by the Bush scene would seem to be in tension with the pleasures of disabled sex and the invention of new and perhaps unexpected or unsanctioned sexual positions.

Of course, there is nothing essentially subversive about a quad rugby player suggesting that he and a partner (female or male) might author, themselves, a variety of sexual scripts. The *process* of interrupting what Brian Keith Axel, in another context, has termed a "national-normative sexuality" is far more vital than identifying supposedly substantive positive disability images (qtd. in Puar 27).[16] Indeed, substantive "positive images" (and identities) will almost invariably be incorporated into the narrative of neoliberalism as it is retold in the near future; that is, in fact, precisely what the Bush scene attempts to accomplish. Put somewhat differently, neoliberalism can accommodate much more easily "the [substantive] best film ever made on disability" than it can ongoing crip processes of disidentification and interruption—interruption, in particular, of the

---

16. Axel is specifically discussing the ways in which torture is used to consolidate national-normative sexuality; Jasbir K. Puar, in an important article on representations of and responses to U.S. military tortures at the Abu Ghraib prison in Iraq, uses Axel to consider the "formulation of national differentiation as sexual differentiation" (27). My argument in this section is that *Murderball* (read generously) flirts with a queer and even potentially feminizing sexual differentiation that would position the men at the center of the film otherwise, but that the film's emphasis on both athletic virility and patriotism essentially rehabilitates them for integration into the national-normative sexuality they might otherwise disrupt. Beyond that, I am suggesting that any "positive images" approach is founded on the desire for integration and national belonging and betrays both the interruptive potentiality of queerness and disability and those subjects, such as Earline Fitzgerald, who are made to figure that interruptive potentiality.

uses to which disability is put in normative and national scripts.

It seems to me that these crip processes are crossing borders and that the protests of *Million Dollar Baby* are more generatively read in this larger context. If earlier, in other words, I took stock of the protests and suggested they had little impact on the issues at hand (the popularity of this one egregious Hollywood film), I would now affirm that they are more productively read through the widespread, increasingly global generation of alternative disabled values and futures.[17] As we celebrate (and hopefully continue to generate) our alternatives to the lessons of an able-bodied, neoliberal primer like *Million Dollar Baby*, it's incumbent upon us to attend to the tensions surrounding current uses of disability in culture. As other, less remarked, disability spectacles of 2005 attest (Hurricane Katrina, Guantanamo, Iraq), disability communities (communities of color far more than the largely white team represented in *Murderball*) can rightfully claim that the bridge to the new world order is still called our back.[18] "Nothing about us without us" always echoing in the background, however (and I imagine we always have yet to recognize just how radical that watch phrase is), we can continue to insist that integration into that order, or any order, is unacceptable if it leaves so many of "us" behind.

---

17. My thinking on the increasingly global generation of disabled values and futures is indebted to David T. Mitchell and Sharon L. Snyder's essay on transnational disability film festivals, "How Do We Get All These Disabilities in Here?" as well as to their important book *The Cultural Locations of Disability*.

18. I am framing my conclusion in this way given that *Million Dollar Baby*, along with the Terri Schiavo case, in many ways became "representative" disability spectacles of 2005; indeed, this essay first appeared as a panel presentation at the Modern Language Association Convention given over to consideration of these two high-profile disability events from that year. I contend that these two events became representative because it is still difficult (in part because of the limitations of identity politics as it has increasingly consolidated in and around disability studies) to perceive certain events—such as Hurricane Katrina or the tortures associated with Guantanamo or other U.S. military prisons—as "disability" events or spectacles.

Works Cited

Davis, Mike. *City of Quartz: Excavating the Future in Los Angeles*. (1990). New York: Vintage, 1992.

Dolmage, Jay and William DeGenaro. "'I Cannot Be Like This Frankie': Disability, Social Class, and Gender in *Million Dollar Baby*." *Disability Studies Quarterly* 25.2 (2005). http://www.dsq-sds.org.

———, eds. "Responding to *Million Dollar Baby*: A Forum." *Disability Studies Quarterly* 25.3 (2005). http://www.dsq-sds.org.

Duggan, Lisa. *The Twilight of Equality: Neoliberalism, Cultural Politics, and the Attack on Democracy*. Boston: Beacon Press, 2003.

Giorgio, Gabriel. "Madrid *en Tránsito*: Traveler's, Visibility, and Gay Identity." *GLQ: A Journal of Lesbian and Gay Studies* 8.1–2 (2002): 57–79.

Hancock, Ange-Marie. *The Politics of Disgust: The Public Identity of the Welfare Queen*. New York: New York University Press, 2004.

Hardt, Michael and Antonio Negri. *Multitude: War and Democracy in the Age of Empire*. New York: Penguin, 2004.

Harvey, David. *A Brief History of Neoliberalism*. Oxford: Oxford University Press, 2005.

———. *Spaces of Global Capitalism: Towards a Theory of Uneven Geographical Development*. London: Verso, 2006.

Hennessy, Rosemary. "¡Ya Basta! We Are Rising Up! World Bank Culture and Collective Opposition in the North." In *World Bank Literature*. Edited by Amitava Kumar. Minneapolis: University of Minnesota Press, 2003. 40–55.

Hockenberry, John. *Moving Violations: War Zones, Wheelchairs, and Declarations of Independence*. New York: Hyperion, 1995.

Hooper, Ed. "Game On!" Review of *Murderball*. *Ragged Edge Online*. February 9, 2005. http://www.ragged-edge-mag.com/reviews/hoopermurderball.html. Accessed October 3, 2006.

Jameson, Fredric. "Postmodernism and Consumer Society." In *The Anti-Aesthetic: Essays on Postmodern Culture*. Edited by Hal Foster. Seattle: Bay Press, 1983. 111–25.

———. *Postmodernism; or, The Cultural Logic of Late Capitalism*. Durham: Duke University Press, 1991.

Johnson, Joel. "*Million Dollar Baby*: After the Awards Hoopla Dies Down." Rev. of *Million Dollar Baby*. *Wolf Moon Press Journal: A Maine Magazine of Art and Opinion*. March 10, 2005. http://www.wolfmoonpress.com/Movies/index.htm. Accessed October 2, 2006.

Klein, Naomi. *Fences and Windows: Dispatches from the Frontlines of the Globalization Debate*. New York: Picador USA, 2002.

Kumar, Amitava. "Introduction." In *World Bank Literature*. Edited by Amitava Kumar. Minneapolis: University of Minnesota Press, 2003. xvii–xxxiii.

Linton, Simi. *My Body Politic: A Memoir*. Ann Arbor: University of Michigan Press, 2006.

Martinez, Elizabeth and Arnoldo García. "What Is Neo-Liberalism?" February 26,

2000. http://www.doublestandards.org/martinez1.html. Accessed October 20, 2006.

Marx, Karl. *A World Without Jews*. (1844). New York: Philosophical Library, 1959.

McRuer, Robert. *Crip Theory: Cultural Signs of Queerness and Disability*. New York: New York University Press, 2006.

————. "Wish You Were Here; or, An Accessible World Is Possible." *ZNet: A Community of People Committed to Social Change*. July 12, 2003. http://www.zmag.org/content/showarticle.cfm?ItemID=3905. Accessed October 20, 2006.

Mitchell, David T. and Sharon L. Snyder. *The Cultural Locations of Disability*. Chicago: University of Chicago Press, 2006.

————. "How Do We Get All These Disabilities in Here?" *Canadian Journal of Film Studies/Revue canadienne d'études cinématographiques*. Special issue on film and disability, edited by Nicole Markotić. Vol. 17, no. 1 (June 2008): 11–29.

————. *Narrative Prosthesis: Disability and the Dependencies of Discourse*. Ann Arbor: University of Michigan Press, 2001.

Movie Mistakes. Mistakes and Corrections for *Million Dollar Baby*. http://www.moviemistakes.com/film4755/corrections. Accessed October 3, 2006.

Puar, Jasbir K. "On Torture: Abu Ghraib." *Radical History Review* 93 (2005): 13–38.

Scott, Allen J. and Edward W. Soja, eds. *The City: Los Angeles and Urban Theory at the End of the Twentieth Century*. Berkeley: University of California Press, 1996.

Smith, Neil. *The Endgame of Globalization*. New York: Routledge, 2005.

Soja, Edward W. *Postmodern Geographies: The Reassertion of Space in Critical Social Theory*. London: Verso, 1989.

Tinkcomm, Matthew. *Working like a Homosexual: Camp, Capital, Cinema*. Durham: Duke University Press, 2002.

Villa, Raúl Homero and George J. Sánchez, eds. *Los Angeles and the Future of Urban Cultures*. Special issue of *American Quarterly* 56.3 (September 2004).

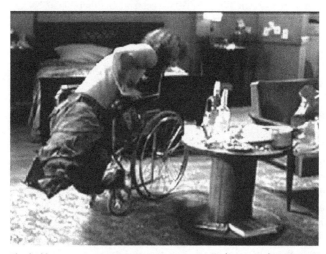

The double-amputee war veteran Lieutenant Dan Taylor (Gary Sinise) lifts himself from a seated position on the floor into his wheelchair. *Forrest Gump.* Directed by Robert Zemeckis. Paramount Studios, 1994.

SHARON L. SNYDER AND DAVID T. MITCHELL

Body Genres

An Anatomy of Disability in Film

Spectacular Disabilities

One of the more memorable scenes from Robert Zemeckis's *Forrest Gump* (1994) concerns the double-amputee war veteran Captain Dan lifting himself from a seated position on the floor into his wheelchair. The scene is pointed for a variety of reasons: First, the capacity to move one's body from the floor to a wheelchair solely with one's arms involves the execution of a substantial feat of strength. Second, the scene provides the viewer with a unique opportunity to stare at the dynamics of a physical transition we rarely witness—particularly from the safe social perspective offered by a movie theatre seat (or one's own furniture). And, finally, a viewer's knowledge of Gary Sinese's able-bodiedness encourages viewers to marvel at the special effects required to simulate amputation in not using one's legs to effect such a transfer.

This essay is excerpted from a chapter in our book titled *Cultural Locations of Disability* (University of Chicago Press, 2006). The book examines cultural spaces set out exclusively on behalf of disabled citizens, for example, charity systems; institutions for the feebleminded during the eugenics period; the rise of an international disability research industry; sheltered workshops for the "multi-handicapped"; medically based and documentary film representations of disability; and current academic research trends on disability in the academy. We characterize these sites as *cultural locations of disability* in which disabled people find themselves deposited, often against their will. At the very least, each of these locales represents a saturation point of content about disability that has been produced by those who share largely debilitating beliefs about the value of human differences. We trace these beliefs back to the eugenics era when disability began to be constructed as undesirable deviation from normative existence. Even in the face of the most benign rhetoric about disabled persons' well-being, these locations of disability have resulted in treatment (both in the medical and cultural sense) that has proven predominantly detrimental to the meaningful participation of people with disabilities in the creation of culture itself.

179

The identification of the latter two layers of imaginative involvement and spectatorial pleasure involved in performances of disability supplies an unanalyzed nexus of viewer identification—or dis-identification, as the case may be. As a witness to this spectacle the viewer is offered a unique opportunity in that the physical prowess of the accomplishment is rivaled only by the technological wizardry of erasing the actual legs of an able-bodied actor. Special effects threaten to overwhelm the more tried-and-true filmic spectacle: a disabled body navigating an environment in its own unique manner.

To interrogate this nexus between spectator and the filmed disabled body as a spectacle, we must inevitably delve into the psychic structures that give meaning to disability as a constructed social space. This space of psychic interaction does not exist universally, but a limited theoretical foray into this well-traversed arena of film criticism should provide opportunities heretofore unrecognized in disability studies.[1] In mainstream fiction film—identified in this essay as U.S.-based productions organized around principles of continuity editing associated with Hollywood industry—disability supplies an important opportunity to feed two seemingly antithetical modes of visual consumption: the desire to witness body-based spectacles and a desire to know an object empirically as an aftereffect of viewing. Whereas mainstream fiction film productions have been exclusively associated with the first viewing position—entertainment through the witness of spectacle—film technology's long historical relationship with the scientific gaze also needs to be theorized.

Throughout the nineteenth and twentieth centuries, what we have called cultural locations of disability have been produced primarily through the scrutiny of disabled bodies as research objects in the investigations of medicine, rehabilitation, and other fields devoted primarily to empiricisms of the body. Film spectatorship borrows from these weighty disciplinary practices in that bodies marked as anomalous are offered for consumption as objects of necessary scrutiny—even downright prurient curiosity. As Elizabeth Cowie contends regarding modes of spectatorship in documentary film, "In curiosity, the desire to see is allied with the desire to know through seeing *what cannot normally be seen*, that is, what is normally veiled or hidden from sight" (28; emphasis added). Disability plays this primary role in most Hollywood film productions in that it provides an opportunity for viewers to witness spectacles of bodily dif-

---

1. The probing of psychic identifications in film criticism has produced a significant body of work, including Teresa De Lauretis's work in *Technologies of Gender* and *Alice Doesn't*; the analyses of Linda Williams discussed at length in this article; Vivian Sobchack's *The Address of the Eye*; William Paul's *Laughing Screaming*; and many others.

ference without fear of recrimination by the object of this gaze. In fact, social conventions of normalcy as products of historical viewing practices are highlighted in mainstream film representations of disability by the cultivation of a belief that one is witnessing a previously secret or hidden phenomenon.

Cowie's repetition of the term "normally" in the above quotation provides a key to theorizing film spectator relationships to the screening of disabled bodies. To a significant degree, film produces interest in its objects through the promise of providing bodily differences as an exotic spectacle. What can "normally be seen" or "what is normally veiled or hidden from sight" secures a privileged position for disabled bodies on film because they promise an opportunity to practice a form of objectifying ethnography. That which is created as off-limits in public spaces garners the capital of the unfamiliar. Film promotes its status as a desirable cultural product largely through its willingness to recirculate bodies typically concealed from view. In this way the closeting of disabled people from public observation exacts a double marginality: *disability extracts one from participation while also turning that palpable absence into the terms of one's exoticism.* Film spectators arrive at the screen prepared to glimpse the extraordinary body displayed for moments of uninterrupted visual access—a practice shared by clinical assessment rituals associated with the medical gaze. Consequently, the "normative" viewing instance is conceived as that which is readily available for observation in culture. To a great extent, film's seduction hinges on securing audience interest through the address of that which is constructed as "outside" a common visual parlance.

In this essay we intend to chart some critical modes of spectatorship generated by conventions of disability portrayal in film. This is not an exhaustive effort by any means, and we do not intend to imply that these are the only viewing positions available. Rather, we intend to identify some significant viewing relationships commonly cultivated in mainstream film. Visual media analysis in disability studies has made some initial efforts to critique filmic portrayals of disability as predominantly negative and stereotypical;[2] yet, in focusing interest exclusively in this area, little attention has been paid to the dynamic relationship between viewers and disabled characters. Since, as we have argued, most people make the majority of their life acquaintances with disabled people only in film, television, and literature, the representational milieu of disability

2. For a critical assessment of this strategy of identifying positive and negative stereotypes of disability in visual media, see our analysis "Representation and Its Discontents," namely, the discussion on pages 17–21.

provides a critical arena for disability studies analysis (Mitchell and Snyder, *Narrative Prosthesis* 52). The analysis of film images of disability provides an opportune location of critical intervention—a form of discursive rehab upon the site of our deepest psychic structures mediating our reception of human differences.

Excessive Film Bodies

To a significant extent this essay owes a debt to the work of feminist film critic Linda Williams. Williams has followed up feminism's efforts to anatomize the complex space that exists between images and their spectatorial reception by audience members. In particular, Williams concentrates—following on the heels of work by film theorist Teresa de Lauretis (*Alice Doesn't*)—on women as imbibers of their own filmed images. Whereas de Lauretis theorized this psychic structure as the site of a "double pleasure" where women identify with both the masochistic objectification of female characters and the sadistic position of the prototypical masculine viewer to whom film is often addressed, Williams probes a variety of genres, and, thus, a variety of potential modes of viewer identification. In essence, Williams's analyses fracture the act of viewing into a rich multiplicity of visual relations based on cross-genre comparison—particularly with respect to films she identifies as existing to elicit extreme bodily sensations in audiences. This attention to cross-genre structures of audience identification allows Williams to de-universalize the more monolithic cast of de Lauretis's influential analysis. Here we want to briefly review Williams's arguments as a predecessor text to our own deliberations. Williams's film bodies provide a key entry into our own speculations about the imagery of disability in mainstream Hollywood visual texts.

In her essay "Film Bodies: Gender, Genre, and Excess," Williams opens by arguing that film bodies play at a critical nexus in film viewing practices. Rather than abstracting the body at a distance, "body genres" such as melodrama, horror, and pornography focus on the production of palpable sensation. Their filmic power depends upon the ability to situate the body in the throes of extreme sensation characterized by stimuli produced by pain, hysteria, terror, or sobbing, in other words, those sensations that involve our bodies in wrenching sensations that might be characterized as excessive. This constitutive excess produced as the key commodity in body genres allows Williams to stipulate heightened somatic involvement as the goal of certain visual genres (although this may also function as the critical product of visual genres high and low as well). In other words, films participating in the body genres target the visceral emotional life of the body both on the screen and in viewing audiences. This analysis situates a phenomenological mode of spectatorship as a process that is critical to the interpretation of cinema and other visual media.

According to contemporary film criticism, a film's success depends upon its ability to generate sensations as well as replicate successful formula plotlines. Hence we can best understand films as *body genres* in that, for example, melodrama, horror, and pornography are experienced primarily in terms of the spectacular moments that generate sensations in the bodies of their viewers (Williams 702). For example, in melodrama a character's loss overtakes audience members, who are also encouraged to experience a similar sensation—usually toward another human being or a body function. In horror films the terror of an unexpected meeting with the villain (often disabled), and anxiety over potential or actual violence, produce an accord of sensations between characters and members of a viewing audience. In pornography, sexual arousal and orgasm performed by the film's characters are likewise intended to produce similar responses for the viewers. Each of these genre formulas depends upon its ability to cultivate an over-identification between viewer and imperiled character on-screen to achieve its desired effects. The body is endangered as a staple plot element in these works, and the degree to which audiences identify with the impending loss of control in their own bodies will determine the ultimate "success" of the film in question. Body films attempt to situate the filmed body in the throes of excessive emotion as an object of mediation for the anticipated viewer's own experience of embodied peril.

What is often deemed "inappropriate" by critics of such films is what Williams defines as "an apparent lack of proper esthetic distance, a sense of over-involvement in sensation and emotion" (5). The viewer surfaces from such film experiences betrayed by a sense of manipulation; audience members find themselves immersed in the "violence" of emotional excess and, in doing so, experience the aftermath of such immersion as a "cheap thrill." One could analyze Williams's analysis as a theory of guilty pleasures in cinema. All these generic forms depend on the portrayal of body spectacle to one degree or another: the horror movie provides violence as a visceral mechanism of terror; the melodrama uses pathos toward bodily loss as the primary tool to evoke intense grief or sadness; and pornographic film involves the explicit portrayal of body functions usually ruled out of bounds by classical cinema. Each form of bodily display provides film viewers with an opportunity to "surrender" to extreme sensations rarely available in our non-film-mediated lives.

Rather than follow certain feminist approaches to such spectacles as condemnatory or as matters of "false consciousness" in female viewers who participate in the consumption of such genres, Williams contends that a multiplicity of viewing spaces exist within such products. In other words, rather than castigate such products as merely replicating the female viewer as "passive victim," body genres offer more than a simplistic formula of masochistic objectification. On the one hand, "identification is neither fixed nor entirely passive" (8); on the other, a viewer's oscillation among positions of power and passivity provides an opportunity to reconcile the *splintering* of self and other—at least for a while. Genre films set a field of signifiers into motion, and viewers try out various vantage points during the story. A pleasure of the multiple is at play in even the most hackneyed of formulas; therefore Williams encourages a more complex examination of "the system and structure" of sensation (2).

In addition, by addressing historically persistent problems such as sexuality, desire, and vulnerability, Williams argues that body genres provide a variety of "temporal structures [that] constitute the different utopian component of problem-solving in each form" (11). By taking up social issues that continue to resonate in the public context as "difficult," body genre films address the defining ambiguity of these problems through a perpetual recycling of their existence within the parameters of their plot structures. Thus, for Williams, the pleasure of horror results from its exposure of adolescent sexuality as not yet fully prepared for an encounter with a monster (as a symbol of insatiable sexual appetite); the investment in melodrama stems from a "quest for connection . . . tinged with the melancholy of loss" (11); and in pornography one might characterize the dilemma as the coincidental encounter between "seducer and seduced" at just the right moment for the pursuit of mutual gratification. In each formula, timing becomes critical to the structural parameters of the genre. The screen bodies "suffer" at the hands of time where pursuits are defeated, deferred, or satiated. The popularity of these plots pivots on their ability to dredge up longstanding (albeit dynamic) social problems that expose viewers to irresolution as a "solution." Thus the "resolution" comes about through the repetition of exposure to a social dilemma that can only be exposed rather than resolved.

To organize her thoughts on the operations at work in body genre films, Williams provides a diagram titled "An Anatomy of Film Bodies" which categorizes the predominating mechanisms at work in each formula. Using bodily sensation as a tool for assessing each genre's opera-tion, the chart anatomizes gendered responses. For the purposes of this essay, what is critical in Williams's anatomy chart is the degree to which the sensations experienced both by bodies on the screen and by the audience coincide. The ecstatic shudder supplied by the horror film, the tears produced by the melodrama, and the orgasm of the pornographic all situate the body as seismic register of the genre film's successful application.

While mapping out the gender of each genre's presumed target audience—melodrama = girls, women; horror = adolescent boys; pornography = men—the diagram also identifies the prototypical affect associated with each formula from sadism (pornography) to sadomasochism (horror) to masochism (melodrama). In each case the dominant production of the gendered viewer reinforces cultural scripts targeted at an audience's relationship to norms of gender and sexuality extant in Western narratives of heterosexuality.

Thus Williams's "anatomy of film bodies" refuses simplistic dismissals of body genre films as crass or merely ideologically duplicitous, while also using their fantasy structures as a means to expose ideologically invested formulas. As she explains in the conclusion of the article, "body genres which may seem so violent and inimical to women cannot be dismissed as evidence of a monolithic or unchanging misogyny, as either pure sadism for male viewers or masochism for females" (12). In doing so, body genres offer an instructive entry into the complex structure of film fantasy within which we participate as members of a media culture.

If such a model can prove instructive for analyses of gendered pleasures and popular myths, we want to argue a similar utility for explorations of disabled bodies as staple characterizations within these popular formulas. Williams's own analysis hits upon a number of conventions pertinent to disability in film without recognizing film's investment in what Elaine Scarry terms the "body in pain" within her own gendered analytical system. Through "An Anatomy of Film Bodies," gender eclipses disability because Williams bypasses an analysis of the body's different pivotal function in the development of each genre.

Because body genres rely so intrinsically on extreme sensation, we argue that disability is certainly as crucial as gender in the primal structuring fantasies that comprise these formulas. In fact, body genres are so dependent on disability as a representational device (a process we have elsewhere termed "narrative prosthesis" [*Narrative Prosthesis* 6]) that each formula can also be recognized by its repetitious reliance on particular kinds of disabled bodies to produce the desired sensational extremes.

Whether it be the "bumbling fool" of comedy (as in the screwball plots of the 1960s that featured later disability telethon sycophant Jerry Lewis), or the disabled avenger of horror (as showcased in any number of psychological thrillers or monster plot formulas), or the long-suffering victim of melodrama such as in the plot of *Dark Victory* (1939) which has Bette Davis's character dying from some indistinct, non-terminal condition (!). Within such an analytical scheme one might also contemplate the various anatomical anomalies that drive pornography plots searching for the ultimate sexual encounter.

In every one of these cases we come upon a familiar body genre formula identified by Williams in her analysis of gender and sensation. Yet one can also identify representations of disability in each of these cinematic scenarios as a key form of embodiment that gives shape and structure to body genre formulas. Quite simply put: *disabled bodies have been constructed cinematically and socially to function as delivery vehicles in the transfer of extreme sensation to audiences.* In doing so, an anatomy of disabled bodies can provide a further deepening of our comprehension of the system and structure of body genres.

An Anatomy of Cinematic Disability

Whereas Williams's essay focuses primarily on the nature of sensations produced by body genres, a full analysis of their impact includes a discussion of the means by which such sensations are produced. This implies not only the undertaking of a theoretical analysis of psychic investments between characters and viewers, but also a scrutiny of the embodied conditions that play host to the generation of sensation in the first place. As a vehicle of sensation, disabled bodies play an important role as either the threatened producer of trauma (such as in the case of the monstrous stalker) or the threat toward the integrity of the able body. The extreme sensations paralleled in screen bodies and audience responses rely, to a great extent, on shared cultural scripts of disability as that which must be warded off at all costs. Bodies are subjugated to their worst fears of vulnerability, and/or the already disabled body is scripted as out of control. The order and mastery associated with the non-disabled body often becomes the threat posed in these film formulas. This fantasy of bodily control among audience members becomes the target of body genres as a fiction deeply seated in the desire for an impossible dominion over our own capacities. What Michel Foucault refers to as the government of the body is at stake wherein individuals are produced as subjects responsible for policing their own bodily aesthetics, functions, and controls (48). In either case the disabled body in body genres surfaces as the locus of tension and the source of excessive sensation.

If productions of body genres display sensations that are, as Williams contends, on "the edge of respectable" (2), then one must contemplate the degree to which disabled bodies are made to demarcate the culturally policed borders of respectability itself. In fact, the designation of extreme sensations might be best characterized as a *response* to the "excesses" of human bodies displayed on the screen. In this manner we are discussing not a fact of bodies but rather a social investment in certain bodies' presumed proximity to abjectness. The "edge" implied by matters of respectability pivots on the fact that questions of social propriety always depend—to one degree or another—on something over which one has little to no control. A body of behaviors or actions deemed inappropriate depends on the degree to which one manages or masks the conditions of one's own materiality. Thus, in Tobin Siebers's terms, the disabled body is expected to engage in public "masquerades" of its own normalcy. "Success" in regard to disability (and all bodies in general) is judged according to one's ability to dissimulate actions or behaviors deemed aberrant and, thus, unrespectable.

The "body genres" relate directly to the degree to which one commands the behaviors and capacities of one's own body. We know that such command is elusive at best, yet the "non-excessive" body is defined by virtue of its ability to oversee and appropriately manage its own by-products. For instance, when John Belushi performs the role of a human "zit" by stuffing his mouth with mashed potatoes and then violently ejecting the contents onto all those around him in *Animal House* (1978), the comedic value of the scene produces a mixture of disgust and laughter that one equates with the essence of "gross" in comedy. The degree to which one experiences this reaction of disgust and laughter may be gendered in Williams's schema, but the vehicle of the sensation is a bodily function gone awry. The performance of a "zit" brings the question of such bodily operations into a public forum that is usually shielded from such discussions as unseemly, while the characterization reveals a bodily "outburst" no longer under the complete dominion of a fully socialized body. Bodies must remain within certain boundaries, and their "leakage" beyond such parameters violates social expectations of propriety (i.e., the appropriate self-mastery of one's bodily functions, fluids, and abilities).

In the chart in figure 1, we adapt Williams's structural dissection of film bodies for disability studies. Whereas her essay focuses on the body

GENRE	COMEDY	HORROR	MELODRAMA
1. Bodily Display	Faked Impairment	Inborn Monstrosity	Maimed Capacity
2. Emotional Appeal	Superiority	Disgust	Pity
3. Presumed Audience	Men (Active)	Adolescent Boys (Active / Passive)	Girls/Women (Passive)
4. Disability Source	Performed	External	Internal
5. Originary Fantasy	Sadism	Sadomasochism	Masochism
6. Resolution	Humiliation	Obliteration	Compensation
7. Motivation	Duplicity	Revenge	Restoration
8. Body Distortion	Malleability	Excess	Inferiority
9. Genre Cycles, "Classic"	Con Artist, Bumbling "Success"	Monster	Long-Suffering

FIGURE 1. Body Genres: An Anatomy of Disabled Bodies in Film

genres of pornography, horror, and melodrama, our own chart substitutes comedy for pornography in order to apply disability to the three foundational genres of film narrative, although, as we mentioned earlier, anomalous bodily anatomies are also on display in pornography as well. This chart details the psychic structures at play in popular Hollywood representations of disability.

From a disability studies perspective, one can readily recognize the significance of disabled bodies to the body genre formula. Rather than a generalized psychoanalytical theory, these plots depend upon the signifying affect of *disabled bodies* as a staple feature of most (we might almost dare to say "all") body genres. Bisecting the columns of three key genre formulas, the chart identifies nine rows of common characteristics found in disability portrayals. The opening category, "Bodily Display," typifies each genre with respect to the source of a character's disability (comedy = performed; horror = inborn/acquired monstrosity; melodrama = maimed capacity). The second row—"Emotional Appeal"—designates the anticipated emotional response toward disability display to which each genre appeals. Row three, "Presumed Audience," characterizes the intended viewers' gender and agency with respect to formulaic disabling spectacles. In "Disability Source," row four, we catalogue the degree of visibility characterizing the representation of disabilities across the three genres. As identified previously, row five ("Originary Fantasy") designates the presumed spectatorial role or affect experienced by viewers in relation to disability portrayals. Row six, "Resolution," refers to most typical forms of erasure that "resolve" the central disabling predicament in the binary cure-or-kill scenarios that all of these genre films take up. Row seven identifies the pervasive motivating force that compels disabled characters into action. "Body Distortion," row eight, lists the most common disability "etiologies" deployed in each body genre. In the final category—"Genre Cycles, 'Classic'"—we have noted the specific genre character types commonly associated with the mechanism of plot formulas.

In other words, every genre develops its own dependency on a specific disability type or two. These types function to give these genres shape and coherency. They become one of the primary means by which genres become recognizable as successful formulaic ventures. Consequently, one issue that this chart helps to establish is the degree to which disability itself is subject to scripted social formulas for its limiting meanings. Like film plots, the disabled body itself can be said to solidify a form of visual shorthand. Its appearance prompts a finite set of interpretive possibilities now readily recognizable to audiences weaned on the grammar of visual media. Without these readable disability formulas, most body genres would be significantly hampered in their sensation-generating objectives.

Consequently, beneath comedy's common portrayal of the disabled body as out of control, the habitual monstrosity of disabled avengers, the maimed capacity of sentimental illness drama, we find a variety of other disability subgenres such as blind "slasher" films that have been recycled for more than four decades now. For example, *Peeping Tom* (1960), *Wait Until Dark* (1967), *Jennifer8* (1992), *Silent Night, Deadly Night III* (1989), *You Better Watch Out*, and even *Afraid of the Dark* (1992) promote identification with visually impaired disabled female bodies in order to induce intense feelings (masochism) of vulnerability in an audience. The genre consistently associates femininity and visual impairment with the sensation of extreme vulnerability that the act of stalking elicits. This repeated plotline produces a web of faulty associations that threaten to turn gender and disability into synonyms for the kind of excessive vulnerability that the situation of being hunted involves. The danger here is primarily one of synecdoche where phenomenologies of disability and gender become synonymous with social acts of terror.

Moreover, the genre of melodrama, or the extra-tissue "weepies," focused on both male and female figures, could hardly exist without award-winning and celebrated disability vehicles such as *The Miracle Worker* (1962), *Dark Victory* (1939), and even *Philadelphia* (1993). In these instances of disability body genres, the predominant, excessive sensation produced often hinges upon the cultivation of the fear of disability that commonly conditions audience ideas of embodiment. Film appeals to viewer concerns about the maintenance of one's bodily integrity, and thus the production of disability serves as a site of visceral sensation where abject fantasies of loss and dysfunction (maimed capacity) are made to destabilize the viewer's own investments in ability. A masochistic relationship between a suffering character and viewer vulnerability is inaugurated.

Nevertheless, these longstanding cinematic deployments of disability have remained undertheorized as a key component of all body genres. For instance, in thriller and slasher films a vengeful character with a disability is socially located as a monster. As a way of responding to socially depreciated situations, the monster secures his (and sometimes her) dire need to wreak havoc on non-disabled worlds as a form of retribution for bodily loss (Longmore). Such a contrivance can be witnessed as the naturalized explanation of the villain's motives in films such as *Touch of Evil* (1958), *Star Wars: The Empire Strikes Back* (1980), *Speed* (1994), *and Richard III* (1955). In turn, audiences undergo a dual structure of identification (sadomasochism) by worrying over their own impending disablement while finding pleasure in the "hunt" as the primary sources of their identification with the imperiled victim's membership among the normative. While there are myriad other combinations and permutations of these identificatory structures critical to the representation of disability (some of which we will discuss here as well), our primary focus will concentrate on the two genres identified above: monstrous thrillers and bumbling comedy films.

Examples of disabled vengeance include *Hannibal* (2001), though the title character himself is ironically exempted from this formula as a further sign of his superiority as a cultured psychotic cannibal. Hannibal's (Anthony Hopkins's) psychiatric dementia is made glamorous—even titillating—in a classic disability hierarchy, by contrasting his figure to that of an even more unbearably repulsive, hyperequipped-power-chair-using, sexual deviant named Mason Verger (Gary Oldman). Audience identification is encouraged to re-orient itself in favor of Hannibal-the-cannibal by rooting for the murderous, and more visibly obnoxious, character to be dumped out of his chair and into a pit of flesh-eating hogs (and the character's personal assistant does oblige this "audience" desire). As an aside it is important to point out that the voracious hog is also a symbol in the family crest of the murderous disabled avenger Richard III. Consequently, the film uses this allusion to Shakespeare—or, perhaps even more likely, the James Bond–like retelling of the drama in Ian McKellen's film version (1995)—as a form of artistic insider lineage that helps to catapult its debased plot to the status of a psychological drama.

If audiences do cheer (or instead resist the film ploy and *grimace*) as the latest hypertech parasite receives his just deserts, we are also surrounded by ear-splitting grunts and chomping on the exegetic sound track to underscore the point that wheelchair users *really are* voracious consumers who burden society with their unproductive bodies. Thus the film stages a form of "just deserts" in feeding Virgil to flesh-eating hogs as an appropriately gruesome punishment for his embodiment of sexual and bodily deviancy. In such a way many screen scenes continue to encourage viewers to free themselves from the shackles of "politically correct" attitudes toward disabled and queer bodies as self-evident markers of pathological aberrancy.

Similarly, examples from the category of comedy body genre cinema, another site for disabled body viewing, also hinges upon narrow ideas about unacceptable bodies that encourage freak-show-like titillation, as well as humor born of an all-too-easy superiority toward each character's bumbling incompetencies. Indeed two such films—*Dumb and Dumberer* and *Stuck on You*—were released in the 2003 film season with promises to mock special schools, "idiocy," and two guys "stuck" together, as in conjoined twins. Such cinematic products promise to heighten prior body sensation exploits by doubling and tripling the forms of abject humiliation (sadism) that the featured characters are willing to undergo, thus giving a new twist to what disability studies critic Martha Stoddard Holmes refers to as the twin structure of Victorian disability plots.

The film field, as usual, seems open to anyone who can get a distributor and corporate backing, and promise to pull in revenues. Despite this limitation on concepts of mass appeal, there have been some films that dramatize a canny awareness about a social model of disability. These exemplars tend to take up disability as a core element of their storyline, as opposed to a series of freak encounters. The best examples of these counter-discursive forays include science fiction and comic-book plots developed in *Gattaca* (1997), much of *Unbreakable* (2000), and some might say *X-Men* (2000) and *X2* (2003). In these films trite attributions of the emotional life of disabled characters—vengeance, innocence, and barely forgivable motives born of tragedy—are swept up into a maelstrom of disability commentary and the plight of postmodern citizenry. As the character of Storm (Halle Berry) in the first sequel to *X-Men* points out to a new mutant:

> STORM: They don't want us so they seek to protect us.
> NIGHTCRAWLER: From whom?
> STORM: Everyone else.

All these films foresee a dystopic future where various incarnations of the gene police provide evidence of a new eugenics on the near horizon of our social context.

Mostly, though, our screens tend to transmit bizarre repetitions and standard excessive reactions to disability experience. In horror film—a genre, as we identify in the chart, where the villain is often represented as disabled—an audience's shared sensations are not cultivated with respect to the disabled characters' emotional experience. And if they are so encouraged, as in the overwrought plot twists of Shakespeare's *Richard III* and its various theatrical and cinematic spin-offs, they will eventually, and gleefully, be exposed, later on, as an unwise audience choice. In fact, inverse correlations to body genres occur if one goes at the topic of representation from a disability perspective: melodramatic elements take up personal intimacy—often with a character's self-denial and repulsion toward a newly acquired disability predicament—whereas horror films are likely to place us in a dreadful encounter with a monstrous, but still human and disabled, character. Hence audience experiences of sensation evoked by characters are not strictly a matter of simple identification; horror encourages emotions that serve to cement longstanding associations of stigma with bodily difference.

Even so, one does not necessarily reject metaphorization while interrogating what David Wills calls "the flaw in the trope of disability." A contest of metaphorical determinism—such as discussions of the overdone overcoming narrative—destine one to nevertheless avoid taking refuge in an "essence" of embodied perspective. What disability studies is engaged in here is a contest of certain forms of metaphor that have dominated the historical canon of disability representations; we are in a visceral battle over images which, as disability studies has asserted, are not outside questions of embodiment. Since disabled people must negotiate a finite repertoire of social meanings (both externally and internally), there are significant stakes in the humanities-based analysis of disability.

For instance, Judith Butler has argued against the existence of a pre-discursive sex prior to a socially inscribed gender. In doing so, Butler does not seek to de-materialize the embodied subjectivity of "women," but rather to privilege a discursive component to embodiment itself. Similarly, in the case of disability, we exist in our bodies by negotiating a cultural repertoire of images that threaten to mire us in debilitating narratives of dysfunction and pathology. By contesting and expanding a representational repertoire of images in culture (even by virtue of shoring up the inadequacies of our current narrative possibilities), we also create space for alternative possibilities for imagining embodied experience itself.

Just as in the key scene in *Crash* (1997) where Rosanna Arquette says, "I'd like to see if I could fit into a car designed for a normal body," disabled people are constantly negotiating a self-image with respect to a normative formula. The goal in disability studies is to leave a permanent mark upon "normative" modes of embodiment—to mar the sleek surface of normativity in the way that Arquette's brace-buckle tears the leather bucket seat of the Mercedes without shame. Such a competition of image and metaphor refuses to distance audiences from the recognition that representation and embodiment are conjoined in a meaningful dependency that disability studies should not sever but deepen.

In the final section of this essay, "Cinematic Interventions," we turn to an analysis of disability documentary cinema as a site of resistance and political revision to the body genres discussed to this point. Our effort here is to forward these alternative film narratives as places where competing disability subjectivities can be forged and explored.

New Disability Documentary Cinema

In contradistinction to most examples of the body genre, we would contend that the current disability documentary cinema constitutes an avant-garde—even the inception of a veritable renaissance—in contemporary disability depictions. In each documentary, one encounters the privileging of disabled persons' voices not simply as a voice added to a growing cacophony of public debates about the meaning of disabled bodies, but also the explicit foregrounding of a cultural perspective informed by, and within, the phenomenology of bodily difference. For ease of definition, in this essay phenomenology means not only the capture of disability perspectives on film but also the meaningful influence that disability has upon one's subjectivity and even cinematic technique itself. Whereas some articles have recognized the former issue (Patterson and Hughes 325–40), we want to focus particularly on the latter, subjectivity and technique, as a means of designating the incarnation of bona fide disability cinema. Last, the third site of a shift in the depiction of disability has to do with the cultivation of disability-identified perspectives that have been formulated within subcultural communities, who are in turn influenced by both international disability rights movements and the area of disability studies.

To exemplify the first point: if we step back for a moment in film history and think about U.S. film that was born during the classical eugenics era, we are struck by the degree to which that era's visual film grammar assumes that an audience will be automatically repulsed and riveted by the display of *any* disability on-screen. For instance, in the public hygiene propaganda film *Are You Fit to Marry?* (1928), near the end of the mother's dream sequence, she imagines an adult version of her disabled baby as father to a strange brood of other disabled children. The pro-eugenics film takes up an explicit argument informed by beliefs about pangenesis in the nineteenth century—in that one kind of disability can (d)evolve into a myriad of other forms of disability. Whereas the adult version named Claude has something akin to cerebral palsy (a nongenetic disorder in and of itself), his progeny have rickets, amputations, feeble-mindedness, and a host of other unspecified maladies. One can only speculate that a psychic response cultivated in 1928 was a viewer's moral and aesthetic recoil in horror at the sight of disability-begetting-disability-begetting-disability.

But in our graduate seminar for students in disabled and disability studies at the University of Illinois of Chicago, viewers tend to find the above scenario ludicrous rather than repulsive. They may chuckle at the misinformed medical notions of an earlier decade, but mostly the students struggle to put themselves back into a mind-set where the mere sight of disability can be turned into a visual rhetoric of horror and distaste. The distinction between these two audiences, one admittedly imagined and projected into the past, says a great deal about the distance one travels in a course on representations of disability and cinema. Film study challenges us to not dismiss a prior era's more pleasurable misinformation, but, more importantly, to trace out a longstanding tradition of representational strategies that continue to inform cinematic technique and influence concepts of "simply native" reactions to bodies. Consequently, even a film now some seventy-five years old can strike a contemporary audience as less farcical than proof of the degree to which new disability cinema must take up combat with a degrading visual inheritance. Documentary, after all, just like horror, melodrama, and pornography, makes bargains to demonstrate "real life" emotions—to bring forth the most credible and empirical insider account of disability truths and existence.

In other words, a course in the history of disability cinema still brings one face-to-face with a sense of the wreckage that can be wrought by generations of repeated representational patterns (such as those identified in our reconfiguring of Williams's "Anatomy of Disabled Bodies in Film" chart) that function to the detriment of disabled people's social identity. At the same time, we study ways that the anticipation of pleasurable information and spectacle for an audience has shifted genealogically across time.

For instance, the scene mentioned above from *Are You Fit to Marry?* exhibits a "grotesque" fantasy about the progeny of the disabled protagonist in a series of medium shots where the mere presence of physical and cognitive disability is intended to be evidence enough of the horrible future that awaits the mother's baby if she allows him to undergo a lifesaving surgery at birth. The medium shot itself proves suggestive of any number of medical textbook photographs where an individual body is used as a stand-in for a generic disability type. Horror, in other words, is mobilized not only in the proliferation of a host of disabled bodies and the consequent social stigma that they bear, but also in the easy appeal to objectifying representational methods in medicine.

In a contemporary disability documentary such as Diane Maroger's *Forbidden Maternity* (2002), one also gains an intimacy with many disabled characters. But in order to counter the eugenics sensation of "something gone awry" in a lineage of defective progeny, Maroger employs a variety of techniques, settings, and dramatic situations that refuse to allow audiences to take up distance from, or distaste of, the presence of disabled bodies. Long shots, close-ups, and nonstandard framing give audiences an intimacy with disabled bodies usually reserved for private or clinical settings. In addition, Maroger also employs a cast of other disabled social intimacies that the documentary's main characters—Nathalie and Bertrand—have consciously sought out as an alternative support network to a repressive familial situation.

So we meet not only the two main characters, who both have cerebral palsy, but also their journalist friend, who has CP as well, and a host of other disabled children who now occupy the institution that they both grew up within. The film assumes a knowingness and comfort with this visual variety of bodily forms that move into and out of the alternative domestic and public space that Nathalie and Bertrand establish. In fact, the object of horror and the sadomasochistic associations that the genre traditionally employs are directly inverted in new disability documentary cinema by virtue of the fact that the audience is situated to respond with repulsion at the debasing mind-set that dominates the characters' interactions with an able-bodied world. Here is the key point: *whereas the proselytizers of the eugenics period denoted the disabled body as the objectionable object within a sea of normalcy, new disability documentary cinema designates degrading social contexts as that which need to be rehabilitated.*

But a mind-set is often difficult to depict, particularly when one seeks to designate a generalized and amorphous dominant perspective about people with disabilities—one that is ubiquitous and yet dispersed through evidence that comes only by way of compiled documents and numerous investigations and paperwork, pieced together incrementally over the course of a lifetime. Surely, as Mark Sherry has demonstrated, disability hate crime does exist, but many of the serious troubles of disability existence can be compiled only through the series of deflections, distrust, and disavowals that are reserved for disabled bodies in apparently separate and contingent moments of excessive care and discrimination.

By and large, *Forbidden Maternity* lingers on details that might seem too inconsequential in its depiction of Bertrand and Nathalie's life. For example, near the middle of the film there's an extended scene shot in the kitchen of their apartment where Bertrand makes salad with a friend who has come over to share dinner with the couple. Whereas Hollywood would rarely "waste" footage in the recording of such a seemingly innocuous scenario, *Forbidden Maternity* recognizes that one of its main oppositions is the mainstream supposition that disabled people are unduly dependent and cannot manage the details of lower-middle-class domestic life. Salad mixing, without some gut-wrenching and dramatic circumstance going on around it, would end up on the cutting room floor of most Hollywood productions. In disability documentary cinema this minutia of detail must be captured as the essence of the argument.

In many ways these films function as the empirical evidence captured visually that sets out to refute, in the same way that a developed qualitative research project can, scientific formulas about the management of disability and our false reliance on a myth of personal independence. The day-to-day details *are the point* because it is at this most basic level of modern existence that bureaucracies have doubted the ability of people with disabilities to manage their own affairs. In this sense the new documentary disability cinema's focus on singular case studies opposes much of today's science on disability, which seeks to generalize management and control schemes for disabled multitudes who are all discounted from the start from being able to coexist with their non-disabled peers. Such a context of systemic doubt and suspicion entails scenes that ask people with mobility impairments to perform their walking gait as "proof" that they need a handicap parking pass or to answer to security guards about their intention to pay for an item just because they are in a wheelchair.

Such a point can also be found in a video such as *When Billy Broke His Head* (1995) where the filmmaker-narrator (Billy Golfus), who has recently experienced a traumatic brain injury, visits a veritable bevy of disabled activists and community members who suddenly populate his social landscape with a variety of previously unfamiliar disability perspectives. For instance, we visit the disabled musician Larry Kegan, who shares the details of his personal dressing habits with the protagonist, and by extension his audience, as a way of further underscoring the complex negotiation of even the most routine rituals of everyday life. Or we ride with Billy sitting next to a woman driver with a neurological disability who navigates the streets of her hometown in her modern equipped van with "only one minor traffic ticket in nine years." Such incidents significantly parallel the salad-mixing scene mentioned above in that they portray disabled people engaged in common activities that become extraordinarily uncommon, and even unlikely, within societies that seek to restrain, segregate, and institutionalize disabled people on behalf of their differences.

When viewers enter into these new disability documentary media landscapes, they discover immediately that routine activities refute the opposition to disabled people's freedom as a denial of the right to pursue lives that are recognizably ordinary. For a generation weaned on spectacular images, gravity-defying special effects, and the digitized erasure of appendages, the new landscape of disability documentary at first strikes one as anything but "spectacular" in comparison to the well-worn formulas of body genres. These films work to unfold arguments that demand a focus upon activities that have been all but ousted from traditional Hollywood fare. Our new disability documentary cinema strives, first and foremost, to make an ordinary life with disability imaginable and even palatable to those of us who have inherited a bankrupt tradition of disability imagery. This demand upon the audiences of new disability documentary cinema involves what the cultural critic Michael Ventura explains as the imaginative leap of identifying with a character who is not "conventionally beautiful": "But the face of Helen Keller was marked by her enormous powers of concentration, while to cast the face of Mare Winningham in the role is to suggest, powerfully, that one can come back from the depths unscathed. No small delusion is being sold here" (177).

What one can also glean from the examples above, and what can be extended to a film such as our first documentary production, *Vital Signs: Crip Culture Talks Back* (1996), are that singular portrayals of people with disabilities are a staple and contrivance of popular genre filmmaking. Whereas in genre film the viewer consumes representations of disability one character at a time and most often follows that lone figure into an either/or resolution of death or cure ("the only two acceptable states" according to the disabled writer Anne Finger), new disability documentary cinema seeks to counter with the portrayal of disability *ensembles* (257).

One could argue that the primary convention of this new documentary genre is the effort to turn disability into a chorus of perspectives that deepen and multiply narrow cultural labels that often imprison disabled people within taxonomic medical categories. The medical model specifies a generalized body type that can be presumably true for all bodies within a classificatory rubric of disorder. While disability documentary films *do not* seek to repress, suppress, or erase the fact of differing biological capacities and appearances (as is sometimes charged in critiques of disability studies), they *do* seek to refute pathological classifications that prove too narrow and limiting to encompass an entire human life *lived*. For instance, in the above-mentioned film *Forbidden Maternity*, Bertrand and Nathalie's disabled journalist friend explains:

> As a person with C.P. I've always had to fight to explain those two letters that were my two letters—the letters that qualified me and always required an explanation. People could see I was disabled. I was obviously mobility impaired given the way my legs were. But when I mentioned "cerebral," they'd say, "cerebral?" From the way you speak one wouldn't guess you're *cerebrally* handicapped. So I'd say, "I'm not cerebrally handicapped. I have cerebral palsy. In other words, when I was born my brain was wounded and this had consequences. In my case, this resulted in walking difficulties. In another person with C.P. it may result in speech impediment or trouble using the hands. That's what *cerebral* means. I never said *mental*. It seems to me you're confusing the words *cerebral* and *mental*.

To confuse the word "cerebral" with the word "mental" is to attempt to malign one form of disability with another. Conditions become stigmatized by virtue of the fact that we allow attributes to endlessly bleed into further disorders. Thus disability exists on a lethal, medicalized continuum where ascriptions of inferiority deepen and further disqualify bodies.

As a result, people with physical disabilities find themselves refuting cognitive "involvements" (such as in the case of CP); and, in turn, people with cognitive disabilities find themselves having to charge those with physical disabilities with a further sedimenting of their own socially derived stigma. However, in either case the effort finds itself impossible because the fates of both groups are historically tethered to each other. Eugenics beliefs used physical disabilities and deformities to reference the "feeblemindedness" residing within, and those who tested below a certain IQ level found themselves standing naked in front of medical personnel searching for the inevitable physical stigmata (Mitchell and Snyder, "Out of the Ashes"). Today, those most likely to be institutionalized, as Frederick Wiseman's "Multi-handicapped" documentary series (1986) about the Talladega, Alabama, institution for Deaf-Blind people demonstrates, are consistently designated as residing among the "multiply disabled."

In addition, while it may seem surprising or even odd to be rehearsing the diagnostic fine points of the multiple permutations of individual experience of a disorder (in a particular environment enfolding a particular body), the point of the new disability documentary cinema is not to refuse impairment (as many contend even in disability studies) (Finkelstein 30–36; Shakespeare 293–300; Barnes 577–80). Rather, these films insist on recognition of a more complex human constellation of experiences that inform medical categories such as cerebral palsy. One must essentially explode the classification's rigid yet often amorphous parameters in order to recognize a more multiple and variegated existence within its boundaries.

To momentarily return to *Vital Signs*, a similar principle is at stake. Rather than foreground a singular voice capable of refuting the inhumanity and derision that disabled people associate with their most inconsequential social interactions, the video orchestrates a panoply of disability perspectives that multiply and exponentially represent what used to be inaccurately referred to as "the disability experience." The point of the film is not merely to present a chorus of voices all working in tandem but rather to capture the diversity, originality, and vitality of vantage points that comprise contemporary disability communities. Thus when the disabled performance artist Cheryl Marie Wade says that "they can have their little telethons as long as we are on there [the television] doing all the other things we do," an alternative perspective from Bob DeFelice promptly counters that "I love telethons. I absolutely love them!" (*Vital Signs*). Like all vibrant subcultures, disability culture is diffuse and orchestrates multiple perspectives, as well as bodies, somatic systems, and minds.

After a showing of *Vital Signs* at a conference of special educators in Chicago, the first respondent in the audience exclaimed, "Wow! All those people are so articulate and in control of their life stories. They're nothing like the disabled people that we see in classes every day." After mulling over the meaning of the comment, we realized the point was that the video paraded a somewhat idiosyncratic and articulate group of disabled people who diverge wildly from the monotonous and misbehaved students who populate special education classes across the country. In response, we argued that disability documentary cinema was not a showcasing of a transcendent point of view but rather a visceral rewriting of the way that we understand disability. The subjects in *Vital Signs* are not about the singular insights of atypical disabled people, but rather about the creativity that sparks and energizes disabled people when they find themselves amongst a community of their peers, performing their knowledge and strategies for an audience that is anxious to learn the fine points of social negotiation in such hostile environments.

What shifts most radically in this scenario is not the persons depicted but the way one comprehends disability experience as the stoke to creativity—as opposed to tragedy, burden, misfortune, and the categories that populate most IEP forms. The new disability documentary cinema changes the terms upon which our understanding of disability experience rests. In *Vital Signs,* the Irish disabled performance artist Mary Duffy explains this dilemma succinctly when she comments, "most people approach me as if: you're a walking, talking disabled person. You're not supposed to talk back." This prototypical and gratuitous exchange highlights the fact that the social expectations of disabled people are so low that even the most cursory interaction promotes shock and disbelief. But the documentary is charged with instilling a new narrative pleasure: the request to have disabled persons with their unique postures, such as Mary Duffy, about disability-based insights and her own body's/life's exemplarity of it.

The follow-up comment to this somewhat disconcerting first observation at the special education conference was from teachers who worried about showing the film to their students for fear that disabled kids would be turned off by being pegged as the "expert" on disability experience. As if they hadn't already been defined as detrimentally different within the normative classroom of most educational settings! In other words, the expressed concern was largely one that struggles with what it means to be singled out and stigmatized for a difference that has been noticed but not openly discussed. What if individual students have acquired a range of knowledge and experience that the teacher lacks? Our own approach to this issue is that without adequate pedagogical contexts about disability history and experience (such as those available in the new disability documentary cinema), disabled students will continue to drift and perform well below many of their non-disabled peers. Indeed in surveys of disabled student achievement in U.S. public education, only students with a developed disabled identity manage to perform at or above the academic level of non-disabled students. Such a fact calls for a redress of our public school curricula that continue to erase disability content from the canon of Western culture. Just as female students and students of color tend to flourish in educational settings that promote the insights of their own communities in history, disabled students will continue to find education largely irrelevant as long as it sidelines their experiences and body differences as insignificant or beside the point.

Cinematic Interventions

In closing we'd like to briefly return to our discussion of disability in historical context. One of the primary insights of the eugenics era was that disability proved to be a uniquely modern phenomenon: we had orchestrated a culture so fast-moving, complex, and demanding that many bodies could not adequately keep up. Yet, despite this accurate depiction of contemporary modern life, the fatal flaw in eugenics theory was that rather than targeting the social context as something in need of repair, disabled bodies themselves became the targeted sites of intervention. Thus efforts at cure, rehabilitation, segregation, prevention—even extermination—dominate the arsenal of eugenics' approaches toward disabled bodies. Disabled bodies were at the forefront of modern innovation: on the frontlines in their experience of how intervention upon the body has become a primary means of redress in the twentieth and twenty-first centuries (hence the proliferation of a vast array of therapies and social services).

Popular film genres, such as those discussed in this essay, developed accordingly by sporting a host of interventions to alleviate individual bodies of their socially derived stigma. In the 1950s, the first starring role for Marlon Brando in *The Men* (1950) featured the wonders of a newly minted rehabilitation industry that could successfully adjust even a paraplegic's incapacitated body; in the 1970s a spate of returning-veterans films foreground sex as the root of an appropriate personal adjustment to postwar disability. Melodramas such as *Forrest Gump* miraculously repair the bodies of double-amputees as a solution to the conundrum that disability has been made to present. As mentioned above, even more recently, horror films such as *Hannibal* promote the expendability of physically disabled bodies to the more fashionable and cultured exploits of "psychotic" cannibalism. All these films trade upon a dominant opposition in the post-eugenics period that is involved in extreme efforts to "fix" disabled people in order to alleviate society of the need to be more inclusive and accommodating of difference.

In contrast, the new disability documentary cinema seeks to target the rightful site of meaningful intervention, namely, a lethal and brutal social context. Rather than identifying different bodies as the appropriate source of intervention, uncomprehending social systems have begun to be targeted as a necessary domain of social commentary in film. All three of our documentary examples cited above foreground disabled bodies while interrogating contemporary social management systems that seek to survey, manage, and control nearly every aspect of their existence. New disability documentary cinema captures uncomprehending interactions between disabled persons and the bureaucracies that ensnare them. In *Forbidden Maternity*, Bertrand and Nathalie must solicit the help of a social worker in order to refute their institutional records that portray both of them as victims of "profound mental deficiencies." In *When Billy Broke His Head*, the narrator must show up at the welfare office in person to get his reduced SSI checks reinstated to the paltry amount of $522 per month. In *Vital Signs*, disabled artists turn their objectifying experiences within the medical industry into social commentaries about the eradication of their humanity in medical theatres and public-stripping clinical settings.

Rather than target the body as the site of intervention, the new disability documentary cinema targets the social services, rehabilitation, and medical industries as a more appropriate site of revision. These films tend to target those institutions that were initially designed to accommodate disability's "endless" differences. Yet, instead of flexible systems, contemporary institutions reveal themselves as efforts in the endless monopolization of all the details of one's existence. They become equal-opportunity sites of discrimination that extract disabled people from pursuing their lives by entrenching them in a morass of legalistic and bureaucratic paperwork. When viewed collectively, these films give one the sense that our post-eugenic era specializes in keeping disabled people busy so that they demand less of the outside world as active participants.

This is a wholly different take from the other world of body genres where people don't want to have their pleasures politicized. All the films that return disabled charges to institutions—or, worse, offer euthanasia—as a meaningful resolution (and we can even offer films with spectacular and complex disability-identified perspectives such as *One Flew Over the Cuckoo's Nest* [1975], *Rain Man* [1988], *Girl, Interrupted* [2000]), summon up assurances about the beneficence of therapists, modern social organizations, and incarcerating stone walls beneath "soothing" adobe façades. Most disability narratives, however experimental, eventually do end up trying to prove that every white coat means well in returning us to safekeeping—on-screen, through a window, where we witness disability experiences managed by comfortable quarters, as if filmed through a soft-focus filter. Such a patronizing impulse is well characterized at the conclusion of *Minority Report* (2002) when the protagonist (Tom Cruise) whisks off his autistic female charge for safekeeping on an island. There, presumably, she will both be shielded from the incomprehensions and exploitative tendencies of able-bodied culture while also finding her feminine passivity redeemed by his sexual interests. And it is in film that we encounter disability largely as a "plight to be conquered" as long as when the lights come up, we don't find the same bodies blocking the aisles on our way back to the theatre lobby.

Works Cited

Barnes, Colin. "Disability Studies: New or Not So New Directions?" *Disability & Society* 14.4 (1999): 577–80.

Butler, Judith. *Gender Trouble: Feminism and the Subversion of Identity.* New York: Routledge, 1999.

Cowie, Elizabeth. "The Spectacle of Actuality." In *Collecting Visible Evidence.* Edited by J. Gaines and M. Renov. Minneapolis: University of Minnesota Press, 1999. 19–45.

de Lauretis, Teresa. *Alice Doesn't: Feminism, Semiotics, Cinema.* Bloomington: Indiana University Press, 1984.

———. *Technologies of Gender: Essays on Theory, Film, and Fiction.* Bloomington: Indiana University Press, 1987.

Finger, Anne. "Helen and Frida." *Kenyon Review* 16 (Summer 1994): 1–7.

Finkelstein, Vic. "Outside, Inside Out." *Coalition* (April 1996): 30–36.

Foucault, Michel. *The Abnormals.* New York: Picador, 2003.

Holmes, Martha Stoddard. *Fictions of Affliction: Physical Disability in Victorian Culture.* Ann Arbor: University of Michigan Press, 2004.

Longmore, Paul. "Screening Stereotypes: Images of Disabled People in Television and Motion Pictures." *Social Policy* (Summer 1985): 31–38.

Mitchell, David T. and Sharon L. Snyder. *Narrative Prosthesis: Disability and the Dependencies of Discourse.* Ann Arbor: University of Michigan Press, 2000.

———. "Out of the Ashes of Eugenics: Diagnostic Regimes in the United States and the Making of a Disability Minority." *Patterns of Prejudice* 36.1 (January 2002). 79–103

———. "Representation and Its Discontents: The Uneasy Home of Disability in Literature and Film." In *Narrative Prosthesis: Disability and the Dependencies of Discourse.* Edited by David T. Mitchell and Sharon L. Snyder. Ann Arbor: University of Michigan Press, 2000.

Patterson, Kevin and Bill Hughes. "The Social Model of Disability and the Disappearing Body: Towards a Sociology of Impairment." *Disability & Society* 12.3 (1999): 325–40.

Paul, William. *Laughing Screaming: Modern Hollywood Horror and Comedy.* New York: Columbia University Press, 1994.

Scarry, Elaine. *The Body in Pain: The Making and Unmaking of the World.* New York: Oxford University Press, 1985.

Shakespeare, Tom. "Defending the Social Model." *Disability & Society* 12.2 (1997): 293–300.

Sherry, Mark. (2000). "Talking about Hate Crimes." *Bent Webzine.* http://www.bentvoices.org/culturecrash/sherry_hatecrimes.htm. Accessed January 3, 2004.

Siebers, Tobin. "Disability as Masquerade." *Literature and Medicine* 23.1 (Spring 2004).

Sobchack, Vivian. *The Address of the Eye: A Phenomenology of Film Experience.* Princeton: Princeton University Press, 1991.

Ventura, Michael. "Report from El Dorado." In *Multi-Cultural Literacy.* Edited by R. Simmonson and S. Walker. St. Paul, MN: Graywolf Press, 1988. 173–88.

Wills, David. *Prosthesis.* Stanford: Stanford University Press, 1995. 36.

Williams, Linda. "Film Bodies: Gender, Genre, and Excess." In *Film Theory and Criticism.* Edited by Leo Braudy and Marshall Cohen. Oxford: Oxford University Press, 1999. 701–15.

Mata Hari (Greta Garbo) descends toward her executioners, as Lt. Alexis Rosanoff (Ramon Novarro), her blind lover, "looks on." *Mata Hari*. Directed by George Fitzmaurice. MGM, 1931.

Coda

We include here as a coda Anne Finger's short story, which serves as a ficto-critical reading of disability and film. By introducing a protagonist (and her friend) observing the film under discussion, Finger implicates readers as both viewers and critics, as some combination of analysis and projected film "topic." Throughout her story, Finger challenges the structures of storytelling as well as presenting a narrative through which such challenges meander. Right from the "opening credits" of the story, Finger projects storytelling itself as metafictional and shows how the story relies on readers and writer agreeing to a contract of suspended belief, mirroring the filmic contract viewers make with the unfolding film. They watch, they remember, they criticize, they enjoy. Through the story, Finger intertwines the role of film critics and film aficionados, and she delineates filmgoers' complicated relationships with the films they love and condemn, the films into which they project themselves, and films that remain eternally problematic.

Blinded by the Light, OR: Where's the Rest of Me?

Anne Finger

A fictional character is limping towards a movie theatre.

A fictional character? Let us give her a name.
Irmgard.
Irmgard? Where did that name come from?
Spat out by my unconscious, which, as Irmgard could tell us, has its own agenda.

For it has occurred to me, in the course of writing that last sentence that Irmgard's mother was a psychoanalyst, as was her mother before her. The name "Irmgard" and the family profession "psychoanalyst" are the tails of a kite, and attached to them, fluttering in the wind of history, is a chain of associations: Vienna, certain books which the grandmother neither burned nor hid, but during those years—for that is the shorthand with which the family refers to World War II—left on a shelf as if she had quite forgotten their existence, the necessary compromises made, etc., etc.

The daughter of this grandmother married, in the 1950s, an American GI-doctor, drawn to his innocence as God must have been drawn to Mary's. She was also, let us be perfectly frank, drawn to the chocolates and nylons and cigarettes from the PX; and spurred into marriage by the intense sexual frustration she suffered in a world de-populated of men; and to the promise he offered of escape from history. She escaped from history all right; in fact, in her new-found home, she was not infrequently called upon to correct a certain confusion that existed in the minds of many between the countries of "Austria" and "Australia."

So Irmgard was born in Kansas in the early 1960s to a mother who had discovered that the charms of innocence soon wear thin. Having finished her residency at the Menninger Clinic, Irmgard's mother left husband and decamped, infant daughter in tow, to Manhattan. She also jettisoned, under the guidance of her own psychoanalyst, a certain European remoteness—it had never occurred to her, until she reached these shores, that parents might be other than emotionally remote—and assumed the guise of a true 1950s Mom, baking cookies in the evenings and experiencing guilt over her divorce and her failure to have breastfed Irmgard.

Along with shortening her clumsy name to Irma, Irmgard declined to go into what was practically the family business. She has become instead a professor of English. She strayed from the fold, but, to be quite frank, not all that far from the fold. Irma would be quite happy if she never again heard the words "unconscious" or "hostility," which, when they issued forth from her mother's mouth, invariably seemed to be uttered with a frisson of Sphinx-like disdain. Add Irmgard to that list of literary daughters who exist in a state of vague and constant irritation at their literary mothers.

But while we have been teasing free that bit of yarn which protruded from the tangled skein of the unconscious, Irma has been limping steadily along in the bright California sunshine, past the man holding a stack of newspapers and singing, in a revivalist-preacher's voice: "Street Spir-rit! Get your Street Spir-rit! Help the home-less. Street Spir-rit!" and the dreadlocked white kids who have seated themselves on the sidewalk in front of the movie theater holding a sign of torn brown cardboard which reads, "MONEY FOR POT, PLEASE."

What causes Irma's limp?

It could be any number of things:

A broken heel on her shoe?

A nasty fall while running—or maybe playing rugby—which has resulted in a sprained ankle?

We all know that disability requires a narrative. (Although my own child, at the age of four, once asked me: How come I'm not disabled? one of his endless childish questions which I found impossible to answer.)

Now Irma is stepping up to the box office and saying, "One disabled, for Mata Hari." Through the invocation of this magic word, "disabled," she pays six dollars for her ticket, instead of nine, and gains admission to this Sunday afternoon movie, part of a series this multiplex is running in one of its mini-theaters, Classics of the Hollywood Cinema.

I am going to give Irma something more than a limp: I am giving her a pair of forearm crutches in fire-engine red. Why? It suits my purposes, I say, as enigmatically as Irma's mother.

"Last theater on your left," the ticket taker says. "The ramp's on your right."

This being a theater built within the past ten years, the ramp is as vis-ible as the stairs, and Irma experiences a momentary frisson of irritation, which she suppresses, her mind not even forming the words, "After all, she means well, even if it's a stupid thing to say."

Now Irma leans against the wall, bending her right leg at an angle, a flamingo-like posture. She is waiting. This act of waiting, which, in the days before her disability, was languorous, tinged with eroticism, a chance for her to exchange with others cool if brief looks of sexual regard, has now become something quite different: No she does not need any door opened for her; yes, she sees the ramp; I'm fine, I'm fine, I'm fine, she sings, her cripple's song.

She waits, and watches with unfocused eyes the passage of people in and out of her field of vision, the candy and popcorn counter opposite. When she was a kid, her eating in the movies was hemmed in by elabo-rate rituals. She allowed herself popcorn, provided that she bit off and slowly masticated each knurl before allowing herself the belly. Using this method of eating, a small container of popcorn would last her through an entire movie, and give her the simultaneous sense of having gorged herself—she had, after all, eaten for two hours without stopping!—and of having her appetites strictly under her control.

When she was twelve or thirteen, she began to buy, instead of popcorn, nonpareils, wafers of chocolate flecked with white spheres of crystallized sugar. While those enormous figures on the screen above her kissed—for she had begun to frequent the sorts of movies where kissing went on— she would slip one of these wafers into her mouth—the speckled side against her tongue, and then press her tongue against the roof of her mouth. Whenever she did this, she would remember once having bitten into a bar of unsweetened baking chocolate she had discovered in the cupboard, and how she had spat and spat, trying to spit the taste from her mouth. As the candy dissolved slowly in her mouth she would feel the chocolate mixing with saliva and streaming down over her tongue, her teeth, wending its way through the caverns and crevices of her mouth. Once a stream of chocolate-drool had escaped from the corner of her mouth, and Eleanor Martin, seated next to her, had said, "Gross!" and then whispered Irma's sin in the collective ear of the other girls: She was drooling! Drooling like an idiot!

But now, a woman with a long white cane is saying, "Irma!"

"Linda!"

The two women kiss, lip on cheek, lip on cheek. Waiting long? *No, just . . . The bus was late. Well, I was already . . . I must have been late, too, because really, I've only been waiting . . . Have you seen this movie before? . . . The Million Dollar Movie, when I was a kid . . . I think I must have been a gay man in a previous life, because . . .*

They have been to the movies together before, these two, so they know the drill: Irma needs the left aisle, and Linda up close.

The lights go down, and the darkness rises up around them, velvet and close.

Irma is arranging herself in her seat. Prior to the amputation of her own left leg, she had heard, of course, of phantom pain. She had imagined it as the body's banshee wail of mourning, as wild and raging as a mother's cry of grief for a lost child, Ronald Reagan's tortured filmic shout: Where's the rest of me? Where's the rest of me? Ahabian, chthonic, frenzied, inconsolable. She hadn't imagined that her loss would be sharp, specific: that certain positions of her upper leg against a movie-theater seat would put pressure on a short-circuited nerve so that she would experience a niggling, slight, but nonetheless annoying phantom itch that wanted scratching. Her amputation did not make her aware of the indifference of the universe—she had already known that perfectly well—but of quirkier things, closer to home: the length of movie seats in movie theatres, for instance.

"Too many previews," Linda grouses, sotto voce.

"I love previews," Irma whispers back. "I wish life could be previews."

Irma feels a pang of disappointment in this comment of Linda's: Linda is a rather new friend, recently hired in another department at the university. Irma has been so excited that at last there's another disabled faculty member—and that it is Linda, who is nearly as acerbic as she is smart—that she had hoped the two of them would agree on everything from the superiority of Black and Green organic chocolate over Scharffenberger to the subject of previews before a film.

The color drains from the screen: MGM's lion roars beneath the motto: *Ars gratia artis.* Words fill the screen: Greta Garbo. Ramon Navarro. Mata Hari. And the music comes up, vaguely oriental and sinuous.

Military men standing in straight lines, banging their drums and blowing into their bugles, a volley of shots, one man slumps dead; another volley of shots, another man slumps dead.

Irma shuts her eyes. Since she has herself become disabled, she has allowed herself to again undertake these exercises, which she used to do as a child: to imagine herself, briefly, blind, or demented. Sometimes she imagines that instead of having had her left leg amputated, she is missing her right. Now, with the eye—that tyrant of the senses—off-duty, she attends to the dialogue on-screen:

Two men volley demands:

"Look, is any woman worth that?"

"Surely you regret having betrayed your country."

With her eyes shut, Irma becomes preternaturally aware, not only of the dialogue, but of the sounds of candy being unwrapped, a persistent and annoying scrich-scrich-scrich—someone rummaging in a plastic carrier bag, perhaps—a dull and distant roar of traffic in the streets beyond.

But with sight asleep, the rich and invisible sensory life going on around it rises to her consciousness. She has rebelled against the sort of Freudian religion in which she was raised, and collects strange tales about psychoanalysis as some lapsed Catholics do about the Church and its saints. She thinks of Freud's early, abandoned obsession with the nose, and wonders if that, not dreams, isn't the true royal road to the unconscious. Despite his obsession with scopophilia, the primal scene, of which he made so much, is far more likely to have come to us via the ear than via our sight.

She opens her eyes, more to mute the intensity of her aural concentration than anything else.

"Come on. Out with it. Who is she? Tell us, you fool," she hears one of the two officials say to a goggle-eyed Byronic man tied to the post, who now utters the Garboesque sentence: "Let me alone."

"Oh, shoot him," says the hardboiled flic, with no more emotion than he would show ordering a glass of wine.

"It's Mata Hari," the detective knows it is: she's bewitched all of Paris.

"Ah well, some dance and some die."

"And some do both."

And then Mata Hari is sauntering onto the stage, past turbaned men who, seated cross-legged on the floor, play a variety of exotic instruments. She is executing a sacramental bump-and-grind before the statue of a multi-armed Balinese god. Small wonder *tout* Paris goes wild for her: after all, she is fleshing out the intercourse between heaven and earth at the heart of the Christian myth, although its representation in that bailiwick is quite a bit more sedate, Mary usually being shown with a look on her face that can be translated as "Oh, dear me!" Whereas Mata Hari—whose name is Malay for Eye of the Dawn—slinks onto stage with a panther step and then starts swiveling her hips and offering herself up, body and soul, to the remote statue who looks down at her in enigmatic silence.

After a bit more narrative filler, the film approaches what Irma has been waiting for, the love scene between Greta Garbo and Ramon Navarro. It's what she remembers from watching this movie with her friend Sharon's mother on the television in their den: how old had Irma been then? Ten or eleven, still slogging through life bent under the weight of the name "Irmgard."

After being downright cruel to the poor lad in the previous scenes—when he, with boyish ebullience, strew flowers at her feet, which she stepped over as if they were trash on the street—Garbo has come to Ramon's quarters in Paris. She stands, lithe as a panther, in her Nefertiti-meets-Catwoman costumes, peeling her gloves slowly off first one finger, then the next, then the next.

Of course, at the age of eleven, a sequined Adrian gown was quite impossible for Irmgard to obtain, as were Mata Hari's bejeweled cloches and sinuous veils and the tiered pagoda crown she wore when dancing: but a pair of gloves, those she could have. After first seeing this movie, she set aside her girlish mittens and wore only gloves. Alone in her bedroom, she would put on her gloves and remove them slowly, finger by finger, freeing, one after another, the five miniature phalluses she carried about with her on each of her two hands. Does she remember this? No, she has squashed it back into the dark corner of the jumbled closet of her unconscious. She is also quite unaware that, as she watches this scene, she is folding and refolding her hands together in her lap.

It's an odd audience that foregoes the lure of sun and air to sit in the darkness on a sunny Sunday afternoon: film buffs and gay men, mostly. Here's Ramon Navarro—he-vamp extraordinaire, Mexican homosexual (the studio described him as being descended from Aztec royalty to make it quite clear he wasn't the kind of Mexican who might tend a viewer's garden or wash her dishes, and explained his bachelor status by his being devoted to his large family of numerous brothers and sisters). Navarro was later in life to be murdered by a pair of male hustlers he'd brought to his home in the Hollywood Hills. He's pretending to be a Russian heterosexual, Lt. Alexis Rosanoff (on film, he doesn't seem to be working very hard on the heterosexual aspect of things; nonetheless, women of the day went gaga for him. Perhaps Irma's mother could answer Freud's question "What do women want?" with "Among other things, somewhat effeminate gay men as fantasy lovers.")

And opposite him? Greta Garbo, who had the habit of referring to herself as a male: *I first came here when I was a young boy . . . I was just a young lad . . . I'm not a normal man, so I can't do what other people do . . .* The Swedish actress portrays a heterosexual Dutch woman, Mata Hari—née Margaretha Geertruida Zelle, a dark orchid among blonde buttercups. A five-year-stint in Sumatra with an officer-husband of the Dutch Colonial Army transformed her into a speaker of Malay, a wearer of a translucent sarong, a woman to whom, when she was in the grip of a typhoid fever, dancing Hindu gods and goddesses appeared. Pictures close to the time of her execution for spying show her to have been plump and forty, with the sort of fleshy arms Irma keeps at bay with daily pumping of weights.

It's the one scene Irma remembers from decades ago. Alexis is gazing at an icon of the Madonna and saying: "My mother made a pilgrimage to the shrine of miracles to get it for me. It's about a hundred miles from our town," and the air in the dark theatre shivers with a sense of lust flavored with ironic detachment.

"What is it supposed to do? Bring you luck?" asks Garbo.

"It guards you from evil," says Ramon. "I had to kneel before the altar and promise mother I would always keep a flame burning in front of it."

"Ra-mon! Ra-mon!" a male voice moans from the back of the theatre.

The actors on the screen, eternally unaware of the audience, march on; although the general laughter that follows that passionate cry drowns out Garbo's next words: "And have you kept that promise?" The film is a rock in a river, and the audience is the water moving around it, sometimes raging, sometimes in doldrums, ever in flux.

Irma, despite her Ph.D. and her own finely developed ironic sensibili-
ties, feels a bit mocked herself, as if the love for sweet Ramon she had
experienced as an eleven-year-old were now being held up for public
ridicule. (Truth to tell, she had remembered the scene as even more high
camp than this: that Ramon's mama had walked not only a hundred
miles to fetch this icon for her boy, but that she had walked on her knees.
In the snow.)

Ramon kneels before Greta, saying: "I love you as one adores sacred
things." When Irma was eleven, it had seemed not only possible but
expected that someday a man would say such a thing to her. But no man
ever had, nor had they thrown flowers at her feet, nor had a total stranger
ever slipped an expensive ring on her finger, etc. No man has ever said of
her, as Alexis said of Mata Hari earlier in the film: "I would give my right
arm to meet her."

And now? Watching this scene is a bit like listening to the Sex Pistols
doing "My Way." Irma experiences both the grandiloquent soar and the
mocking of the grandiloquent soar.

The stump of Irma's amputated leg starts to throb. She shifts position, easing her weight from her left cheek to her right and then back
again, pressing the places where her flesh joins her prosthesis. It took her
a while, after her amputation, to master the art of sitting for any length
of time, and during that period she developed a critical strictness that
would have made her mother proud. Her mother had once regarded a
row of women on the beach, reading murder mysteries and romances,
and sneered, "I myself should prefer to stare at the horizon." Irma had
been intolerant of self-indulgent theatrical productions and dance performances that sought to dazzle the audience with a fiery show. On the
other hand, she championed any production, filmic or theatrical, which
made her forget her pain. But now, she has become adept at the hundreds
of minute accommodations her body must make in the course of an evening; she will even remove her prosthesis if her comfort warrants it.

Irma glances at Linda, who is staring at the screen, and wonders what
she sees. Linda is what is variously called legally blind, low vision, imperfectly blind.

Spies standing in the rain; secret passageways; 1917 versions of high-
tech spy-gear; a traitor who may be a double-agent and must be done
away with: and then, the chief German spy, with his Leninesque goatee,
is calling "Jacques," and disability limps on-screen. The poor word—
"limp"—it is called upon to cover so many differing gaits, from a stiff-
legged hesitation to this clumping lurch. All the film shows of Jacques as
he enters the frame is a close-up of his lower legs. One of his feet might

belong, perhaps not to a romantic lead, but to Rosanoff's orderly or to one of the twelve men of the firing squad, or to the in-sync marching soldiers. His other leg is shortened, his shoe has an enormous wedge on the bottom of it. Clearly he is one who might say he was born *deform'd, unfinished, sent before my time/Into this breathing world, scarce half made up.* Off he gallumps, Carlotta screams, wicked Mata scarcely winces.

And Irma?

The smooth flow of the narrative broke when Jacques's feet entered the frame. Surely, she saw this scene when she watched the movie decades before? But it left no marker, no trace. She feels a kinship with the girl she once was, who imagined that someday she, dressed in a sequined gown, would be taken into the arms of a man like Ramon Navarro, who would say to her: I adore you, as one adores sacred things. But what of the girl who saw that crippled foot and took so little notice of it that it left no trace in her memory? That girl is the enemy of the woman she is now.

Sometimes friends ask her if she dreams of herself as "you know— the way you were. Before." In her dreams she is inside herself. It is a bit like asking herself if she dreams of herself as white. She supposes in her dreams she is an amputee: she certainly isn't otherwise, but then again, she's not particularly aware of it.

It's daydreams where things get tricky: those theatrical productions of her mind where she is simultaneously within and without, not just the star, but also the audience; the writer, director and producer, gaffer and best boy, too. Her mind always hesitates, there's a brief hiccup in the fantasy while she inserts her gait, her prosthesis, her bright red pair of crutches.

More fabulous clothes, more threats of betrayal; more hurried assignations. And then Mata Hari, whose heart has been made of ice, finds it melting: she is going to be saved by the love of a good man.

Not just any good man, it turns out: the love of a good disabled man. For plucky Lieutenant Rosanoff, as he carries the secret missives back to Russia (a country which Mata pronounces, her mouth caressing each syllable, as Russh-ee-a) has been shot from the sky, and in his tumble to earth has been blinded—although fortunately and miraculously remaining unscathed in every other fashion.

Mata goes to see him at the hospital, and there disabled bodies abound: maimed soldiers displaying their stumps, somnambulant shell-shocked veterans, blind men who stare with catatonic wisdom into the void, etc., etc., etc., etc. And here is Alexis, lying abed with a magnificent white bandage wrapped around his head (exhibiting his new and heroic lack).

And then the film marches towards the final moments, when Alexis and Mata's love proves as true as it is doomed: there's Mata in the courtroom, on trial for treason, looking very Joan of Arc in the dock; of course, Alexis, being blind, all this can be kept from him. When he's brought to her in the final moments of her life, he thinks he's visiting her at a sanitarium, that she's off to the operating room rather than off to the firing squad; and then Mata's blissful moment as she is led off, glowing with the light of true love.

As the words, "The End," appear on the screen, Irma leans over, picks up her crutches from where they have been lying on the floor, and Linda's cane snaps open.

Filmography

"Academy Awards." *The Kids in the Hall.* The Comedy Network. Directed by
  Michael Kennedy. Season 3, episode #304. First aired CBC, January 21, 1991.
Adada Directed by Im Gweon-taek. Munyea, 1987.
Afraid of the Dark. Directed by Mark Peploe. Fine Line Pictures, 1991.
Alien. Directed by Ridley Scott. 20th Century Fox, 1979.
Animal House. Directed by John Landis. Universal, 1978.
The Apartment. Directed by Billy Wilder. MGM, 1960.
Are You Fit to Marry? John E. Allan, Inc, 1927. Also issued as *The Black Stork* 1917.
As Good as It Gets. Directed by James L. Brooks. Tristar, 1992.
As Is. Directed by Michael Lindsay-Hogg. Warner Bros., 1986.
At First Sight. Directed by Irwin Winkler. MGM, 1999.
The Aviator. Directed by Martin Scorcese. Warner Bros., 2004.
Beaches. Directed by Garry Marshall. Touchstone, 1988.
The Best Years of Our Lives. Directed by William Wyler. MGM, 1946.
The Big Combo. Directed by Joseph H. Lewis. Pioneer, 1955.
The Big Heat. Directed by Fritz Lang. Columbia, 1953.
The Big Parade. Directed by King Vidor. MGM, 1925.
The Big Sleep. Directed by Howard Hawks. Warner Bros., 1946.
Blink. Directed by Michael Apted. New Line Cinema, 1994.
The Blue Dahlia. Directed by George Marshall. Paramount, 1946.
Born on the Fourth of July. Directed by Oliver Stone. Universal, 1989.
The Brasher Doubloon. Directed by John Brahm. 20th Century Fox, 1947.
Breaking the Waves. Directed by Lars von Trier. Zentropa Film Entertainment, 1996.
Breathing Lessons: The Life and Work of Mark O'Brien. Directed by Jessica Yu. Inscru-
  table Films production in conjunction with Pacific News Service, 1996.
Citizen Kane. Directed by Orson Welles. RKO, 1941.
Coming Home. Directed by Hal Ashby. MGM, 1978.
Crash. Directed by David Cronenberg. Fine Line Pictures, 1996.
Dancer in the Dark. Directed by Lars von Trier. Zentropa Film Entertainment, 2000.
Dark Victory. Directed by Edmund Goulding. Warner Bros., 1939.
Double Indemnity. Directed by Billy Wilder. Paramount, 1944.

Dragonwyck. Directed by Joseph L. Mankiewicz. 20th Century Fox, 1946.

Dr. Jekyll and Mr. Hyde. Directed by John S. Robertson. Paramount, 1920.

Dumb and Dumberer: When Harry Met Lloyd. Directed by Troy Miller. New Line Cinema, 2003.

An Early Frost. Directed by John Erman. Wolfe Video, 1985.

The Elephant Man. Directed by David Lynch. EMI Films, 1980.

L'enfant sauvage (The Wild Child). Directed by François Truffaut. Les Films du Carrosse, 1969. United Artists, 1970.

Fallen Sparrow. Directed by Richard Wallace. Fox Hills, 1943.

Fight Club. Directed by David Fincher. 20th Century Fox, 1999.

Forbidden Maternity (Maternité interdite). Directed by Diane Maroger. Athenaise Productions, 2002.

Forrest Gump. Directed by Robert Zemeckis. Paramount, 1994.

Freaks. Directed by Tod Browning. MGM, 1932.

F**k the Disabled: The Adventures of Greg Walloch. Directed by Eli Kabillio, 2002.

Gaby: A True Story. Directed by Luis Mandoki. Tri-Star Pictures, 1987.

Gattaca. Directed by Andrew Niccol. Columbia, 1997.

Gilda. Directed by Charles Vidor. Columbia, 1946.

Girl, Interrupted. Directed by James Mangold. Columbia Tristar, 1999.

Hannibal. Directed by Ridley Scott. MGM/Universal, 2001.

He Who Gets Slapped. Directed by Victor Sjöström. MGM, 1924.

The Hunchback of Notre Dame. Directed by Wallace Worsley. Universal, 1923.

I Am Sam. Directed by Jessie Nelson. New Line Productions, 2001.

Ice Castles. Directed by Donald Wrye. Columbia Tristar, 1978.

The Idiots. Directed by Lars von Trier. Zentropa Film Entertainment, 1998.

In the Gloaming. Directed by Christopher Reeve. Home Box Office Network, 1997.

In a Lonely Place Directed by Nicholas Ray. Columbia, 1950.

"It is fine! EVERYTHING IS FINE!" Directed by Crispin Hellion Glover and David Brothers. Volcanic Eruptions, 2007

Jennifer8. Directed by Bruce Robinson. Paramount, 1992.

Johnny Belinda. Directed by Jean Negulesco. Warner Bros., 1948.

Johnny Guitar. Directed by Nicholas Ray. Republic Pictures, 1954.

Kiss of Death. Directed by Henry Hathaway. 20th Century Fox, 1947.

Kramer vs. Kramer. Directed by Robert Benton. Columbia, 1979.

The Lady from Shanghai. Directed by Orson Welles. Columbia, 1948.

Laura. Directed by Otto Preminger. 20th Century Fox, 1944.

Magnificent Obsession. Directed by Douglas Sirk. Universal, 1992.

The Maltese Falcon. Directed by John Huston. Warner Bros., 1941.

The Manchurian Candidate. Directed by John Frankenheimer. M.C. Productions, 1962.

Mata Hari. Directed by George Fitzmaurice. MGM, 1931.

The Men. Directed by Fred Zinnemann. Republic Pictures Home Video, 1950.

Mildred Pierce. Directed by Michael Curtiz. Warner Bros., 1945.

Million Dollar Baby. Directed by Clint Eastwood. Warner Bros., 2004.

Ministry of Fear. Directed by Fritz Lang. Paramount, 1944.

Minority Report. Directed by Steven Spielberg. 20th Century Fox, 2002.

The Miracle Worker. Directed by Arthur Penn. MGM/UA, 1962.

Moby Dick. Directed by Lloyd Bacon. Warner Bros., 1930.

Mulan. Directed by Tony Bancroft and Barry Cook. Disney Pictures, 1998.

Murderball. Directed by Dana Shapiro and Henry Alex Rubin. Velocity/Thinkfilm, 2005.

My Left Foot. Directed by Jim Sheridan. Palace/Granada Films, 1989.

My Life. Directed by Bruce Joel Rubin. Columbia TriStar, 1993.

Norma Rae. Directed by Martin Ritt. 20th Century Fox, 1979.

Oasis. Directed by Lee Chang-dong. East Film, 2002.

One Flew over the Cuckoo's Nest. Directed by Milos Forman. Warner Bros., 1975.

Out of the Past. Directed by Jacques Tourneur. RKO Eagle Lion, 1947.

A Patch of Blue. Directed by Guy Green. Turner, 1965.

Peeping Tom. Directed by Michael Powell. Astor, 1960.

The Penalty. Directed by Wallace Worsley. Samuel Goldwyn, 1920.

The Phantom of the Opera. Directed by Rupert Julian. Universal, 1925.

Philadelphia. Directed by Jonathan Demme. Columbia Tristar, 1993.

Pocahontas. Directed by Mike Gabriel and Eric Goldberg. Disney Pictures, 1995.

Psycho. Directed by Alfred Hitchcock. Paramount, 1960.

The Raging Moon (aka *Long Ago, Tomorrow*). Directed by Bryan Forbes. EMI Films, 1970.

Rain Man. Directed by Barry Levinson. MGM, 1988.

Ray. Directed by Taylor Hackford. Universal, 2004

Rear Window. Directed by Alfred Hitchcock. Universal, 1954.

Rebecca. Directed by Alfred Hitchcock. Selznick Pictures, 1948.

Richard III. Directed by Laurence Olivier. London Films, 1955.

Ride the Pink Horse. Directed by Robert Montgomery. Universal, 1949.

Scent of a Woman. Directed by Martin Brest. City Light Films, 1992.

The Sea Beast. Directed by Millard Webb. Warner Bros., 1926.

The Sea Inside. Directed by Alejandro Amenábar. Fine Line Features, 2004.

Seventh Heaven. Directed by Frank Borzage. Goldwyn, 1927.

Shallow Hal. Directed by Bobby and Peter Farrelly. 20th Century Fox, 2001.

Silent Night, Deadly Night III: Better Watch Out! Directed by Monte Hellman. Quiet, 1989.

Six Days Seven Nights. Directed by Ivan Reitman. Touchstone Pictures, 1998.

Snow Cake. Directed by Mark Evans. An independent film release, 2006.

Somewhere in the Night. Directed by Joseph L. Mankiewicz. 20th Century Fox, 1946.

Son of the Sheik. Directed by George Fitzmaurice. United Artists, 1926.

Sorry, Wrong Number. Directed by Anatole Litvak. Paramount, 1948.

Speed. Directed by Jan de Bont. 20th Century Fox, 1994.

Spellbound. Directed by Alfred Hitchcock. MGM, 1945.

The Spiral Staircase. Directed by Robert Siodmak, 1945.

Star Wars: Episode V—The Empire Strikes Back. Directed by Irvin Kershner. 20th Century Fox, 1980.

The Station Agent. Directed by Tom McCarthy. An independent film release, 2003.

Stepmom. Directed by Chris Columbus. Columbia Tristar, 1998.

Strangers on a Train. Directed by Alfred Hitchcock. Warner Bros., 1951.

Stuck on You. Directed by Peter and Bobby Farrelly. 20th Century Fox, 2004.

The Sweet Hereafter. Directed by Atom Egoyan. New Line Home Video, 1998.

Terms of Endearment. Directed by James L. Brooks. Paramount, 1983.

They Live by Night. Directed by Anthony Mann and Nicholas Ray. Warner Home Video, 1949.

Thieves Highway. Directed by Jules Dassin. Criterion, 1949.

Touch of Evil. Directed by Orson Welles. Universal, 1958.

Unbreakable. Directed by M. Night Shyamalan. Buena Vista, 2000.

Vertigo. Directed by Alfred Hitchcock. Paramount, 1958.

Vital Signs: Crip Culture Talks Back. Directed by David Mitchell and Sharon Snyder. An independent film release, 1996.

Wait Until Dark. Directed by Terence Young. Warner Bros., 1967.

Walk on the Wild Side. Directed by Edward Dmytryk. Columbia, 1962.

The Waterdance. Directed by Neal Jimenez and Michael Steinberg. A No Frills Film Production, 1992.

Whatever Happened to Baby Jane? Directed by Robert Aldrich. Warner Bros., 1963.

When Billy Broke His Head . . . and Other Tales of Wonder. Directed by Billy Golfus. Independent Television Service, 1995.

Whose Life Is It Anyway? Directed by John Badham. MGM, 1981.

Wit. By Margaret Edson. Adapted for film by Emma Thompson and Mike Nichols. Directed by Mike Nichols. Home Box Office Network, 2001.

X-Men. Directed by Bryan Singer. 20th Century Fox, 2000.

X2: X-Men United. Directed by Bryan Singer. 20th Century Fox, 2003.

You Better Watch Out. Directed by Lewis Jackson. Academy Entertainment, 1980.

Notes on Contributors

TIMOTHY BARNARD is Visiting Assistant Professor of American Studies, Film Studies, and English and Coordinator of Mellon Projects in the Humanities at the College of William & Mary. He has presented his research on masculinity, modernity, and Hollywood at annual conferences of the Modernist Studies Association, the Modern Language Association, the American Historical Association, the American Studies Association, and the Association of Literature on Screen. For the past three years he has also been serving as the director of William & Mary's annual Global Film Festival.

JOHNSON CHEU is Fixed-Term Assistant Professor in Writing, Rhetoric, and American Cultures at Michigan State University. His research into disability has appeared in *Disability/Postmodernity: Embodying Disability Theory* (Continuum, 2002), and *Bodies in Commotion: Disability and Performance* (University of Michigan Press, 2005). Recent work appears in the collection *Difference on Display: Diversity in Art, Science, and Society* and is forthcoming in "Bloodlust and Dust: Essays on the HBO's *Carnivale*" and "On the Verge of Tears: Why the Movies, Television, Music, and Literature Make Us Cry." He is currently editing an anthology of film criticism on representations of diversity in Disney entertainment.

SALLY CHIVERS is Associate Professor and Chair of Canadian Studies and English at Trent University. In addition to her first book, *From Old Woman to Older Women: Contemporary Culture and Women's Narratives* (The Ohio State University Press, 2003), she has published works on the portrayal of disability, aging, and gender in film; the Canadian disability movement; directors Thom Fitzgerald and Akira Kurasawa; author Margaret Atwood; and Canadian road trips. Her publications have appeared in the following: *Canadian Review of American Studies; Tessera;* and a number of book collections including *Group*

Politics and Social Movements in Canada (Broadview Press, 2007), *Adventures of the Spirit* (The Ohio State University Press, 2007), *Great Canadian Film Directors* (University of Alberta Press, 2007), and *Unfitting Stories: Narrative Approaches to Disability, Disease and Trauma* (Wilfrid Laurier Press, 2007). Her forthcoming book, *The Silvering Screen: Old Age & Disability in Cinema* (University of Toronto Press, 2010) is on aging and disability in cinema.

PAUL DARKE is Director of the Outside Centre, a UK Disability Arts organization that produces the Wolverhampton Disability Art and Disability Film festivals. He is an internationally respected academic, writer, and cultural critic who has written and created extensively around the issue of identity and culture. He is also the originator of Normality Theory (see http://www.darke.info). He earned his Ph.D. from the University of Warwick examining disability and its cultural specificities and impact. More recently he has produced *Motion Disabled* with the artist Simon McKeown (see http://www.motiondisabled.com) and is working on "The Chair" (a Holocaust memorial to disabled people; see http://www.the-chair.com).

MICHAEL DAVIDSON is Distinguished Professor of American Literature: Poetry, Cultural Studies, Gender Studies, Disability Studies at the University of California, San Diego. He is the author of *The San Francisco Renaissance: Poetics and Community at Mid-Century* (Cambridge University Press, 1989); *Ghostlier Demarcations: Modern Poetry and the Material Word* (University of California Press, 1997); *Guys like Us: Citing Masculinity in Cold War Poetics* (University of Chicago Press, 2003); and *Concerto for the Left Hand: Disability and the Defamiliar Body* (University of Michigan Press, 2008).

HEATH DIEHL is Instructor in the General Studies Writing and University Honors Programs at Bowling Green State University. His recent articles have appeared in *Studies in the Literary Imagination* and *Journal of the Midwest Modern Language Association*. He is the author of the book *Stages of Sexuality: Performance, Gay Male Identity, and Public Space(s)*.

ANNE FINGER is an independent scholar, creative writer, and leader in the field of disability studies. Her short story collection *Call Me Ahab*, which won the Prairie Schooner Book Prize in Fiction, was published in fall 2009 by the University of Nebraska Press. Among her other books are *Elegy for a Disease: A Personal and Cultural History of Polio* (St. Martin's Press, 2006), a memoir, and *Bone Truth* (Coffee House Press, 1994), a novel.

EUNJUNG KIM is a postdoctoral fellow of Vulnerability Studies in the School of Law and the Race and Difference Initiative at Emory University. Her essays have appeared in *Wagadu: Journal of Transnational Women's and Gender Studies*, in the *Canadian Journal of Film Studies*, and in the book collection *Intersectionality and Beyond: Law, Power and the Politics of Subjectivity* (Routledge-Cavendish, 2008). She has also published widely on women with disabilities in South Korea.

NICOLE MARKOTIĆ is Associate Professor in the Department of English Language, Literature, and Creative Writing at the University of Windsor. She is the author of the books *Connect the Dots* (1994) and *Minotaurs & Other Alphabets* (Wolsak & Wynn, 1998); the novella *Yellow Pages* (Red Deer Press, 1995)—a book about Alexander Graham Bell and the oppression of Deaf culture; as well as her most recent novel, *Scrapbook of My Years as a Zealot* (Arsenal Pulp Press, 2008), which features disabled characters as well as a scene set in one of the Nazi killing hospitals. Her published articles include "Disabling the Viewer: In Tod Browning's Freaks" (in *Screening Disability*), "Widows and Orphans" (in *Biting the Error*), and "Icarus, Gods, and the 'Lesson' of Disability" (*Journal of Literary Disability*). She was an editor for Red Deer Press for six years and has edited special issues for such literary journals as *Canadian Journal of Film Studies/Revue canadienne d'études cinématographiques, Open Letter,* and *Tessera.*

DAWNE McCANCE is Distinguished Professor of Religious Studies and Editor of *Mosaic: a journal for the interdisciplinary study of literature* at the University of Manitoba. She is the author of *Medusa's Ear* (State University of New York, 2004), a study of the trope of female deafness in the philosophy of the Western research university, and more recently, *Sleights of Hand: Derrida Writing, Derrida on Religion,* and a forthcoming book, *Critical Animal Studies.*

ROBERT McRUER is Professor of English at George Washington University. His most recent book, *Crip Theory: Cultural Signs of Disability* (New York University Press, 2006), won the prestigious Alan Bray Memorial Book Award from the GL/Q Caucus for the Modern Language Association. He is the author of *The Queer Renaissance: Contemporary American Literature and the Reinvention of Lesbian and Gay Identities* (New York University Press, 2006). He is also co-editor, with Abby L. Wilkerson, of *Desiring Disability: Queer Theory Meets Disability Studies,* a special issue of *GLQ: A Journal of Lesbian and Gay Studies;* and, with Anna Mollow, of the forthcoming anthology *Sex and Disability* (Duke University Press, 2010).

SHARON SNYDER AND DAVID MITCHELL have been making documentary films about disability history, art, and culture since 1994. Their production company, Brace Yourselves Productions, promoted a community ethos in the creation of independent films that featured multiple interpretations of embodied differences articulated by persons with disabilities. Their low-budget film productions have been the recipients of international awards, including the Grand Prize from Rehabilitation International, a Directors' Award from Superfest, a Bronze Apple Award from the National Education and Media Association, as well as Best of the Festival awards from Moscow's Breaking Barriers festival. Retrospectives of their film works have been featured at Toronto's Abilities Arts Festival and at Munich's "The Way We Live Festival" for their influence on other disability films. While on the faculty at the University of Illinois, Chicago, they developed courses for a Ph.D. and an M.S. degree in disability studies and for the infusion of disability studies into undergraduate coursework. These courses include Representation and Disability; Eugenics in America; Disability, Gender, Race, and Sexuality; Disability and Culture; Introduction to Disability Studies (core requirements toward a degree); Visualizing the Body; and Disability and Film Traditions, among others. They have published three books—*The Body and Physical Difference: Discourses of Disability* (University of Michigan Press, 1997), *Narrative Prosthesis: Disability and the Dependencies of Discourse* (University of Michigan Press, 2000), and *Cultural Locations of Disability* (University of Chicago Press, 2006)—and served as senior editors on the five-volume *Encyclopedia of Disability* (Sage, 2005). More recently Snyder and Mitchell edited and contributed essays to the spring 2010 issue of *The Journal of Disability and Cultural Studies* which features new scholarship on the theme "The Geo-Politics of Disability." This work is the foundation for their next book project on disability and the geopolitical imagination—a study exploring the impact of the forces of neo-liberal "rescue" on self-definition and group affiliation. Currently they are the recipients of a multiyear grant from the U.S. Department of Education on disability studies curriculum development, with the goal of improving outcomes for students with disabilities at universities. The grant is being implemented by the Institute on Disabilities at Temple University where David Mitchell serves as Executive Director.

Index

aberrancy, pathological, 191
able-bodied vs. disabled position, 68n2, 69
able-bodiedness, 179, 196; compulsory, 48–49, 171n15; emergence of, 161n1; exploitative tendencies of, 203; heterosexuality and, 153; naturalization of, 161n1; norms of, 153; sexuality and, 147; threat to integrity of, 186
ableism, 52, 72, 78
ableist gaze, 62
ableist notions of primacy of seeing, 74
absent presence, 25–26
AccSex Network, 144
Afraid of the Dark, 189
agency, 1, 26, 27, 123
Aldrich, Robert: *Whatever Happened to Baby Jane*, 47n6
Algren, Nelson: *Walk on the Wild Side*, 47–48, 59–60
Alien, 73
allegory, 112, 121n11; vs. analogy, 112n6, 120
Allen, Nick, 141n6
alternative cinema, 8
"alternative phallic heterosexual narrative," 139n5
Althusser, Louis, 9, 10, 11; "problematic," 9, 11
American Theater, 111, 111n5
amputation, depiction of in film, 23–40, 194
analogy, 121–22, 125; allegory vs., 112n6, 120; self-reflexive, 125

analysis, formal, medical practice and, 115–19
"anatomy of film bodies" (Williams), 184–88, 195
Anders, Glenn, 48
Andrews, Dana, 46
Animal House, 187
anti-disabled ethos, 159
antimedicalization, 98
anti-nationalism, 159–75
Apartment, The, 53n13
apparatus theory, 79n12
Are You Fit to Marry?, 194–95
asexuality, 151–52, 154; problematization of, 139n5
As Good As It Gets, 171n15
As Is, 110n2
assimilation, minority group, 71
At First Sight, 8n15
audience: able-bodied, 14, 72, 132; embarrassment of, 101; male vs. female, 35–37; response of 5, 186, 196; sensation, 186, 192; spectatorship, 72n9, 76n11
authenticity, *158*, 164; fabricated, 162
autobiography, 86–87
Aviator, The, 166
Axel, Brian Keith, 174

Baclanova, Olga, 131
Badham, John: *Whose Life Is It Anyway?*, *96*, 97–106
Baer, Ulrich, 89
Barashe, Moshe, 70n5

225